GUIDE TO THE
GENERAL ELECTION

CONDITIONS OF SALE

GUIDE TO THE
GENERAL ELECTION

R. L. LEONARD

A PAN ORIGINAL

Foreword by
DAVID BUTLER

PAN BOOKS LTD : LONDON

First published 1964 by
PAN BOOKS LTD
8 Headfort Place, London S.W.1

PRINTED AND BOUND IN ENGLAND BY
HAZELL WATSON AND VINEY LTD
AYLESBURY, BUCKS

CONTENTS

FOREWORD

The importance of elections is taken for granted but the nature of elections is little understood. Nationwide voting every four or five years is an essential safeguard of democracy and liberty – that, at least, is an axiom of contemporary democratic faith. But there is remarkable ignorance on the vital questions: what do elections really accomplish? what factors decide elections? and even, how are elections conducted? Anyone who studies carefully the press reports on by-elections will be struck by the self-confident but quite unproven assertions about what matters in electioneering. Few reporters are bold enough to say that campaigning takes the form of a traditional and often empty ritual, which, like all rituals, has become surrounded by hallowed myths.

No one – not the politicians, nor the professional party workers, the pollsters or the psephologists – knows with any certainty what does decide elections. The experts are only really confident about some of the factors that have far less influence than is popularly supposed, or even no influence at all.

One of the reasons why I welcome Mr Leonard's lucid and reliable account of the electoral process in mid-twentieth century Britain is that, while it sets out so clearly what is beyond dispute, it does not pretend to answer the central questions to which there is, as yet, no definitive answer. Why do people stay loyal to their parties? why do they switch? what specific government or party policies or outside circumstances lead them to change or to change back their vote?

Politicians and journalists spend a great deal of effort planning or analysing how votes may be influenced. The speculation on the subject is fascinating: sometimes it may hit on the truth but often it is far wide of the mark. Mr Leonard's book will help people to judge better than before between the rival theories that are propounded. It also has the down-to-earth virtue of providing the simplest and best account of the technicalities of electoral law and practise that I have encountered.

DAVID BUTLER

Nuffield College,
Oxford.

ACKNOWLEDGEMENTS

The author wishes to thank the following authors and publishers for permission to reprint copyright material: Mr Alfred J. Junz and the Hansard Society for Parliamentary Government for the table on page 20, which originally appeared in *The Student Guide to Parliament*; Mr Richard Rose and *The New Society* for the table on page 47. Mr D. E. Butler, Mr Richard Rose and Macmillan & Co. Ltd for the tables on pages 98 and 151, which are taken from *The British General Election of 1959;* the Liberal Party for the summary of election offences contained in Appendix 7; National Opinion Polls Ltd and Social Surveys (Gallup Poll) Ltd for the figures on which the diagrams in Appendix 4 are based; J. Whitaker and Sons, Ltd for Appendix 10, which is reproduced from the 1964 edition of *Whitaker's Almanack*, amended to November 1963.

He is greatly indebted to Mr Butler not only for contributing the foreword but also for numerous helpful suggestions which have greatly improved the book in many particulars. The responsibility for any errors remains that of the author alone.

He would also like to thank Mrs Susan Huggett who typed much of the manuscript and, above all, his wife who typed most of the rest and without whose encouragement this book would never have seen the light of day.

CHAPTER ONE

INTRODUCTION

'THE DISADVANTAGE of free elections', Mr Molotov once remarked to Ernest Bevin, 'is that you can never be sure who is going to win them.'

Perhaps, unconsciously, he had put his finger squarely on the feature which makes democratic systems of government so *interesting*. For it is the uncertainty which attends nearly every general election, at least in the United Kingdom, which adds spice to what might otherwise be regarded as a rather tiresome civic duty.

It is this, possibly, which explains a persistent paradox in British politics: that whereas only a tiny minority – probably less than 1 per cent – take an active part in politics between elections, well over three-quarters turn out to vote, without any compulsion, whenever a general election is held. Yet, the choice which is presented to the thirty million or so electors who record their votes at elections, is largely determined by the few thousands who take a continuing part in the activities of the political parties. It is they alone who participate in the selection of Parliamentary candidates and it is they who have a *direct* influence on the policies adopted by the political parties.

At every general election about two million young men and women are entitled to vote for the first time. It is in the hope that it will be of assistance to some of them, and also to those older voters who are perhaps puzzled or uncertain about particular aspects of the electoral system, that this book has been written.

A rather conspicuous gap does seem to have been left by the many able authors who have written on British elections. There are several excellent manuals on election law which are of invaluable assistance to election agents and others engaged professionally in the conduct of elections, but are too bulky and complex to appeal to the general reader. The series of books on post-war general elections, sponsored by Nuffield College, Oxford[1] and such scholarly works as D. E. Butler's *The Electoral System in Britain since 1918* are more likely to find their way into his hands, and they contain a mine of useful information, expertly and agreeably presented. So far, however, little has been published about British elections which has been addressed specifically to the voter. It has seemed to the present author that there was scope for a book which explained the complexities of the electoral system in a simple manner and which also contained an account of how the political parties are organised, both locally and at a national level, how their Parliamentary candidates are chosen and how the policies which they put before the electorate come to be adopted.

This book is addressed to voters who support all political parties and to those who remain uncommitted. The author is not lacking strong political opinions, but in this work he has attempted throughout to describe *how* the system works rather than explain *why* he approves or disapproves of its different features.

The greater part of this book was written during the summer and autumn of 1963. Parts of it, especially Chapter 13, are devoted specifically to the 1964 general election. How soon will the remainder of the book be out of date? This is difficult to predict, for the two most distinctive features of the British electoral system are its antiquity and its capacity for evolution. One or two of its features date back to the earliest elections to the House of Commons in the thirteenth century, a great many stem from the eighteenth and nineteenth centuries. Yet during 1963, alone, two important changes were made – peers were permitted to vote and to stand for election if they disclaimed their titles, and the rights of servicemen to obtain a discharge to fight elections were restricted. So, though some parts of the electoral law remain intact for centuries, others are liable to be

1. See Appendix 8 on p. 204.

amended at virtually any time. The great majority of amendments are of a minor character.

The ancient origins of many of the laws governing elections are a considerable benefit, in so far as they engender a sense of continuity and a greater readiness to respect their observance than might otherwise exist. But in a quickly changing world, there are disadvantages in operating a system largely designed for an earlier and more leisurely age. It may be questioned whether it is a good thing that political parties, which play so predominant a part in the fighting of elections, are hardly mentioned in the whole body of electoral legislation. The law regarding radio and television broadcasts at elections is also notably ill defined.

On balance, therefore, the author would be pleased if this book became out of date sooner rather than later. But, he is more than doubtful whether this will in fact happen, as most previous legislative changes in this field have only been introduced many years after the need for reform has become manifest.

CHAPTER TWO

WHEN ELECTIONS ARE HELD

APART FROM the result, the principal uncertainty about a British general election is its timing. Unlike in the United States and the great majority of democratic states, outside the Commonwealth, there is no fixed date for British Parliamentary elections.

There is, however, a limit on the length of life of the House of Commons. In 1694 it was set at three years, which was increased to seven years in 1715. Under the Parliament Act of 1911 it was reduced to five years, which is the present limit. During both World Wars annual Prolongation of Parliament Acts were passed at the expiry of this limit to avoid the inconvenience of a war-time election, but though such a measure would theoretically be possible in peace time it is inconceivable that it would be attempted.

No peace-time Parliament has in fact run its full five years, as Table 1 shows:

Table 1

General Election	Duration of Parliament		Original Government majority
	Years	Days	
1918	3	265	263
1922	—	361	79
1923	—	266	None
1924	4	159	225
1929	2	105	None
1931	3	356	425
1935	9	200*	247
1945	4	189	186
1950	1	213	6
1951	3	183	16
1955	4	104	60

* Duration extended by annual Acts of Parliament during 1939–45 war.

Except in the case of a minority government or one with a very small majority (as in 1950) it will be seen that most Parliaments have continued for a period of between three and four and a half years. Unless an election is precipitated by a Government defeat on a vote of confidence in the House of Commons (which has not occurred, otherwise than to a minority Government, since 1886), it is in effect the Prime Minister who decides the date of a general election.

In theory the Sovereign may refuse the advice of the Prime Minister to dissolve Parliament. In practice she could not refuse any but the most frivolous request. Especially after a Parliament has passed its half-way mark, the Prime Minister may safely recommend a dissolution at any time.

The decision is his alone. In earlier times the agreement of the Cabinet was always sought, but in 1918 Lloyd George successfully set the precedent, which has never since been challenged, of not consulting his Cabinet on this decision. The Prime Minister may seek the advice of a number of senior colleagues, but is by no means bound by it. It is known that both in 1950 and in 1951, several senior Cabinet Ministers disagreed with Mr Attlee's decision to go to the country.

When there is a coalition government the Prime Minister has less freedom of choice in the matter, unless his own party actually possesses a majority in the House of Commons. Thus in 1945, the Labour and Liberal Parties would have preferred an election to be deferred until October but the Prime Minister, Winston Churchill, insisted on a July election and his view prevailed.

Numerous factors influence prime ministers in their choice of general election dates. The economic situation, the state of the government's legislative programme in the House of Commons, the need for the country to be represented at important international negotiations by a government with a fresh mandate from the people. This list could be extended indefinitely, but there is little doubt that the principal factor was neatly summed up by Lord Poole, then joint chairman of the Conservative Party, in a speech at Newcastle in June 1963. 'The Prime Minister is likely to have a general election', he said, 'at the time when he thinks he is most likely to win it.'

The Prime Minister's prerogative of effectively choosing the date of general elections is a powerful weapon for the Government and a serious handicap to the Opposition. It has moreover assumed greater significance during the past decade when public opinion polls have provided a far more accurate and sensitive barometer to the relative standing of the political parties than existed in earlier periods. Traditionally, by-elections had been the main measure of political support, but the results of these can often be misleading. Thus in 1880, on the strength of two Conservative victories in by-elections at Liverpool and Southwark, Lord Beaconsfield went to the country and saw his party go down to defeat.

Mr Macmillan was, in 1959, the first Prime Minister to capitalise on the new precision with which public opinion polls enable a Prime Minister to choose a favourable moment for a dissolution, but he will assuredly not be the last. To have much hope of winning an election, under present conditions, it seems to be necessary for the Opposition party to lead the Government in popularity for three consecutive years, short of an error of judgment by the Prime Minister.

But though the Prime Minister's advantage appears immense, his area of choice is more limited than is immediately obvious. For in practice there are normally only a limited number of dates between which to choose.

The winter months are normally excluded from consideration for climatic reasons, April is reserved for Budget legislation, early May for local elections, Easter and Whitsun must be avoided and the period from mid June to mid September is the holiday season. This leaves late spring and early autumn as the only occasions normally seriously considered for electioneering. Apart from 1945, when the election was held on the earliest practicable date after the German surrender, 1950 has been the only occasion since 1923 when the election has been other than in late May or October or early November. It may be safely assumed that the great majority of future general elections will take place in one or other of these two short periods.

Table 2—Dates of General Elections

1924	Wednesday	29 October
1929	Thursday	30 May
1931	Tuesday	27 October
1935	Thursday	14 November
1945	Thursday	5 July
1950	Thursday	23 February
1951	Thursday	25 October
1955	Thursday	26 May
1959	Thursday	8 October

Over the last thirty years, general elections and the great majority of by-elections have been held on a Thursday, which is generally considered to be the least inconvenient day of the week for the purpose. There is no reason to believe that this practice will not continue. Before 1918, polling had been spread over a fortnight or more and results in the first constituencies to poll were already known when voters in other constituencies went to cast their votes. This was sometimes alleged to cause a 'bandwagon' in favour of the party which made early gains. The only recent occasion when voting has been 'staggered' was in 1945 when, because of local holiday arrangements, twenty-three seats in the north of England and Scotland polled one or two weeks later. But as none of the votes in this election were counted until three weeks after the original polling day, to allow for servicemen's votes to be sent from overseas, there was no risk of a 'bandwagon' being created on that occasion.

Dissolution of Parliament is effected by Royal Proclamation, but it is customary for the Prime Minister personally to break the news with a statement giving notice of the dissolution and stating briefly and in non-controversial terms the reasons for going to the country at that particular time. In 1951 and 1955 Mr Attlee and Sir Anthony Eden made brief broadcasts announcing their decision. In 1959 Mr Macmillan, reverting to an earlier custom, contented himself with a statement released from Downing Street on 8 September, in the following terms:

> The Parliament elected in May 1955 is now in its fifth year. A General Election must therefore take place either this autumn or early next year. From the point of view of home affairs there is no reason why a General Election should not be held this autumn. But the date of the election must also be considered and decided in the light of the world situation. Important international negotiations lie ahead. It is clearly right that the people should have the opportunity of deciding as soon as practicable, who are to represent them in these negotiations.

Polling day is seventeen days (excluding Sundays and Bank holidays) after the date of dissolution, and by giving ten days' notice of dissolution, Mr Macmillan's announcement came exactly one month before the election. This was ten days more than legally necessary, but was shorter notice than had been given in any other post-war election.

In so far as the Government has the advantage of fore-knowledge in making its preparations, it may be presumed to gain by giving as short notice as possible. On the other hand, there is nowadays usually so much advanced press speculation, that the Opposition is not likely to be caught napping.

As soon as Parliament is dissolved, the Lord Chancellor is ordered by Royal Proclamation to issue writs for the holding of fresh elections throughout the country. The writs are issued as soon as practicable following the Royal Proclamation and are sent to the Returning Officers in each Parliamentary constituency. The Returning Officer is the person appointed to organise the conduct of elections and in England he is normally the sheriff of the county, the mayor of the borough or the chairman of the urban district in which the constituency is situated. In Scotland he is the sheriff and in Northern Ireland the under sheriff. The

Returning Officer appoints a Deputy Returning Officer, normally the Clerk of the Council, who in fact carries out most of the duties of the office.

Not later than four o'clock in the afternoon of the second day after the writ has been received the Returning Officer must publish, normally by means of posters outside public buildings and on commercial advertising sites, notices of election stating the place and times at which nomination papers must be delivered and the date of the poll. The election will only then be officially in train, though most people concerned in it will already have been extremely busy with their preparations for several weeks past.

CHAPTER THREE

THE VOTERS

THE FRANCHISE is enjoyed by all British subjects and citizens of the Republic of Ireland, with few exceptions, over the age of twenty-one. The only other qualification required is that of residence.

Thus, British Parliamentary elections are based on the principal of universal franchise. It was not always so, indeed it was only the abolition of plural voting (by university graduates and occupiers of business premises) by the Representation of the People Act of 1948, which finally established the principle of one man, one vote.

Like most developments in the British constitution, progress towards universal suffrage had been slow and gradual. Prior to 1832, voting was a privilege reserved for a mere 5 per cent of the population and it required five Acts of Parliament spread out over a period of one hundred and sixteen years for the transition from oligarchy to democracy to be effected.

The growth of the British electorate since 1832 is shown in Table 3 and in Figure 1.

Table 3—Growth of the Franchise

Representation of the People Acts	Provisions relating to voters' qualifications	Total Electorate	Percentage of population over 20 years of age
Prior to 1832	Counties —40s. freeholders. Boroughs—various and unequal franchises.	509,000	5
1832	Counties —40s. freeholders, £10 copyholders, £10 leaseholders, £50 tenants at will. Boroughs—£10 householders.	720,000	7

1867	Counties	—40s. freeholders, £5 copyholders, £5 leaseholders, £12 tenants at will.	2,231,000	16
	Boroughs	—All occupiers of rated dwelling houses, lodgers occupying £10 lodgings.		
1884	Counties and Boroughs	—A uniform franchise for householders and lodgers, giving a vote to every man over 21 who had a home.	4,965,000	28
1918	Men	—Abolition of property qualification in counties. Qualification by either six months' residence or the occupation of a £10 business premises.	19,984,000	74
	Women	—Enfranchised at the age of 30. Plural voting by university graduates and the holders of the business premises qualification restricted to two votes including the one for residence.		
1928	Women enfranchised at 21. Male and female adult suffrage.		29,175,000	96·9
1948	University constituencies and all plural voting abolished. 'One man – one vote.'		34,915,000	96·7*

* The elimination of plural voting led to an apparent but not a real reduction in the percentage qualified to vote. This table is taken from *The Student Guide to Parliament* by Alfred J. Junz, Hansard Society, 1960.

Apart from minors and aliens, the following categories of people are ineligible to vote:

Peers, or Peeresses in their own right, who have not disclaimed their titles. Irish peers are entitled to vote, as are the wives of all peers.

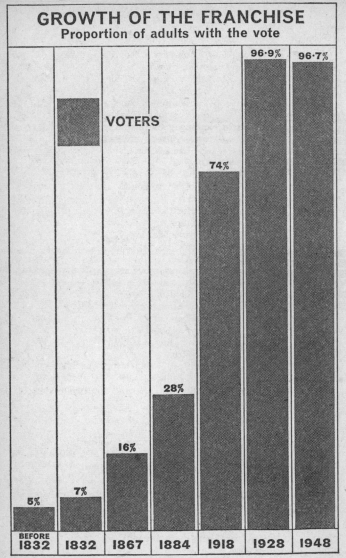

GROWTH OF THE FRANCHISE
Proportion of adults with the vote

VOTERS

96·9%   96·7%

74%

28%

16%

7%

5%

BEFORE
1832   1832   1867   1884   1918   1928   1948

Figure 1

Persons of unsound mind, who may, however, vote 'during lucid intervals'.

Felons. A person sentenced for treason or felony to a term of imprisonment exceeding twelve months is disqualified while serving his sentence.

Persons convicted of corrupt or illegal practices in connection with elections (see p. 116 below and Appendix 7) are ineligible to vote for five years from the date of conviction.

Although adults not in any of the above categories are qualified to vote they may not do so unless their names appear on the Register of Electors. This is prepared annually and the Registration Officer for each Parliamentary constituency is required by law to make 'sufficient enquiry' to ensure that it is accurate. The Registration Officer is appointed by the Home Secretary and is normally the Town Clerk or the clerk to the council of the principal local government area (county or urban district) in which the constituency is situated. In Scotland the Registration Officer is the assessor of the county or large burgh of which the constituency forms part. The Registration Officer is the same person as the Deputy Returning Officer, who is responsible in practice for the organisation of elections in the different constituencies.

To be included in the register one must be resident in a constituency on a qualifying date, 10 October, in England, Wales and Scotland. In Northern Ireland it is necessary to have been resident at the same address for three months before the qualifying date. This is to prevent residents of the Irish Republic crossing the border for a short period only and registering as voters. During weeks preceding the qualifying date the Registration Officer supplies forms, usually by means of a house-to-house canvass, to heads of households, requiring them to fill in details of all members of the household (including lodgers) who are eligible to vote. Any person who refuses to comply or who gives false information is liable on summary conviction to a fine not exceeding £20.

In addition to eligible voters over the age of twenty-one

on 10 October, persons whose twenty-first birthday occurs between then and the following 15 June should be included on the form. They will be registered as 'Y' voters, but will be ineligible to vote at any election that takes place before the following 2 October. This means, in practice, that a high proportion of voters do not become eligible until nearer their twenty-second than their twenty-first birthdays.

A further special category are Service voters. These are marked on the register with an initial 'S' and, in addition to members of the armed forces, include persons employed in the service of the Crown outside the United Kingdom and the wives of service voters who are residing outside the United Kingdom to be with their husbands. Service voters are eligible to vote either by proxy or by post.

Non-resident occupiers or owners of business premises or land, whose rateable value is not less than £10 a year are entitled to vote in local elections, providing they do not have a residential qualification in the same local government area. Since 1948, however, there have been no business voters in Parliamentary elections.

On 28 November each year a provisional register is published by the Registration Officer and is displayed in post offices, public libraries and other public offices until 16 December. The provisional register is in three parts. List A is the register already in force, compiled at the end of the preceding year. List B is the list of proposed additions to the register, consisting of newly qualified voters, those who have changed their addresses or those whose voting status has changed (e.g. by ceasing to be Y voters) from the previous year. List C is a list of proposed deletions from the register – consisting of those who have died or moved away or, again, those whose voting status has changed.

During the period that the provisional register is open to inspection claims and objections may be made to the Registration Officer, in respect of inaccurate entries or omissions. It is especially important that newly-qualified voters or those who have changed their address during the previous year should check that they are included in the provisional register; but there is no guarantee that voters who had been included in the previous years' register will be included in the next. If the head of the household has inadvertently failed to make an accurate return the voter might be included wrongly in the list of proposed deletions. There is also a possibility, on rare occasions, of a clerical error by the staff of the Registration Officer. The vast majority of voters who do not bother to check the provisional register each year nevertheless find, when they come to vote, that they have been properly registered. On the other hand, thousands of qualified voters at each general election find that they are not on the register and it is then too late to do anything about it.

Claims and objections may be made on or before 16 December (or 17th if the 16th is on a Sunday) on a form obtainable from the Registration Officer, who is entitled to make enquiries and to require proof of age or nationality from claimants.

The final register which consists of the former list A, with the entries from list B incorporated and those from list C removed, together with amendments arising from successful claims and objections, is printed shortly before 15 February, on which day it comes into force and remains valid until 14 February of the succeeding year. The Parliamentary register incorporates that used for local government elections, the franchise for which is, except for the difference explained on page 24, the same.[1] Copies of the register in each constituency are normally available for inspection in public libraries and certain other public offices and free copies are provided for the agents of political parties and to Parliamentary candidates. Registers, or parts thereof, may also be purchased from the Registration Officer by members of the general public for 1s. plus one penny for every hundred, or part, names.

The register is divided into polling districts (each of which is distinguished on the register by an initial letter or

[1]Peers are also permitted to vote in local government elections.

letters). Polling districts are devised by the Registration Officer to give each voter the minimum distance practicable to travel to cast his vote. They vary in number between a mere handful of voters (sometimes less than a dozen) in remote hamlets to over 5,000 in densely populated areas in the centres of cities. The most usual number of electors in polling districts in towns is, however, between 1,000 and 2,000.

There are normally between one and a dozen polling districts in each Ward (the local government electoral area in towns), several of which normally comprise a borough constituency. In country areas each village would be a separate polling district and towns and larger villages would be subdivided. Within each polling district the electors are listed in street order. Each entry consists of, reading from left to right, the voters' electoral number (counting from 1 in each polling district), his surname, first Christian name, the initials of any other Christian names and the number or name of the house. Within each household the names are given in alphabetical order, and there is no indication whether women are married or single.

Special categories of voters are indicated by letters printed in bold type immediately preceding the voter's surname, as follows:

Y – Young voters who may not vote in elections before 2 October.

S – Service voters.

L – not entitled to vote at Parliamentary elections.

C – not entitled to vote at county council elections.

R – not entitled to vote at rural district elections.

A bold J, printed, after the elector's name signifies that he is eligible for jury service.

A portion of the 1962 register for polling district N of the Millbank Ward of the Cities of London and Westminster constituency is reproduced in Figure 2.

Certain persons who would find it difficult or impossible to vote in person may claim the right to appoint a proxy or to vote by post. Proxies may be appointed by service

(Marsham Street, S.W.1)—*cont.*

3974	Mallalieu, Betty M.	42
3975	Mallalieu, Edward L.	42
3976	Chapman, Edward J.—J	43
3977	Y—Chapman, Jacqueline M.	43
3978	Chapman, José E.	43
3979	Vickers, Joan H.	44
3980	Thornehill, Freda G.	45
3981	Ells, Dagnall G.	46
3982	Ells, Joan	46
3983	Morrissey, Kathleen	46
3984	Owen, Grace	47
3985	Owen, Humphrey F.—J	47
3986	Hamlyn, Ralph A.	48
3987	Hillingdon, (Lady) Sarah	49
3988	L—Hillingdon, (Lord)	49
3989	Channing, Lily M.	50
3990	Foster, Edwin T.—J	50
3991	Hubbert, David	51
3992	Hubbert, Eleanor	51
3993	Cunningham, (Sir) John	52
3994	Hannay, Dorothy M.	52
3995	Foord, Dorothy M.	55
3996	Foord, Edward J.—J	55
3997	Foord, Edward S.	55
3998	Owen, Violet	55
3999	Neilson, Ethel C.	56
4000	Neilson, George C.	56

Figure 2

voters who are likely to be abroad or at sea on account of their employment on polling day. Application to appoint a proxy, must be made, on an appropriate form, at least twelve days before polling day. Two proxies are named on the form, the second of whom would be entitled to vote on behalf of the elector only if the first proxy indicates within five days of being approached by the Returning Officer that he is unable to act on behalf of the absent voter. A proxy records the vote at the same polling station at which the absent voter would otherwise be entitled to vote.

Postal votes may be claimed for an *indefinite period* by those unable, or likely to be unable, to go to vote in person, because of:

(1) The general nature of their employment, service or occupation (for example, long-distance lorry drivers and merchant seamen).
(2) Blindness or other physical incapacity (a doctor's signature is needed on the application form).
(3) No longer residing at the qualifying address (unless they still reside in the same borough, urban district or rural parish).
(4) Having to make a journey by sea or air.

In addition a postal vote may be claimed for a *particular election only*, by reason of:

(1) Service as a member of the Reserve or Auxiliary forces.
(2) Employment on date of Poll as a Constable, or by the Returning Officer.
(3) At a General Election being a candidate or a candidate's spouse in some other constituency.
(4) At a General Election being a Returning Officer, Deputy Returning Officer or Acting Returning Officer, or being employed by a Returning Officer, in some other constituency.

A service voter, even though he has appointed a proxy, may apply to vote by post, or may vote at his polling station personally if a ballot paper has not already been issued to his proxy.

Any proxy voter who himself falls into one of the above categories may apply to vote by post.

Applications for postal votes must be made, on the appropriate form, to the Returning Officer of the constituency at the latest by the twelfth day before the date of the poll. This is also the last day on which applications to cancel postal and proxy votes may be made. Applications by returning officers' staff and by constables may, however, be accepted by the Returning Officer even after the twelfth day. It is highly advisable, however, for people eligible to vote by post to make arrangements well in advance. Delay can be experienced in obtaining the appropriate form and, where necessary, getting it signed by a doctor, and at every election many voters who would be eligible find that they have left it too late to apply. The importance of the postal vote, especially in closely contested constituencies is touched on in Chapter 11, below.

In copies of the election register supplied to polling stations postal voters are marked in ink on the register with the letter 'A' and voters with proxies are marked 'B'.

An absent voters list, including the addresses to which postal voting forms must be sent, is compiled by the Returning Officer and is available for inspection at his office. A copy of the list is supplied free of charge, on request, to each candidate or his election agent.

Although considerable efforts are made by Registration Officers to ensure the accuracy of the election register, it is an imperfect instrument. It is already four months old when published and sixteen months old at the end of its life. Thus at all times large numbers of dead people are on the register while people who have moved are not registered in respect of their current address (probably only a minority of these apply for a postal vote or travel back to their previous neighbourhoods to register their votes on polling day).

Some years ago the Government Social Survey made a study of the accuracy of the election register. They found that when compiled it was 96 per cent accurate (i.e. 96 per cent of electors were registered in respect of the address in which they were actually living on the qualifying date). By the time the register was published it was only 94 per cent accurate. There was thereafter a cumulative loss of $\frac{1}{2}$ per cent per month, due to removals, until at the last month that the register was in force its degree of accuracy was only 87 per cent.

The 1948 Representation of the People Act provided for two registers to be compiled each year, but in 1949 as an economy measure the number was reduced to one. The apparent effect of this has been to disfranchise anything up to an additional 3 to 4 per cent of the population at any one time.

The total number of registered voters is now nearly 36 million, including nearly 300,000 Y voters and about 300,000 service voters. Over 31 million are in England and Wales, 3½ million are in Scotland and 900,000 in Northern Ireland. Almost 28 million, or 78·8 per cent, actually voted in the 1959 general election.

CHAPTER FOUR

CONSTITUENCIES

THE HOUSE OF COMMONS has at present 630 members, each of whom is the representative of a single member constituency. The origin of the different constituencies is diverse. Some constituency names, particularly those comprising medium-sized provincial towns, go back several hundred years, though the precise boundaries of the constituencies are unlikely not to have been altered at some time. The large majority of constituencies have in fact been delineated within the last fifteen years.

The basis of representation in the House of Commons was, with few exceptions, two members for each county and two for each borough from 1264 to 1832. No attempt, however, was made to ensure that members represented equal numbers of voters and enormous discrepancies in the size of constituencies had developed long before the 1832 Reform Act. Medieval boroughs which had declined almost to nothing retained their right to elect two members, while large cities, such as Manchester, Leeds, Sheffield and Birmingham, which had grown up during the seventeenth and eighteenth centuries, had no separate representation. It has been estimated that by 1832 the largest Parliamentary constituency had more than 100 times as many electors as the smallest. In 1832 and again in 1867 the worst anomalies were removed, but no systematic attempt was made to redraw the electoral map on the basis of approximately equal constituencies.

In 1885 a much more thorough redistribution was undertaken and the ratio between the largest and smallest constituency was reduced to 8:1. The Representation of the People Act of 1918 went one stage further and reduced the disparity to a maximum of 5:1. The 1885 Act also replaced the great majority of two-member constituencies with single member seats, though the last of the two-member constituencies did not disappear until 1950.

Although the principle of approximately equal constituencies had been accepted in 1918, no provision was made to correct anomalies caused by future movements of population. Thus by 1939, the rapid growth of suburban fringes to London and other major cities had produced a large number of constituencies with an excessive number of electors, while depopulation of city centres and of remote rural areas had left many other constituencies with tiny electorates.

The Speaker's Conference on Electoral Reform in 1944 recommended the establishment of permanent machinery for the redistribution of seats, so that major anomalies should not again arise. An Act of the same year established four Boundary Commissions, one each for England, Wales, Scotland and Northern Ireland which should make a general review of constituency boundaries at intervals of not less than three nor more than seven years. Each commission consists of three members and each is chaired by the Speaker of the House of Commons, though his role is largely nominal.

The first reports of the Commissions were, with one major amendment (mentioned below), approved by the House of Commons in 1948 and came into effect at the 1950 general election. They provided the first systematic delineation of constituencies which had ever been attempted, and of the 625 seats which made up the 1950 Parliament only 80 had retained their boundaries untouched.

In November 1954 the Commissions produced their second reports which came into force in time for the 1955 general election. The recommendations which they made were much less far-reaching than in 1948. Altogether, major alterations were suggested to 172 constituencies and minor alterations to 43, and the creation of five additional seats was recommended.

The proposals of the Commissions, and particularly

those of the English Commission were greeted with a storm
of protest. There was general agreement, with which the
Commissions themselves concurred, that if redistribution
had previously been too infrequent it now erred very
much on the other side.

Two groups of people were particularly incensed by the
effects of this second redistribution within barely five years
– Members of Parliament and active party workers in the
constituencies. MPs of all parties were agreed that the
normal hazards of political life were severe enough, without
adding the further hurdle of a fresh bout of redistribution
every five years or so. For a stiff hurdle it proved in a number of cases: safe seats were to become marginal or even
hopeless, and marginal seats might become safe for the
other side.

In 1950, of the seventy members who lost their seats at
least half could blame redistribution, partly or wholly for
their defeat. In 1955 at least eleven members were in the
same position. Sir Frank Soskice (Labour) and Sir Ralph
Assheton (Conservative) were double casualties, losing their
seats through redistribution on both occasions.

The inconvenience which redistribution brings to mem-
bers of local political organisations was well described by
Sir Kenneth Thompson, Conservative MP for Liverpool,
Walton, in a speech in the House of Commons on 15
December 1954. He said:

> We in the House are compelled to face the facts of political
> life. Political party organisation consists of the little constitu-
> ency club, a polling district committee, a ward organisation, a
> constituency organisation all pyramiding up from the modest
> humble, unobtrusive men and women who . . . do the slogging
> day-to-day work of a political party. . . . Every time a unit is
> taken from the electorate of a constituency, every time a
> boundary line is altered by however much or however little,
> some Mrs Jones is chivvied out of this organisation and hived
> off to what is to her a foreign land, where there are a lot of
> people who do not speak her language. At the whim – if that
> is not an offensive word – of the Boundary Commission, she is

expected to accept this as her lot and destiny and the pattern of her future political activity.[1]

The strong reaction to the 1955 redistribution led to amending legislation being passed by the House of Commons in 1958 which extended the period between general reviews of constituencies to a minimum of ten and a maximum of fifteen years. This means that the next general review will not be made before the end of 1964 nor later than the end of 1969. The power to make recommendations at any time to cover individual anomalies has been maintained.

The statutory rules under which the Commissions operate are few and simple. The total electorate is divided by the number of constituencies to secure an electoral quota, and the number of electors in each constituency should 'be as near to the quota as is practicable'. Boundaries of local government areas should be respected but may be crossed if necessary to avoid 'excessive disparities' from the quota. However, the Commissions might depart from the rules 'if special geographical conditions, including in particular the size, shape and accessibility of a constituency, appear to them to render a departure desirable'. The number of constituencies in Scotland and Wales must not be less than 71 and 35 respectively and in Great Britain not substantially greater or less than 613, while Northern Ireland is to have 12 seats.

This allocation gives more than their proportionate share of seats to Scotland and Wales, presumably as a sop to their national susceptibilities; conversely Northern Ireland has less than its proportionate share, because its domestic affairs are dealt with by the Northern Ireland Parliament at Stormont.

Of the 630 seats in the present Parliament 511 are in

1. Quoted by D. E. Butler in an article 'The Redistribution of Seats', *Public Administration*, Summer 1955, which is much the fullest account of the procedure and effects of redistribution yet to appear. See also *The Electoral System in Britain since 1918*, Oxford University Press, 1963, by the same author.

England, 36 in Wales, 71 in Scotland and 12 in Northern Ireland. At the 1959 general election the largest constituency Antrim South (in Northern Ireland) had an electorate of 93,634 – nearly four times as large as the smallest, the Western Isles (in Scotland) with an electorate of 25,178. However, all but 24 constituencies had electorates within the range of 35,000 to 75,000, the average constituency containing about 56,000 electors. No English constituency now has fewer than 35,000 electors.

The rapid growth of new towns and housing estates in recent years has led to a considerable expansion of the electorates of certain constituencies and this suggests that the English Boundary Commission may have to make interim recommendations to create a handful of extra seats before the next general review of constituencies. In 1955, for instance, no constituency outside Northern Ireland had more than 80,000 voters – by 1959 there were two and the 1962 register revealed four more and the prospect that several others would soon be in the same category, while several constituencies would before long expect to have more than 100,000 voters. At the same time the smallest seats were getting smaller and by 1961 Ross and Cromarty had replaced Western Isles as the smallest constituency.

Table 4—Changes in the electorate in certain large and small constituencies

	1955	1959	1962
Epping	68,184	83,647	90,996
Billericay	58,872	78,328	90,854
Hornchurch	77,041	87,544	90,024
Hitchin	62,258	75,493	83,787
Horsham	59,776	76,618	82,434
Arundel	69,034	75,601	81,168
Kettering	69,764	74,696	77,744
Merioneth	27,472	26,435	26,688
Orkney and Zetland	27,868	26,435	25,651
Western Isles	24,856	25,178	24,923
Ross and Cromarty	25,750	25,350	24,280

The political impartiality of the Boundary Commissions is unquestioned, but their work certainly has a considerable effect on the fortunes of the political parties and some of their decisions, and particularly those of the English Commission, have been the cause of fierce controversy.

Until 1948 there was an accidental pro-Labour bias in the electoral system. The effect of this was that the Labour Party needed to poll fewer votes than the Conservatives to secure any given number of seats in the House of Commons. Thus in the 1929 general election Labour polled 266,981 fewer votes than the Conservatives, but secured 28 more seats. As a result of the 1948 redistribution the pro-Labour bias disappeared and a similar bias in favour of the Conservatives has been introduced into the system. Accordingly, in the 1951 general election the Labour Party obtained over 200,000 more votes than the Conservatives, but had 26 fewer seats in the House, and the Conservatives were able to form the Government. This bias was not removed by the subsequent redistribution in 1954–5.

To some extent the anti-Labour bias is fortuitous, due to the heavy concentration of Labour voters in mining and other predominantly industrial areas, while the Conservative vote is more evenly spread out. This disadvantage has, however, been compounded by the action of the English Boundary Commission, which decided in 1948, without any statutory authority, to give preferential treatment to rural voters in comparison with urban on the grounds of the 'advantages of accessibility and convenience' enjoyed by the latter. This led them to recommend county constituencies with an average electorate of only 55,360 voters, while their recommended borough constituencies had an average electorate of 61,442.

When these recommendations were debated by the House of Commons Mr Attlee's government proposed the creation of seventeen extra borough seats, which lowered the average borough electorate to 57,833 – though this meant that borough constituencies still had over 2,000 more voters on average than county seats. In 1954–5 the

English Commission's report, approved *in toto* by the House of Commons, further widened this differential to nearly 4,000. As the Conservatives are stronger in rural areas and Labour in the towns this action of the English Boundary Commission, however well-intentioned, had unfortunate political effects. While there is a good case for a small number of thinly populated counties in North Wales and the North of Scotland to receive special treatment in order that the physical size of constituencies should not become so enormous as to make the task of representing them almost impossible, there is surely no justification for a general discrimination against the urban voter.

In fairness to the Commissions it must be said that the political effects of their recommendations cannot always be accurately predicted. In 1948 it was widely anticipated that the Conservatives would gain considerably from the proposed changes and this did indeed prove to be the case. In 1954-5 it was again anticipated that the Conservatives would benefit (and the late Aneurin Bevan accused them of gerrymandering; an accusation which Sir Winston Churchill had made against Labour, with even less justification, in 1948), but when the results of the 1955 general election were analysed it was apparent that the political effect of redistribution had been so negligible that it was impossible to determine which party had benefited.[1]

While detailed criticism can be made of the recommendations and procedures of the Boundary Commissions,[2] in general the difficult problem of delineating constituencies appears to have been solved more satisfactorily in Britain than in many other countries and accusations of gerrymandering are rare.

All Parliamentary constituencies are now territorial ones, though from 1603 to 1950 representatives of the Uni-

1. See *British General Election of 1955* by D. E. Butler, p. 157.
2. See in particular J. F. S. Ross, *Elections and Electors*, Eyre and Spottiswoode, 1955; and D. E. Butler, *The Electoral System in Britain since 1918*, op. cit.

versities (elected by post by graduates) sat in the House of Commons (and four representatives of the Queen's University, Belfast, still sit in the Northern Irish Parliament at Stormont). University representation was abolished in accordance with the principle 'One man, one vote' by the Labour Government of 1945–51. This step was opposed by the Conservative Party at the time and a pledge to restore the University seats was given by Sir Winston Churchill. When a Conservative government was elected, in 1951, however, no attempt was made to redeem that pledge, and two years later Sir Winston announced that the question was to be dropped.

The method of election within each constituency is the simplest ever devised. Each voter has one vote which he records by marking an X against the candidate of his choice on the ballot paper. The candidate who polls the largest number of votes in the constituency is elected, even if he is supported by only a minority of the voters.

Where three or more candidates are in the field this is of course quite a common occurrence, and in the 1959 general election 73 out of 630 Members were elected with a minority vote. In 1945 and 1950, when many more three- and four-cornered fights took place, 203 and 186 Members respectively were in the same position.

Where support for three candidates is very evenly balanced it is possible for a member to be elected with not much more than one-third of the votes, as happened in the Caithness and Sutherland constituency in 1945, when the result was as follows:

E. L. Gander Dower (Con.)	5,564	(33·47%)
R. McInnes (Lab.)	5,558	(33·43%)
Sir A. Sinclair (Lib.)	5,503	(33·10%)
Con. majority	6	

A more recent example was the South Dorset by-election in November 1962. Here the result was:

Guy Barnett (Lab.)	13,783	(33·5%)
Angus Maude (Con.)	13,079	(31·8%)
L. Norbury-Williams (Lib.)	8,910	(21·7%)
Sir Piers Debenham (Ind.)	5,057	(12·3%)
Paul Burn (Ex-serviceman)	181	
Michael Fudge (Ex-serviceman)	82	(0·7%)
J. C. O'Connor (Ex-serviceman)	45	
Lab. majority	704	

It is of course theoretically possible in multi-sided contests for a candidate to be elected with considerably less than one-third of the votes. This has, however, never happened, at least in modern times, though in a by-election for the former Combined English Universities constituency in 1947, contested by five candidates, the winning Conservative polled just over 30 per cent of the votes.

The combination of single-Member constituencies and a 'first past the post' method of voting leads to considerable discrepancies between the proportion of votes polled by parties and the number of seats which their candidates obtain in the House of Commons. Between the two larger parties this normally has the effect of exaggerating the majority obtained by the more successful and thus ensuring a larger majority for the government in the House of Commons than could mathematically be justified. The only recent occasions when this has not occurred were in 1950 and 1951 when, in closely contested elections, the bias against the Labour Party, described above on p. 36, offset the tendency of the system to favour the larger party. Had the Labour lead in votes been a little larger on these two occasions Labour would undoubtedly have benefited from this tendency. The proportions of votes and of seats won by the three main parties since 1945 are shown in Table 5.

It is clear from a glance at the Liberal performance that third parties are very much under-represented under present conditions. They are likely to remain so unless they poll at least 30 per cent of the total vote or their support is concentrated in regions or individual constituencies, instead of being fairly evenly distributed throughout the country as has been the case with the Liberals.

The apparent injustice of the system led to demands in the period between the First World War for the introduction of a system of proportional representation (or P.R.), as practised in a number of other countries. The only system which ever enjoyed much support among British opinion is that of

Table 5—Percentage of seats and votes won by the parties

| | 1945 | | 1950 | | 1951 | | 1955 | | 1959 | |
	votes	seats	votes	seats	votes	seats	votes	seats	votes	seats
Labour	48·1	62·2	46·1	50·4	48·8	47·2	46·4	44·0	43·8	40·9
Conservative	40·2	33·2	43·5	47·7	48·0	51·3	49·7	54·5	49·4	57·9
Liberal	9·0	1·9	9·1	1·4	2·5	1·0	2·7	1·0	5·9	1·0

the single transferable vote in multi-member constituencies (returning, say, three to seven members). Under this system, if in a six-member constituency the Conservative candidates polled half the votes, the Labour candidates a third and the Liberals a sixth the Conservatives would get three seats, Labour two and the Liberals one. Over the country as a whole this system would still tend to benefit large parties and penalise small ones, but to a lesser extent than does the present system.

Proportional representation was almost adopted in 1918, but support for it thereafter rapidly declined except, understandably, in the Liberal Party. Since the Second World War, however, the Liberals have tacitly conceded that they are unlikely to rally popular support for this measure and it is no longer a major item in their programme. Although various systems of P.R. work perfectly effectively in a number of countries (Ireland, West Germany, Sweden, etc.), it is extremely unlikely that it will ever be adopted in Britain where coalition government, which seems to be the inevitable concomitant of P.R., is heartily disliked in peace time. The truth is that only small parties, which are heavily penalised under the present system, are likely to favour P.R. If one of them became a large party, with the prospect of power, it would clearly be doing so well under the present system that it would be likely to lose its enthusiasm for change. This is, in effect, what actually happened in the case of the Labour Party which forty years ago tended to support P.R.

A less drastic reform of the voting system, the alternative vote, was actually approved by the House of Commons both in 1918 and 1931. This provided for single-member constituencies, but if the leading candidate polled only a minority of the votes the lowest candidate would drop out and his second preference votes would be transferred until the winner emerged with more than 50 per cent of the votes. But defeat of the measure in the Lords in 1931, followed by a change of government prevented it coming into force, and since then nothing further has been heard of this proposal.

Although in recent general elections every one of the 630 constituencies has been contested the real battle is invariably confined to a much smaller number of seats. More than half the seats are so securely held by one or the other party that their loss is almost inconceivable. The numbers of constituencies which actually change hands at each general election is small; in 1959 only 35 out of 630. Even in 1945, a 'landslide' year, only 227 seats changed hands out of 640, little more than a third.

This figure must represent virtually the maximum number of seats which are at all likely to change hands at any one general election. Far more frequently it is to be expected that less than 100 seats would change hands, but at most elections 100 gains for the opposition party would be more than enough to ensure victory. (Up to 1945, it was usual for a larger number of seats to change hands at general elections, but there are few signs of a return to such conditions.)

In practice, constituencies are regarded as falling into three categories: safe, hopeless and marginal. A safe seat held by one party is of course a hopeless seat for the other. Of the 630 seats in the present House of Commons about 400 may reasonably be regarded as safe for one side or the other. It is impossible to give the exact definition of a safe seat, but a reasonable working assumption is that any constituency with a majority of 6,000 or more is unlikely to change hands at a general election.[1] In the average size constituency the loss of such a majority would mean that more than seven voters out of every hundred had changed their minds in the same direction. Such a heavy turnover of votes is unusual in British conditions.

Of the remaining 230 or so constituencies with majorities of less than 6,000 about half are at present held by the Conservatives and half by the Labour Party. These are the marginal seats which are won or lost at general elections, and as the general trend in all constituencies is normally in the same direction it is singularly unlikely that more than half of these would in fact change hands at any particular general election. Given the small movement of opinion at the last three general elections, it is in fact only those with a majority of less than 3,000–4,000 which have appeared to be seriously marginal.

While the important contest in the great majority of constituencies has for the past forty years been between the Labour and Conservative candidates there are a few constituencies where this has not been the case. There have in recent general elections been not much more than a dozen constituencies in which Liberal Members have been elected or in which Liberal candidates have represented a strong challenge to the sitting member. There are also three constituencies in Northern Ireland which have been represented in recent Parliaments by Irish Nationalist

1 The only one to have done so since 1945 is Darlington, which had a Labour majority of 6,107 in a three-cornered fight in 1950 and which returned a Conservative with a majority of 813 in a straight fight in 1951. In by-elections more dramatic changes are liable to occur and in 1962 three constituencies with larger majorities than this changed hands – Orpington, Middlesbrough, West and South Dorset.

Members of one type or another. The other nine Northern Ireland constituences are safe Conservative seats, but in most of these too the main opposition is provided not by the Labour Party but by the Nationalists.

Nothing is static in British politics and over the years safe seats have become marginal and marginal ones safe. This is partly due to the movement of population, partly to the effect of redistribution and partly to changes in political opinion. Each new Parliament elected alters the status of different constituencies. In the 1959 general election the Conservatives made a net gain of twenty-three seats. But the effect on the electoral map was far greater than this. The great majority of safe Conservative seats became yet safer, some Conservative marginals moved into the safe category, some Labour marginals became Conservative marginals, hitherto safe Labour seats became marginal and safe Labour seats had reduced majorities. If Labour were to win the 1964 general election this whole pattern would be reversed.

CHAPTER FIVE

POLITICAL PARTIES – NATIONAL

ALTHOUGH THEIR existence is ignored in virtually all the laws and regulations governing the conduct of elections, it is the political parties which give them shape and purpose. The overwhelming majority of Parliamentary candidates are party adherents, and it is an exceptionally rare event for an independent candidate to secure election.

In this chapter and the next the organisation of each of the three major parties, together with that of minor parties who have put up candidates in recent general elections, is examined in some detail. Before discussing the individual parties it should be noted that there is a common pattern in the organisation of all three parties.

Each party is made up of three elements – the Parliamentary Party, comprising the MPs and peers who belong to the party concerned, the party bureaucracy and the mass membership throughout the country. The third element is discussed in Chapter VI, the first two are dealt with here.

Of these three elements it is the Parliamentary Party which is dominant in each party. This is explicitly recognised in the Conservative Party and also, though to a lesser degree, in the Liberal Party. In both these parties strong Parliamentary groups existed long before either a bureaucracy or a mass membership organisation was formed. The latter were set up, in the mid nineteenth century specifically to provide support for the Parliamentary party and to ensure the continued election of MPs representing the party concerned. In the Labour Party the mass organisation was set up first. In the early days of this century when there were only a few Labour MPs they were clearly subordinate to the extra-Parliamentary organisation of the party. But, at least from 1924 onwards, when the first

minority Labour government was formed, the Parliamentary Labour Party has secured for itself in practice, though
not formally, a dominance comparable to that of the
Parliamentary Conservative Party and superior to that of
the Parliamentary Liberal Party.

In all three parties then, it is the leader of the party in
the House of Commons who is recognised as the leader of
the whole party, even though the other elements in the
party have had no direct part in the election of the leader.
The members of the Parliamentary Party – full-time
professional politicians in daily contact with each other
for eight months of the year – have little difficulty in mono-
polising the most important policy decisions. This is less
true of the Labour Party, particularly when it is opposition,
but even here it is fair to say that it is only when there is a
crucial division within the Parliamentary Party that the
views of non-Members of Parliament, as expressed through
the Party Conference, begin to count and occasionally to
prevail.

The party bureaucracy in the Conservative Party is under
the direct control of the Leader. In the Labour and Liberal
parties it is responsible to the elected representatives of the
mass membership. Because many of these elected representatives are also Members of Parliament the Parliamentary Party exercises a considerable indirect influence
over the bureaucracy and clashes of interest are rare. It is
undoubtedly true that responsibility for the party machine
is much more widely diffused in the Labour and Liberal
parties, in practice as well as in theory, than in the Conservative Party.

The party bureaucracy consists of a headquarters in
London and a series of regional offices throughout the
country. The Conservative and Labour headquarters face
each other from different sides of Smith Square in Westminster – the Conservative headquarters is called the
Central Office, the Labour one Transport House. This is
actually the headquarters of the Transport and General
Workers' Union, the Labour Party being tenants of part of

the building. The Liberal Party headquarters is round the corner in Victoria Street, where they are tenants of numbers 54, 56 and 58. The nearness of all three headquarters to the House of Commons emphasises their close relationship to their respective Parliamentary parties.

The functions of the party bureaucracy are manifold. They are responsible for publishing a constant stream of pamphlets and leaflets for distribution through the constituency and local branches of the party. These range from the crudest propaganda handouts to sophisticated discussion pamphlets on policy, intended for the use of study groups within the party. Posters and other propaganda material are also produced in great quantities, and a steady supply of advice and information is supplied to constituency party secretaries who seldom experience a week without receiving at least one communication from head office.

Each party maintains a research department, one of the important functions of which, especially when the party is in opposition, is to brief its spokesmen in 'the House of Commons on the wide range of subjects on which they are called upon to speak. This department is also responsible for much of the material contained in the party publications, though it is the publicity department which actually prepares them.

An increasingly important function in recent years has been the supervision of the party television and radio broadcasts and both the Labour and Conservative parties maintain a mock television studio in which their MPs and prospective candidates can be put through their paces. The bureaucracy is also responsible for organising speaking tours by prominent MPs and supplying speakers on demand for a very large number of speaking engagements throughout the country, both at election time and between elections.

The organisation department, which is responsible for maintaining an efficient vote-winning machine throughout the country, is the least glamorous but perhaps the most essential section of the party headquarters. The organising staff, through its regional offices, keeps a fairly tight rein on the full-time constituency agents, although most of these are actually employed by the constituency parties. Not only is the organisation department concerned that the constituency and local parties should be in a constant state of readiness to fight elections, it is also responsible for ensuring that the selection of Parliamentary candidates should proceed according to the party rules. If there is any irregularity it is their function to bring the constituency party into line.

Other head office departments deal with such matters as local government, international and Commonwealth affairs (including relations with like-minded political parties in other countries), and the raising of funds.

Although each party headquarters undertake the same tasks, the efficiency with which they are performed varies considerably. The Conservative Party not only has a much larger staff, but because it pays considerably higher salaries is able to attract better qualified people to its employ and enjoys a far lower turnover of employees than the Labour Party. The Liberal Party's staff is substantially smaller than that of the Labour Party, but its salary scales are rather higher, though less than those of the Conservatives.

Table 6 shows how the size of the staff of the three parties varies and is a rough guide to the thoroughness with which they are able to perform their tasks.

Table 6—The Staffs of the Parties

	Conservatives Eng. and Wales		Labour Britain		Liberals Eng. and Wales	
	A	C	A	C	A	C
General HQ Staff	39	86	12	45	5	22
Agents						
National office	9	12	7	9	3	3
Regional offices	60	60	38	24	10	10
Constituencies	520	?	208*†	?	64*†	?
Research	25‡	17	12	6	4	3
Publicity	24†	28	9*†	5	3	2

* Plus part time volunteers   A = administrative
† Plus paid part time staff.   C = clerical
‡ Independent of general headquarters.

The maintenance of the party bureaucracy is an expensive business and the difference in the size of the staffs of the three parties is undoubtedly a direct reflection of their financial resources.

The most recently published balance sheet of the Labour Party shows the annual income for 1962 as £310,000. In the same year the Liberal Party income was some £74,000, an increase of nearly £30,000 over the previous year. The Conservative Party resolutely refuses to publish its accounts but its income clearly cannot be less than double that of the Labour Party and probably is many times larger.

The party bureaucracy is entrusted with the task of organising the annual Party Conference which provides the sole opportunity for the members of the mass organisation to give collective expression to their views. The three conferences are held in rapid succession, first Liberal, then Labour, then Conservative, in September and October each year at one of the small number of seaside resorts which have the facilities to house such a gathering. The most popular are Blackpool, Scarborough, Brighton and Llandudno. Each conference receives a report on the work of the party bureaucracy during the year and a Parliamentary report, and then proceeds to debate a large number of policy resolutions which have been sent in by constituency parties or, at the Labour conference, by trade unions.

The Conservative conference is a cumbrous affair with some 4,500 delegates and acts as little more than a party rally. It has no formal power to do more than proffer 'advice' to the Leader, and the number of occasions when it has had any apparent influence on party policy is extremely small. The Labour Party conference has about 1,200 delegates of whom perhaps 800 come from constituency parties, and the remainder from trade unions. As the constituency delegates represent less than one million members while the trade unionists represent over five million, the latter have a predominating influence on the voting, though spokesmen from the constituency parties enjoy the lion's share of the speech making. It is the Labour

Party conference which decides the policy of the party and especially the election programme on which it is to fight. Theoretically, therefore, its influence is immense. In practice, however, the Parliamentary leadership consistently enjoys the support of several of the larger trade unions and this normally guarantees it a majority at the conference. It is only when one or more of the normally 'loyalist' trade unions disagrees with the Parliamentary leadership, as happened on the issue of defence policy in 1960, that the leadership runs a serious risk of defeat.

The majority of delegates to a Labour Party conference undoubtedly sincerely believe that they are there to frame the policy of the party and the debates are vigorous and lively. And the great amount of time and trouble which both the Parliamentary leadership and many busy trade union leaders devote to the conference is strong evidence that its influence, though less than decisive, is far from negligible.

The Liberal Assembly has in theory considerably less power than the Labour Party Conference. However, the absence of a trade union block vote and the small number of Liberal MPs means that the Parliamentary leadership of the Liberal Party is in a far weaker position in relation to its party conference, and this undoubtedly increases the influence of the conference. Although on paper the Liberal Assembly has little more power than the Conservative conference, in practice its influence on its Parliamentary leadership is at least as strong as that of the Labour Party conference. When a party is in Government the power and prestige of Ministers inevitably detracts from the influence of the party conference; this is true of all parties.

The Conservative and Unionist Party is the oldest and most resilient of British parties. Its origins go back at least 300 years to Stuart times and the earlier name, Tory Party (still widely used by friends and foes alike), dates from 1679. 'Tory' was an Irish word meaning brigand, and it was applied to the King's supporters, who were supposedly willing to use Irish troops against Englishmen to enforce the succession of James II. Tories were supporters of the Crown and drew their support principally from the squirearchy and the clergy.

The name Conservative was adopted following the Reform Act of 1832. Some thirty years later, finding themselves in a permanent minority in the then politically dominant urban middle class, the party, under the inspiration of Benjamin Disraeli (later Lord Beaconsfield) set out to form the basis of a mass party. Local Conservative Associations were formed in many constituencies to secure the election of Conservative MPs. The 1867 Reform Act, which gave the vote to most of the urban working class, gave added impetus to this development and in the following three years the party took on substantially its present shape.

The Liberal Unionists, who broke away from the Liberal Party in 1885 because of their opposition to Irish Home Rule, finally amalgamated with the Conservative Party in 1912, hence its present unwieldy name.

Conservatives in Scotland and in Northern Ireland normally call themselves Unionists and Ulster Unionists respectively, but the term is infrequently used in England and Wales.

Three distinct elements make up the modern Conservative Party. The Parliamentary Party, the National Union and the Central Office. They are linked at the apex by the Leader, who enjoys very considerable formal power, much more than his Labour or Liberal counterparts. The most influential of the three elements is undoubtedly the Parliamentary Party, which is composed of all Members of Parliament who take the Conservative Whip. The management of the Parliamentary Party is the responsibility of the Chief Whip, who is appointed by the Leader of the Party.

From the Parliamentary Party and the Conservative Peers, the Leader chooses his Cabinet when a Conservative government is in power; when in opposition he appoints a 'shadow cabinet'.

The Parliamentary Party has a number of specialist committees on Defence, Foreign Affairs, Trade and

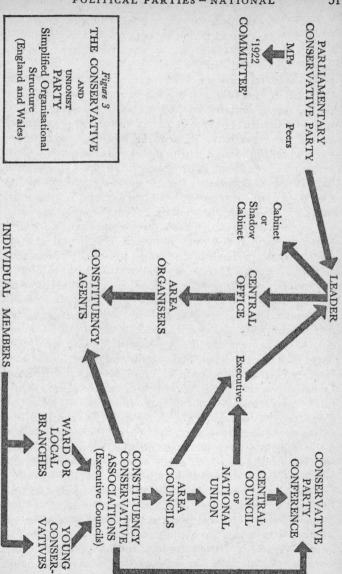

Figure 3
THE CONSERVATIVE
AND
UNIONIST
PARTY
Simplified Organisational
Structure
(England and Wales)

Industry, Agriculture, etc. When the Party is in opposition the committees are attended by both front and back bench Members, when in Government they are comprised entirely of back bench Members.

An unofficial body which wields considerable power is the '1922 Committee' (known as such because it was originally formed on the initiative of the back bench Members elected to the Parliament of 1922). This committee, known formally as the Conservative Members' Committee, meets every week while Parliament is sitting and consists, when a Conservative government is in power, of all the Conservative back bench Members. Its Chairman, who is elected by the Committee, is a prominent back bencher and his is a most influential voice in Party affairs. When Conservatives are in opposition the 1922 Committee comprises the entire Parliamentary Party, and the back bench influence is diluted by the presence of the leading front bench Members.

The National Union of Conservative and Unionist Associations, which dates from 1867, is the body representing the mass following of the Conservative Party throughout the country. It is a federation of constituency associations, and its annual conference is, in effect, the Annual Conference of the Conservative Party. Despite its name, it includes only Associations in constituencies in England, Wales and Northern Ireland; a parallel organisation, the Scottish Unionist Association, being responsible for Scotland.

The governing body of the National Union is the Central Council, a cumbrous body of some 3,000 members, on which every constituency has five representatives and which meets once a year in London. Its Executive Committee, with about 150 members meets about every two months, and is an important political body. Most of its more routine administrative work is normally delegated to its General Purposes Sub-Committee, which meets monthly.

The Executive of the National Union has a series of advisory committees on various aspects of organisation – local government, Parliamentary candidates, Young Conservatives, Women, etc. – and these committees are normally reproduced at Area and Constituency levels. The National Union has twelve Provincial Area Councils on which the constituency associations are directly represented and which meet once a year. The National Union is not responsible for organisation — its function is to act as a two-way channel of communication between the Leader, the Parliamentary Party and the rank and file members in the constituencies.

Organisation is the responsibility of the Central Office, which was established by Disraeli personally in 1870. Its direction has since remained firmly under the control of the Leader who appoints its Chairman[1] (normally a Cabinet Minister or leading Parliamentary figure) and other officers. The General Director of the Conservative Central Office, who is responsible to the Chairman and is, in effect, his full-time deputy, is also traditionally the Honorary Secretary of the National Union and the Central Office Agent in each of the Provincial Areas is also the Honorary Secretary of the Area Council of the National Union.

An unofficial body, the Bow Group (founded in 1957), and modelled, to a great extent, on the Fabian Society, does a great deal of independent research on policy matters. Although its members, who are all under thirty-five, are all Conservatives and it enjoys friendly relations with the Party organisation, it has no formal link with it.

The Leader of the Conservative Party is nominally elected by a meeting consisting of all the Conservative Members of the House of Commons and of the House of Lords, all prospective Parliamentary candidates and the Executive Committee of the National Union. In fact there has never been a contested election, the leadership being decided by a process of informal consultation between the leading Party figures in both Houses of Parliament and only one name is put before the meeting for formal endorsement.

When a Conservative Government is in power the Sovereign is normally advised to send for whoever is desig-

1 From April to October 1963 there were two joint-Chairmen — Mr Macleod and Lord Poole.

nated even before the meeting to elect the new Leader has been convened. On the resignation of Sir Anthony Eden in January 1957, the Queen was advised by Sir Winston Churchill and Lord Salisbury to send for Harold Macmillan, in preference to R. A. Butler, as the new Conservative Prime Minister. This process of involving the Sovereign in the selection of a political leader was widely criticised at the time, and some Conservatives felt that on future occasions their leader should be chosen by vote. Thus Mr Humphry Berkeley, MP, said on 3 July 1963: 'The most satisfactory way of electing a leader would be through a secret ballot of the Conservative MPs.' Lord Poole, the joint chairman of the Conservative Party, also expressed concern at this time about the adequacy of the traditional method of 'evolving' a leader. But no change was effected and when, in October 1963, Harold Macmillan announced his forthcoming resignation in the midst of the Conservative conference, ten days of the most intensive canvassing and speculation ever known in British politics ensued before the Queen, on the advice of the retiring Prime Minister, sent for the Earl of Home; the most fancied candidate, R. A. Butler, having again been passed over.

Although Lord Home was quickly accepted by the majority of the party the degree of dissatisfaction at the manner of his selection was far greater than ever before. As *The Economist* put it on 26 October 1963: 'the arguments for the Conservatives abandoning their secret processes, and resorting next time to some more open election of a leader are overwhelming'. Nothing has yet been done, however, to bring about a change in the traditional system. Once elected, the Leader has an enviable security of tenure. He is not required to submit himself for periodic re-election and remains in office until his death or resignation.

The Conservative Party has always been one of the two principal parties of the State. In the period from 1832 to 1916 Conservative and Liberal governments alternated in power, though the Liberals had the lion's share of office. Since then the Conservatives have been the normal

'Government Party' and have held power either separately or in coalition for all but nine of the last thirty-seven years.

The Conservative Party has not published membership figures for some years, but it is believed to have between two and three million members. It is organised in each of the 630 constituencies and normally nominates Parliamentary candidates for all but a handful of seats. In the 1959 general election there were 625 Conservative candidates, and in 1955, 623.

The National Liberal Party

In 1931 a group of twenty-five MPs split off from the Liberal Party and allied themselves to the Conservatives, adopting the title of Liberal National (changed to National Liberal in 1948). A Liberal National group continued to function in the House of Commons until the early 1950s, but it became less and less distinct from the Conservative Party. Although a handful of MPs and candidates still style themselves as Conservative and National Liberal, or in some similar manner, there is no discernible difference between them and 'ordinary' Conservatives.

The *Labour Party* differs from all others in possessing a large affiliated membership (mostly trade unionists) in addition to its individual members. In fact for the first eighteen years of its existence it was impossible to become an individual member of the Labour Party.

The Party was formed, under the title of the Labour Representation Committee, at a conference in London on 27 February 1900. The conference was convened by the Trades Union Congress, following a resolution passed at the TUC conference the previous year. It was attended by representatives of sixty-seven trade unions and three small socialist organisations (the Independent Labour Party, the Social Democratic Federation and the Fabian Society). The purpose of the organisation established at this meeting was to secure the representation of 'working-class opinion' in the House of Commons 'by men sympathetic with the aims and demands of the Labour movement'. In the early years the Labour Representation Committee (which became the Labour Party in 1906) did no more than co-ordinate the political activities of its affiliated organisations and all Labour candidates at that time were financially sponsored by one or other of these affiliates.

Success at first came slowly to the new party. Only two Labour MPs were elected in the 1900 election (one being J. Keir Hardie who had been the driving force behind the creation of the Party). But in the period from 1906 to 1923 the Labour Party progressively replaced the Liberals as one of the two principal parties, becoming the official Opposition in 1922 and forming its first (minority) government in 1924.

In 1918 the party adopted a new constitution which, with a number of subsequent amendments, is still in force today. This at last made provision for individual membership of the party and the creation of constituency Labour Parties throughout the country followed immediately after. The 1918 constitution also specifically committed the party for the first time to Socialist objectives.

The Parliamentary Labour Party is made up of Labour MPs and Peers, though the latter are few in number and wield little influence. Each year when Labour is in opposition it elects, by ballot, a Leader, Deputy Leader, Chief Whip, and a Parliamentary Committee (or Shadow Cabinet) of twelve members in the Commons and three in the Lords. Unlike in the Conservative Party, whenever a vacancy occurs for the leadership it is invariably contested. On the last occasion, in February 1963, Harold Wilson obtained 115 votes, George Brown 88 and James Callaghan 41, on the first ballot. As no candidate had obtained a clear majority, a second ballot was held between the two leading candidates, and Harold Wilson emerged as the leader by 144 votes to 103. Once a leader has been elected he may find, as did Clement Attlee (Leader from 1935 to 1955), that he is never challenged for re-election. On the other hand, Hugh Gaitskell (Leader from 1955 to 1963), was challenged

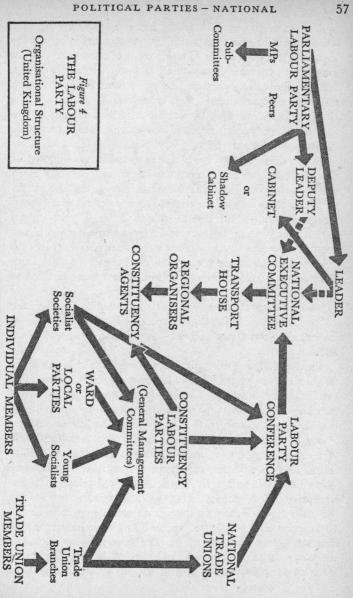

Figure 4
THE LABOUR PARTY
Organisational Structure
(United Kingdom)

both in 1960 and 1961. It is clear, therefore, that the Leader of the Labour Party enjoys less security of tenure, at least in theory, than his Conservative counterpart and his powers are certainly less. When in Government, however, Labour does not require its Leader or other officers to offer themselves for annual re-election and the Leader, as Prime Minister, appoints his own Cabinet. In Government, therefore, a Labour leader is no less clearly in command than his Conservative counterpart.

The leader of the Party is also, when in opposition, Chairman of the Parliamentary Party and presides at its weekly meetings. Policy and Parliamentary tactics are discussed at these meetings and are frequently put to the vote, which is binding on the Leader and the Parliamentary Committee. When Labour is in Government the Parliamentary Labour Party elects a back bench Member as Chairman and it comes to resemble more closely the Conservative 1922 Committee, though Ministers are entitled to attend and to vote, and frequently do so.

The party bureaucracy is not controlled, as in the case of the Conservative Party, by the Leader, but by a National Executive Committee elected by the Labour Party Conference.

This committee, normally known as the NEC, consists of 28 members of whom 26 are elected by the conference. The other two are the Leader and Deputy Leader of the Parliamentary Labour Party, and their ex-officio membership of the NEC is the only direct link which the Parliamentary Party has with the party organisation as a whole. Of the 26 elected members of the NEC, 12 are elected by the trade union delegates to the conference, 7 by the constituency party delegates and 1 by the delegates of socialist and co-operative organisations. Five women members and the Treasurer are elected by the whole conference, but as the trade unionists' votes predominate, the constituency party delegates have little influence on the election of these six members. In practice, a majority both of the seven constituency party representatives and the five women members have invariably been Members of Parliament.

The NEC, which normally meets monthly, appoints the General Secretary who is the chief official of the party and who is responsible to them for the running of Transport House and of the party machine in the country. The NEC and its various sub-committees are also responsible for making appointments to other senior posts in the party bureaucracy.

In 1962 the Labour Party had 768,000 individual members and 5,528,000 affiliated members. The latter belonged to 86 trade unions which had affiliated nationally to the Party, one Co-operative Society (the Royal Arsenal) and three small socialist organisations (the Fabian Society, the Jewish Socialist Labour Party (Paole Zion) and the Socialist Educational Association.)

Among the affiliated trade unions are the six largest unions – the Transport and General Workers' Union, the Amalgamated Engineering Union, the National Union of General and Municipal Workers, the National Union of Mineworkers, the Union of Shop, Distributive and Allied Workers and the National Union of Railwaymen, and most of the other larger unions representing manual workers. The most important unions not affiliated to the Labour Party all represent white collar or professional workers, e.g. the Civil Service unions and the National Union of Teachers. Some white collar unions, such as the Clerical and Administrative Workers' Union are, however, affiliated to the party.

The unions pay an affiliation fee of ninepence per member per year, the same sum as is paid to the national party by constituency Labour parties. As the affiliated membership is so much larger, however, the unions contribute by far the larger part of the party's funds at national level. The affiliation fees are not paid from the general funds of the union but, by law, must come out of a special political fund from which members may contract out if they do not wish to support the Labour Party financially. The political levy, as it is called, usually amounts to about fourpence a month and it is paid by just over four-fifths of the members of the affiliated trade unions.

The Fabian Society, which has been affiliated to the party from the beginning, is an independent socialist research organisation, whose principal function is the publication of books and pamphlets studying current political, economic, and social problems from a democratic socialist viewpoint. Although it is an affiliated body it expresses no collective viewpoint within the party and in practice its relationship to it is very similar to that of the Bow Group to the Conservative Party. The Fabian Society, founded in 1884, restricts its membership to those 'eligible for membership of the Labour Party'. This means, in effect, that non-members of the Labour Party may join, provided they are not members of other political parties.

Although it has been one of the two major parties since 1922, the Labour Party has hitherto been markedly less successful than the Conservatives in securing office. In 1945 Labour was returned with a large majority in the House of Commons and formed a government which continued in office, introducing major legislative changes in a great many fields until the general election of October 1951, though it lost most of its majority in the general election of February 1950.

Minority Labour governments were in power in 1924 and in 1929–31, dependent on Liberal support in the House of Commons. Labour Ministers also took part in the wartime coalition governments of 1916–18 and 1940–5. For all the rest of its life the Labour Party has been in opposition, and this factor is undoubtedly reflected in its constitution which, unlike that of the Conservatives, is more fitted to a party in opposition than in government.

The Labour Party normally contests every seat at general elections, except for a few county constituencies in Northern Ireland.

The *Co-operative Party*, founded in 1917, has been formally allied to the Labour Party since 1926. It has agreed not to put up candidates in opposition to Labour candidates and the only Co-operative nominees who are put forward are those selected by constituency Labour Parties as Labour candidates. They are normally designated as Co-operative and Labour candidates, but otherwise are indistinguishable from other Labour candidates. The Co-operative Party has branches in more than half the Parliamentary constituencies. Co-operative Societies with eleven million members are affiliated to the party, but it is doubtful whether it has more than 10,000 individual members. It sponsors its candidates financially in the same way as the trade unions (see Chapter VII). Its local branches are affiliated to constituency Labour parties, and it is financed more by contributions from the political funds of Co-operative Societies than by the subscriptions of its members.

In 1959 the Co-operative Party agreed with the Labour Party to limit the number of its sponsored candidates to thirty. The table below shows the number who have been nominated at recent general elections.

Table 7—Co-operative Party candidates

Year	Candidates	Elected
1945	33	23
1950	33	18
1951	37	16
1955	38	18
1959	30	16

The *Liberal Party* has roots which go back as far as those of the Conservatives. It grew out of the old Whig Party, which dated from the debates in 1679 over the attempted exclusion of the Duke of York, later James II, from the succession. The Whigs probably derived their name, which was at first meant contemptuously, from the Whiggamores, a body of Scottish Presbyterian insurgents who had marched on Edinburgh in 1648. The Whigs became identified as the party of those wishing to assert the authority of Parliament over that of the Sovereign and, later, as the advocates of Parliamentary reform through extension of the franchise.

In the years following the Reform Act of 1832 the new name of Liberal Party gradually replaced the old. Unlike 'Tory', the term 'Whig' passed completely out of common usage by the end of the century.

Under the leadership, successively of Palmerston and Gladstone, the Liberal Party dominated the Parliamentary scene during the greater part of the Victorian era. In 1886, however, it suffered a major setback through the defection of the Liberal Unionists over the issue of Irish Home Rule. In 1906 a Liberal government was elected with an immense majority, but during the next fifteen years the Liberals were replaced by the Labour Party as one of the two main parties, a process which was aided by a bitter division between the supporters of the last two Liberal Prime Ministers, Asquith and Lloyd George. The decline of the Liberal Party continued unabated until the early 1950s when it was reduced to a mere six seats in the House of Commons. Since then it has shown signs of revival and has substantially increased its vote at by-elections, though in 1963 it could still boast of no more than seven MPs.

The Liberal Party has a more complicated organisational structure than either of the two larger parties and many fairly senior members of the Liberal Party are often at a loss to describe it accurately. The Leader of the party is elected by the Liberal MPs and, as in the other parties, is recognised as leader of the whole party.

The extra-Parliamentary organisation of the party is known as the Liberal Party Organisation and it is run according to a constitution adopted in 1936.

At its apex is the Liberal Assembly, or party conference, which meets once a year and to which each constituency Liberal association sends delegates. The size of the Assembly has fluctuated with the fortunes of the Liberal Party but in recent years there have been about 800 delegates. The Assembly elects by ballot the officers of the party and its representatives on the Liberal Council. This body, with between 100 and 200 members, meets four times a year and is responsible for policy decisions between meetings of the

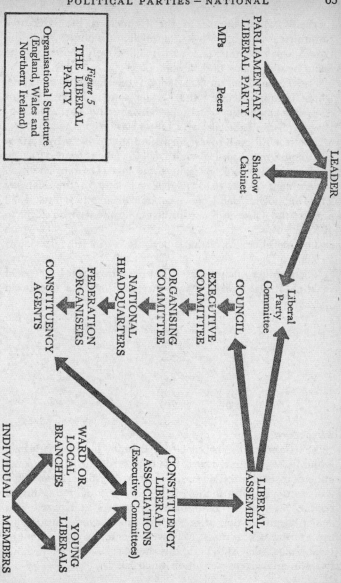

Figure 5
THE LIBERAL PARTY
Organisational Structure
(England, Wales and
Northern Ireland)

Assembly. Subordinate to the Council is the Executive Committee, of some 30–40 members, of whom 9 form the Organising Committee, which effectively controls the Party headquarters and bureaucracy.

The Council is represented on the Party Committee, which is appointed by the Leader and is responsible for co-ordinating policy decisions between the Parliamentary Party and the Liberal Party Organisation.

The last Liberal government, led successively by Campbell-Bannerman and Asquith, held office from 1910 to 1916. Liberals took part in the Lloyd George coalition government from 1916 to 1922, briefly in the Ramsay MacDonald national government from 1931 to 1932 and in the Churchill coalition government from 1939 to 1945.

The membership of the Liberal Party in June 1963 was 278,000.

The number of candidates that have been put in the field by the Liberal Party in post-war elections has fluctuated widely.

Table 8—Liberal Party candidates since 1945

Year	Candidates	Elected
1945	306	12
1950	475	9
1951	109	6
1955	110	6
1959	216	6

Minor parties

The *Communist Party* of Great Britain, founded in 1920, is the most prominent of the minor parties with a national following. It claimed a membership of 34,568 in June 1963, with some 1,200 branches. It employs about one hundred people either in its London headquarters at Kings Street near Covent Garden or on organisational work throughout the country. Communist MPs were elected to Parliament in 1922, 1924, 1935 and 1945, but the party has been without Parliamentary representation since 1950.

Table 9—Communist Party candidates since 1945

Year	Candidates	Elected
1945	21	2
1950	100	0
1951	10	0
1955	17	0
1959	18	0

The *Welsh Nationalist Party* (or Plaid Cymru), with headquarters in Cardiff, polled more votes than any other minor party in the 1959 general election, though it has never won a Parliamentary seat. Founded in 1925, its programme is self-government for Wales. It claims a membership of 15,000 of whom barely 2,500 are fully paid up. Its greatest strength lies in the Welsh-speaking areas of North and West Wales.

Table 10—Plaid Cymru candidates since 1945

Year	Candidates	Elected
1945	8	0
1950	7	0
1951	4	0
1955	11	0
1959	20	0

The *Scottish National Party*, whose headquarters are in Glasgow, was founded in 1928 with the aim of securing self-government for Scotland. Its only Parliamentary seat, Motherwell, won at a by-election in April 1945, was lost three months later in the 1945 general election. Its membership in August 1963 was 12,000, organised in about one hundred branches.

Table 11—Scottish National Party candidates since 1945

Year	Candidates	Elected
1945	8	0
1950	4	0
1951	1	0
1955	2	0
1959	5	0

The *Sinn Fein*, the political branch of the now disbanded terrorist organisation, the Irish Republican Army, was founded during the First World War. In the 1918 general election it won 69 out of the 103 Irish seats which it contested. Since the establishment of Northern Ireland, it won one Parliamentary constituency in 1922 and 1923 and then seemed to have passed into history. In 1955 and 1959 it reappeared, however, and contested all twelve seats in Northern Ireland mostly nominating convicted terrorists as its candidates. Two were elected in 1955 but were later disqualified as felons (see p. 84, below). It draws its support from strongly Roman Catholic areas.

Various other *Irish Nationalist* candidates have contested Northern Irish seats, and from 1922 to 1955 between one and three constituencies were continuously represented by Irish Nationalist Members, who usually refused to take their seats in the House of Commons.

The *Independent Labour Party* (ILP) was formed in 1893 and was one of the founding bodies which established the Labour Party in 1900. It remained affiliated to the Labour Party until 1932 and, at its peak in 1929, had thirty-seven Members of Parliament. Since 1932 its membership has declined to a few hundred and the only area in which it has retained much support has been in Glasgow, where it continued to be represented in Parliament until 1950. The ILP's policy is strongly internationalist and, though anti-Communist, it is well to the left of the Labour Party.

Table 12—ILP candidates since 1945

Year	Candidates	Elected
1945	5	3
1950	3	0
1951	3	0
1955	2	0
1959	2	0

The *Union Movement* of Sir Oswald Mosley was founded in 1948 as the successor to his previous British Union of Fascists. The party contested one constituency in 1959.

A wide variety of *Independent* candidates, often wearing bizarre labels, offer themselves at each general election and at occasional by-elections. In 1955 there were 23 independent candidates and in 1959, 17. Few independent candidates poll more than a few hundred votes, except when one or other of the two major parties does not contest the constituency (a rare event). The only independents who have been elected since 1945 have been returned with the, more or less, open support of the Conservative Party. Thus, Sir David Robertson, a former Conservative MP for the same constituency, was elected for Caithness and Sutherland in 1959 and Mr G. Forrest, who later took the Conservative whip, was elected for Mid-Ulster in a by-election in 1956. The only other Members to be elected since 1945 without being official party nominees were the Speakers of the House of Commons who, in 1950 and 1955, were elected without opposition from the political parties in the constituencies which they had formerly represented as Conservatives.

CHAPTER SIX

POLITICAL PARTIES – LOCAL

THE NATIONAL organisation of the political parties monopolise publicity in the press and on radio and television, but it is the local branches with which the voter is likely to come into contact.

Both the Conservative and Labour parties have branches in each of the 630 constituencies (although the Labour Party may have no effective organisation in a few of the county constituencies in Northern Ireland). The Liberal Party's coverage is less comprehensive, but in July 1963 it had some sort of organisation in 475 constituencies.

A constituency party (or association as it is called by Conservatives and Liberals) is not normally the nearest the parties get to the grass roots. Local branches are organised at ward level in towns and cities and in villages and small towns in country areas. Here, however, the two main parties' coverage is less complete. In hopeless constituencies in industrial towns, and especially in mining areas, there are some constituencies where the Conservative ward organisation is rudimentary or non-existent. In the counties too, there are many villages and small towns without any Labour organisation. Liberal organisation below constituency level is extremely patchy. In some constituencies they match or even better the coverage of the larger parties. In probably a majority of constituencies, however, there is no Liberal organisation below constituency level.

It is the ward or local party, at least in the Conservative and Labour parties, which is the basic level of party organisation. The ward party is the actual unit to which party members belong; it is responsible for recruiting new members and collecting subscriptions and for the great majority of party members it is the only organ of the party with which they have any contact.

The typical ward or village party meets every month, usually in the house of one of its members, sometimes in a hired school room or village hall, occasionally on party premises. The number of members varies enormously, both according to the size of the electorate in the area covered (which will range from a tiny village to a large ward in a city with anything up to fifteen to twenty thousand electors) and the strength of the party in the area. In practice, the membership is unlikely to be less than half a dozen nor more than 1,500. The great majority of members do no more than pay their subscriptions to the party, when they are called on at their homes. The attendance at most ward or local party meetings is likely to range between six and forty, averaging between 5 and 20 per cent of the members in most towns, though in country areas the percentage attendance is likely to be considerably higher.

The minimum subscription to each of the parties is small and has not changed since pre-war days. The Labour Party asks for six shillings a year from its members and the Liberals five shillings, while Conservatives are let off lightest of all. Their minimum subscription is two shillings and six pence. The subscription to the Conservative and Liberal parties is normally collected by an annual visit to the member's home. In most areas the Labour Party made arrangements, in the past, for the monthly or even weekly collection of smaller amounts. With the fall in the value of money, however, such arrangements are now an exception. Most Labour members now subscribe quarterly or half-yearly, while an increasing proportion make a single annual payment. The collection of subscriptions is mainly carried out on a voluntary basis by keen party members, though all three parties resort in many areas to paid collectors who may also receive a percentage of the amount that they collect. There is a great deal of inefficiency in the machinery for collecting subscriptions and it is apparent that each party loses a substantial amount each year because of this. It has, for instance, been estimated that, of the Labour minimum subscription of six shillings, no more than four shillings and sixpence is, on average, collected. Many branches with a potentially larger membership refrain from attempting to recruit new members because of a lack of volunteers to act as collectors.

The minority of party members who attend the monthly meeting of the party often find only a small part of its agenda is devoted to political matters. Many ward meetings, particularly in the Labour Party, have a speaker to address them on a subject of national importance and there may be a resolution to discuss on the social services or a foreign policy issue. It is equally likely, however, that the agenda will consist almost exclusively of administrative matters, particularly those concerned with fund raising. It is not unusual for a local party to spend more time discussing who is to look after the sweet stall at the party's jumble sale than it devotes to considering possible resolutions for the annual conference of the party. It follows from this that local party branches are as much social as political affairs and the sense of comradeship at this, the lowest level of party politics, is strong.

In areas in which parties are not strong, local and ward parties often have an ephemeral existence depending for their existence primarily on the enthusiasm of one or two members who provide the impetus for the others. A loss of interest on the part of one or two individuals, or their removal from the neighbourhood, may cause the branch to collapse altogether and go out of existence. Then, after an interval of perhaps several years, an enthusiastic newcomer will start things up again and with the aid of old and un-reliable records will call on long dormant members and try to rekindle their interest.

Even in areas in which a party is strong its local branches will not necessarily be flourishing. The absence of challenge from the other side may breed apathy and the party organisation, however strong on paper, may be sickly and lethargic. It is in marginal constituencies, where there is a constant electoral challenge, that the local parties on both sides are most likely to be large and active organisations.

There is a wide variation in the nature and circumstances of local branches. Differences within each of the three main parties are often greater than those between them. At this, the lowest level of organisation, the procedures and functions of branches of all political parties are very similar, so much so that there is no need here to distinguish between them. The only consistent difference is that there is less political discussion in Conservative than in Labour or Liberal branches, but even to this general rule there are manifold exceptions.

Depending on its strength and its circumstances, a local branch will have a number of officials. The minimum is normally a Chairman, Honorary Secretary, and Honorary Treasurer, though in very small branches even these offices might be doubled up. There are normally also one or more Vice-Chairmen and a number of other functional offices, of which Canvassing Officer, Social Secretary, Membership Officer, Literature Secretary, and Raffle Officer or Tote Organiser are most common. There may also be an assistant secretary and, in the case of the larger and more active branches, an executive committee whose membership would include most or all of the officers listed above.

The most active members of the branch will also be delegates to the managing body of the constituency party, known as the Executive Council in the Conservative Party, the General Management Committee (GMC) in the Labour Party and the Executive Committee in the Liberal Party.

It is this body which contains the hard core of militants, usually of between twenty and one hundred attending members (though the nominal membership may be higher), who keep the wheels of the party organisation turning throughout the country. At this level there is a notable difference between the parties. The managing body of a Conservative or Liberal constituency association will contain, in addition to representatives of ward and local branches, delegates from women's organisations and of the Young Conservatives and Young Liberals respectively. A Labour GMC similarly contains representatives from wards, Young

Socialists and Women's Sections but will also include delegates from affiliated organisations – trade unions, co-operative organisations and, perhaps, a local Fabian Society. For every individual member of the Labour Party there are five affiliated members and the nominal membership of a great many GMCs is made up predominantly of the delegates from affiliated bodies. Many of these are inactive, and it is very rare for there to be a majority of delegates of affiliated organisations among those actually attending. On special occasions, such as the selection of a Parliamentary candidate, however, it sometimes happens that a meeting of a GMC is crowded out by an influx of unfamiliar delegates who may never appear again.

The governing bodies of constituency parties are important and influential organisations. They are responsible for fighting elections, both Parliamentary and local government, and for all practical purposes are the voice of the national party within their own areas.

Most of them meet monthly and, as in the case of local branches, much of their time is devoted to discussing financial and administrative matters. Constituency Labour parties, particularly those which are strongly left wing, frequently pass resolutions of a political nature, which are sent to Transport House for consideration by the National Executive Committee. Protests at the actions or omissions of the party leadership or of Transport House officials are also frequently registered, with little apparent effect. Liberal and Conservative associations make their views known to their respective head offices with far less frequency.

Constituency parties elect delegates to the annual party conference, who may or may not be instructed on how to cast their votes on the most controversial issues to be debated at the conference. It is usual for each constituency party to send one resolution to the annual conference, though here again the right is more often asserted by Labour parties than by Liberal or Conservative associations. The most important *political* act of constituency parties is undoubtedly, however, the selection of Parliamentary candidates. This is discussed in detail in Chapter VII.

The ward and local parties are, in most respects, definitely subordinate to the constituency parties. Each constituency party has a full panoply of officers – Chairman, Vice-Chairman, Honorary Treasurer, Secretary, Assistant Secretary, and numerous other people designated to do specific tasks. In the Conservative and Labour parties, sub-committees of the constituency party's governing body, known respectively as the Finance and General Purposes Committee (Conservative) and the Executive Committee (Labour) are responsible for the day-to-day running of the constituency party. Conservative constituency organisations normally have several other standing sub-committees and make provision for both Young Conservatives and women members to be largely represented on all organs of the party.

The principal function of constituency parties is to maintain an electoral organisation in a constant state of readiness. Constituency parties able to maintain a full-time agent find this a much more manageable task. The Conservatives are much better placed in this respect. In the summer of 1963 they employed 520 agents in England and Wales alone, some of whom were responsible for one constituency only and the rest shared responsibility for two, three or four neighbouring constituencies. At the same time the Labour Party had 208 agents in the field and the Liberals about 70, in the whole of Great Britain. The Conservative and Labour figures have remained constant for about a decade, but the Liberals have achieved a threefold increase since 1959.

Most agents earn between £600 and £1,300 a year, the rate of pay in the Conservative Party being higher than in the Labour and Liberal parties. It is the two latter, however, that experience the greatest difficulty in paying their agents' salaries, and many Labour and Liberal agents spend a great deal more of their time running money-raising schemes, the main purpose of which is to meet their own salaries. They then have little time left over for organising work. The headquarters of the Conservative and Labour

parties have a limited amount of money at their disposal to
help constituency parties to employ agents. Their money
is channelled into the marginal constituencies: other constituency parties wishing to employ an agent are expected
to pay their own way.

Full-time agents normally act as secretaries to the constituency parties which employ them.

The activities of constituency parties between elections
are varied. Among the most important are to keep the name
and activities of its Member of Parliament or prospective
Parliamentary candidate continually in the public eye.
(Candidates are invariably known as *prospective* candidates
in the period until the general election campaign begins.
Otherwise money spent on the candidate's activities
between elections might be legally chargeable to his election expenses, which are restricted by law. See Chapter
XII.)

The traditional method of doing this is the public meeting. With the spread of television and other mass media
interest in public meetings has declined in the post-war
period, though there is some recent evidence that it is now
increasing. Nevertheless, few constituency parties in borough
constituencies now organise more than four public meetings
a year and many do far less. The meetings, normally
addressed by the MP or prospective candidate and two or
three other speakers, are publicised through posters, local
newspaper advertisements and by the delivery of leaflets.
When one of the speakers is a nationally known figure
considerable extra effort may be put into planning the
meeting. In some areas a great deal of apathy is encountered
and the hard core of active party members will make up
by far the greater part of the audience. In other areas
good attendances are obtained, and lively meetings may
be expected if 'the opposition' turns up to have its say. It
seems likely that many constituency parties take an unduly
defeatist view of the public demand for meetings and that
if they took the trouble to organise them well, to obtain
competent and varied speakers and to publicise them widely

and in good time, they would get better attendances than they imagine.

Most Members of Parliament and some prospective candidates hold regular 'surgeries' to which their constituents may come with their personal problems. Pensions and housing are the subjects which recur most frequently, but an extremely wide range of problems are referred to MPs for their help and advice. Often it is a question of referring the constituent to the proper authority – the National Assistance Board, the Housing Department of the local Council or the Public Health authority. Sometimes, however, a Member can be of direct assistance by taking up a case personally with a Minister or asking a question in Parliament. This 'welfare work' of MPs is one of their most important activities and it consumes an increasing proportion of their time and energies. In so far as Members of Parliament have a personal vote, it is more likely to be built up laboriously over the years through diligent application to the personal problems of constituents than by any more flamboyant action or gesture.

The agent or secretary will always be on the look out for other ways of pushing his MP or prospective candidate into the limelight. If a local organisation – a church or youth club, a dramatic society, a rotary club or any one of a hundred others – wants somebody to open a bazaar, distribute prizes or make a speech (quite often on a non-political subject) he has just the man for the job. The value of such assignments for prospective candidates lies at least as much in the report which will follow in the local newspaper as in the activity itself.

Most constituency parties organise membership drives from time to time in which their members call from house to house, usually in what are regarded as favourable areas, trying to persuade people to join. Little time is normally wasted on attempting to convert 'hostile' elements, but any one who shows interest will be carefully fostered. In such cases a further visit by the Parliamentary candidate or party secretary may well be arranged.

A different sort of canvassing is designed to provide a reliable record of the voting intentions of the electorate. The purpose is to obtain a 'marked register', so that the party has a good idea of where its support lies when the election is due. Copies of the election register are cut up and stuck on hard boards – and party members are asked to mark 'F', 'A' or 'D' against the name of each voter after calling at their houses. These abbreviations stand for 'For', 'Against' and 'Doubtful'. The proceedings at each house are crisp and seldom long prolonged. Most canvassers adopt an apologetic stance and mumble something along these lines: 'Good evening, Mrs Jones? I'm calling on behalf of the . . . Party. We wonder whether we can rely on your support at the next election.'

The response to this enquiry is varied, but rudeness is extremely rare. 'Yes, you can depend on us' or 'We always vote on the day' are likely rejoinders from party supporters. 'I'm afraid we're on the other side' or 'You've called at the wrong house, old chap' are the limits to the hostility which the average canvasser can expect to encounter. There *are* voters who will say: 'If I had a hundred votes I wouldn't give one to your lot' or even 'If you come this way again I'll set my dog on you', but they are few and far between.

A subsidiary object of house-to-house canvassing is to discover invalids and other people who would be eligible for postal votes, so that they may be helped to claim them. Relatively few voters take this initiative themselves, without prompting from their party. The party which organises the largest number of postal votes in a marginal constituency may find that this has made all the difference between victory and defeat. There is no doubt that the Conservatives are more alive than the other parties to the need to build up a large postal vote and that they have hitherto enjoyed much greater success in this sphere.

Elections to local authorities absorb a great deal of the time and money of many constituency parties. Outside London they take place every year in May, with county council elections every three years in March. In London the local authority elections are also once every three years. Local elections help parties to keep their electoral organisation in a state of readiness for the general election and the canvassing results help the party to maintain an up-to-date 'marked register'.

It can happen, however, that excessive preoccupation with local government matters can hinder a constituency party's ability to fight an effective general election campaign. The more able members may have become aldermen or councillors and may devote so much time to council affairs that they have little to spare for the party. If the party controls the town council, unpopular decisions by the council, such as raising council house rents, may adversely affect the party's electoral appeal at a Parliamentary election.

The ownership or tenancy of premises can have a similarly two-edged effect on a constituency party. Parties employing a full-time agent obviously need premises to provide an office in which he can work and to store the party records. It is a great advantage, too, to have a hall in which to hold meetings and to use as committee rooms at election time. And a permanent headquarters acts as a focus for a wide variety of party activities. There is danger, however, that if the premises are used extensively for social activities the political work of the party will suffer. In such circumstances the premises may be a heavy drain on the party's funds without producing any equivalent benefit to its electoral prospects.

Money raising is a perennial problem for constituency parties. Few of them derive sufficient income from subscriptions and donations to meet even their most essential commitments. The gap is met in nine cases out of ten by appeals to the gambling instinct. There are a few parties, where the Nonconformist conscience is strong, which succeed in rising above such expedients. But the Colne Valley Labour Party, which raises £500 a year through a gift day, run along the lines of a Church Harvest Festival, is all but unique. In all three major parties it is normally the raffle or whist drive, the bingo session, the football pool or tote scheme which keeps the local branches solvent. The income which constituency parties derive from such sources varies from a few pounds to about £10,000 per annum. The latter amount is rarely reached but a large number of parties make between £500 and £2,000 out of their fund-raising schemes.

There is no published information about the funds of constituency parties, but seventy different parties sent their balance sheets for the year 1962–3 to the present author in response to an enquiry which he made while compiling this book. This enquiry revealed an average income for Conservative associations of £3,100, for Labour parties of £2,000 and for Liberal associations of £690. It seems likely that the figure for the income of Conservative associations revealed by this sample is rather on the low side.

An indication of the main sources of income and expenditure of a moderately prosperous constituency party is given by the following imaginary income and expenditure account:

Expenditure	£	*Income*	£
Agent's salary	800	Subscriptions	450
Clerical help	300	Football competition	1,200
Agent's expenses	200	Dances	125
Rent and office charges	200	Bazaar	180
Postage, telephone	125	Derby draw	200
Stationery	100	Financial appeal	80
Publications	75	Miscellaneous	65
Subscription to Head Office	100		
Depreciation of Equipment	50		
Local elections	100		
General Election fighting fund	170		
Miscellaneous	80		
TOTAL	£2,300	TOTAL	£2,300

Each of the parties has youth organisations which are made up of branches formed on a constituency basis or to cover a smaller area within a constituency. The branches are represented on the governing bodies of constituency parties.

The Young Conservatives, with some 120,000 members in 1,600 branches, are much the largest and most powerful of the three organisations. Many of the branches are primarily social organisations but Young Conservatives, particularly in suburban areas, provide much of the manpower for canvassing teams and other electoral activities. There is no doubt that they represent a valuable asset to the Conservative Party.

The Young Socialists have about 22,000 members in 760 branches. More political than their Conservative counterparts, they often embarrass the Labour Party by embracing policies well to the left of the leadership. Many branches play an important part in the party organisation, particularly at election times, but overall the Young Socialists have undoubtedly proved less of an asset to their party than have the Young Conservatives to theirs.

The Young Liberals have rather less than 15,000 members in about 500 branches. If allowance is made for their smaller membership, their contribution to the work of the Liberal Party is very comparable to that of the Young Socialists to Labour.

CHAPTER SEVEN

CANDIDATES

WHO IS ELIGIBLE

NO SPECIAL qualifications whatever are legally required of Parliamentary candidates; the only positive requirements are those which also apply to voters – that is, to be a British or Commonwealth subject or a citizen of the Republic of Ireland, and to have reached the age of twenty-one. It is not even necessary to be on the election register, and 'Y' voters may be candidates before they have qualified to vote providing they have passed their twenty-first birthday.

There are, however, a number of disqualifications which together exclude a large number of people from being elected. People in the following categories are disqualified:

Peers. English and Scottish peers, unless they have renounced their peerage during their lifetime. Irish peers are not disqualified.

Clergy. Clergy of the Church of England or the Church of Ireland, Ministers of the Church of Scotland and Roman Catholic priests. Clergy of the Church of Wales and nonconformist ministers are not disqualified.

Aliens, but those who have acquired British citizenship through naturalisation are eligible, as are citizens of Commonwealth countries.

Members of Legislatures outside the Commonwealth. These would normally be excluded as aliens, but the effect of this provision is to disqualify the exceptional case of people with dual nationality and members of the Seanad and Dáil of the Republic of Ireland.

Certified Lunatics.

Bankrupts. Undischarged bankrupts are disqualified from six months after the date of adjudication and remain so until either the bankruptcy is annulled or a grant of discharge is awarded, accompanied by a certificate that the bankruptcy was not due to misconduct.

Felony. Following conviction, felons are disqualified and remain so until they have served their sentence or received a free pardon.

Corrupt and illegal practices at elections. Persons convicted of such practices may be disqualified for varying periods (see Appendix 7).

Much the largest number of people disqualified from membership of the House of Commons, however, are those who hold *offices of profit under the Crown*. This includes sheriffs, judges, civil servants and a very wide and varied list of office-holders, many of whom receive only nominal remuneration for their services.

Before 1957 there was an immense degree of confusion as to what actually constituted an office of profit. Members elected to the House of Commons who performed public service, such as membership of Rent Tribunals, found to their dismay and astonishment that they were disqualified from membership of the House and liable to pay extremely high monetary penalties (£500 per day) for sitting and voting in the House. Ten members found themselves in this position between 1945 and 1955, and in nine cases the House passed emergency legislation to validate their position. In the other case, Mr C. Beattie, the member for Mid-Ulster in 1955, had to vacate his seat and a by-election was held to replace him.

The confusion which existed before 1957 was due to the fact that the different disqualifying offices had resulted from over 100 Acts of Parliament enacted over a period of 250 years and there was no list of these offices to which would-be candidates could refer to see whether they were disqualified. The position was clarified, however, by the 1957 House of Commons Disqualification Act which contained two schedules one listing specific offices which do disqualify, the other listing those which do not.

It is highly advisable for all would-be candidates to

study these lists before accepting nomination – as there is now little excuse for candidates who transgress through ignorance.

It should perhaps be added that though civil servants are disqualified from membership of the House of Commons, schoolteachers, employees of nationalised industries and local government employees are all eligible.

Armed Forces. The final category of people disqualified from membership of Parliament are members of the armed forces. It has, however, been normal for a serviceman seeking nomination to be discharged. In 1962, an ingenious soldier, Malcolm Thompson, who had been refused a discharge in order to enrol as a university student, offered himself as an independent candidate at a by-election at Middlesbrough West and consequently secured his demobilisation. Later the same year twelve more servicemen followed his example, several of them discovering that they did not even have to be nominated (and thus have to pay a deposit of £150) to secure their discharge; it was sufficient just to apply for nomination papers.

By the end of the year, when further by-elections were expected at Colne Valley and Rotherham, it appeared that the trickle of servicemen using this means to obtain a cheap and easy discharge was threatening to become a flood. No less than 174 requests were received for nomination papers at Colne Valley and 493 at Rotherham. A Select Committee of the House of Commons reported that the problem was a most complex one and that it would take much care and thought to devise a permanent solution. As a temporary expedient, to meet the need to proceed with the by-elections already pending, it recommended the appointment of a small advisory committee which would vet applications by servicemen wishing to be candidates and would advise the appropriate service Ministers whether to grant a discharge.

This recommendation was approved by the House of Commons in February 1963 and a committee consisting of two Queen's Counsel and six former MPs was appointed by the Home Secretary. Its function was to examine the application of each would-be candidate (who would normally be personally interviewed by the Committee) and decide whether he had genuine Parliamentary ambitions. The unsatisfactory nature of this expedient was soon apparent. Of the twenty-six servicemen who actually applied to the Committee in connection with the Colne Valley and Rotherham by-elections only one was recommended for discharge. But as soon as he had secured his demobilisation he announced that he had changed his mind and did not offer himself as candidate.

Since then there have been only a handful of applicants, but at a general election with 630 seats to be filled it might prove extremely difficult for the committee to function properly if there were a large number of applicants. It is therefore highly desirable that a more satisfactory permanent procedure for dealing with this knotty problem should be devised before the next general election takes place. However, in July 1963, the Select Committee reported that it was still unable to suggest a permanent solution to the problem and recommended that the advisory committee should continue to function.

Although all the above categories disqualify from membership of the House of Commons, there is in practice no means of preventing a disqualified person presenting himself as a candidate. The responsibility of a returning officer in vetting a nomination is confined to ascertaining that the nomination form has been properly filled in and signed by the requisite number of electors. He is not required to satisfy himself that the candidate is not a disqualified person.

In practice, no political party would normally agree to support a candidate known to be disqualified,[1] and few disqualified people would consent to nomination. Occasionally, however, such a candidate is nominated as a gesture. Thus in 1955 and 1959, as also on earlier occasions,

1. Though the Rev. R. C. Gaul, a clergyman of the Church of England, was nominated as a Liberal candidate at Louth in 1951 and at Grantham in 1955.

several candidates serving prison sentences were nominated by Sinn Fein in Northern Ireland constituencies. In 1955 two of them were elected, Mr Thomas Mitchell for Mid-Ulster and Mr P. Clarke for Fermanagh and South Tyrone. In 1961 Mr Anthony Wedgwood Benn (the former Lord Stansgate) successfully contested a by-election in his constituency of Bristol South-East, although disqualified at that time as a peer.

In the event of a disqualified person being elected, it is open to his defeated opponent to apply to the Judicial Committee of the Privy Council to have his election declared void. When this has occurred, the Committee has held that if the facts leading to the disqualification had been generally known to the electors, those who have voted for the disqualified candidate should be deemed to have thrown their votes away, and the runner-up has been declared elected in his place. This indeed happened in the cases of both Mr Clarke and Mr Wedgwood Benn. In the case of Mr Mitchell, however, the defeated candidate did not petition the Judicial Committee, but the seat was declared vacant by a resolution of the House of Commons. In the ensuing by-election Mr Mitchell was again elected, and on this occasion his Ulster Unionist opponent, Mr C. Beattie, secured the seat by virtue of an election petition. But his triumph was short-lived, as mentioned on page 81, he was found to hold an office of profit and had to vacate the seat. So in this minor comedy of errors it took one general election, an election petition and two by-elections to secure an eligible member for Mid-Ulster in the 1955 Parliament.

Where a disqualified person has been elected, without the facts leading to the disqualification being generally known to the electorate, the runner-up is not elected in his place, but a by-election is held to find a successor. This occurred in Belfast West in 1950, when the Rev J. G. MacManaway, a clergyman of the Church of Ireland, was elected, and it was not established until later that he was disqualified.

How Candidates are Chosen

The procedures of the three main political parties for selecting candidates differ in a number of important details, but are basically similar. In each case the selection is the responsibility of the local constituency party and the influence of the party headquarters is relatively minor.

A pamphlet published by the Conservative Central Office for the guidance of local associations states: 'Subject to certain simple Party rules each association has complete freedom to select the man or woman of its choice.' There are well-established procedures within the Conservative Party which limit, however, the degree of local variation in methods of selection.

The Executive Council of a Conservative association wishing to select a new candidate appoints a selection committee, usually of about six members, who would be amongst the most influential and senior members of the association. The Chairman of the association is invariably included unless, which is not infrequently the case, he has ambitions to be selected himself. The purpose of the selection committee is to consider all the possible aspirants for the candidature and reduce them to a small number from which the Executive Council may make its choice.

The constituency chairman is expected to obtain from the Central Office a list of names of suitable people, together with biographical details. One of the vice-chairmen of the National Union, assisted by the Standing Advisory Committee on candidates, is responsible for maintaining an official list of approved potential candidates from among whom a number of names would be sent. Any member of the Conservative Party may apply to be included on the official list, and he is then interviewed by the Vice-Chairman or by members of the Standing Advisory Committee, and, if approved, his name is added to the list.

Together with the names obtained from Central Office, the selection committee considers any members of the constituency association who have expressed an interest in the candidature and also the names of Conservatives who may have written asking to be considered. If it is a safe Conservative seat there may be a large number of these and it is not uncommon for a selection committee to have over a hundred names from which to choose.

The selection committee quickly whittle this number down to about seven or eight, and in the case of a safe seat few of the applicants would have much chance of surviving to this stage unless they were nationally known figures, were obviously extremely well qualified or were personally known to a member of the selection committee.

The seven or eight people chosen are invited to attend to be interviewed by the selection committee which then chooses normally two or three names from whom the Executive Council may make its final choice. Occasionally, however, when the selection committee decide, in the words of the Central Office pamphlet, that 'a candidate is available whose record is so distinguished and whose qualifications are so outstanding that his adoption is practically a foregone conclusion' only one name is put forward to the Executive Council.

Before this stage is reached the names of any of the surviving nominees who are not included on the approved Central Office list are submitted to the standing Advisory Committee for endorsement. If endorsement is refused and the constituency proceeds to select a nominee in spite of this, he is not regarded as an official party candidate at the ensuing election. Cases of an association selecting a candidate who has not been previously approved, are, however, extremely rare.

The nominees put forward by the selection committee attend a selection conference of the Executive Council. Each makes a short speech (normally limited to a period varying between 10 and 30 minutes) and answers questions put to him from the floor. A secret ballot is then held to choose who will be the candidate. There is no provision in the party rules as to the conduct of this ballot. It is possible for the nominee leading on the first ballot to be chosen forthwith, even though only a minority may have voted for him. It is far more usual, however, for an exhaustive ballot to be held, with the bottom candidate falling out if no overall majority is obtained on the first ballot.

The Executive Council's choice is submitted for approval to a general meeting of the whole association. This is normally a formality, but there have been occasions in which the Executive Council's choice has been challenged at this stage and another name substituted.

Money nowadays plays no significant part in the selection of Conservative candidates. This has not always been so. Up till 1948 it was very common for Conservative candidates to defray the whole of their election expenses and in addition to pay a large annual subscription to the constituency association. Consequently wealth was a prerequisite for potential Conservative Members, with very few exceptions.

The shock of defeat in 1945, however, led to a comprehensive reappraisal of the organisation of the Conservative Party following the report of a Committee presided over by Sir David Maxwell Fyfe (now Lord Kilmuir). Its recommendations, which were accepted by the party, have fundamentally altered the financial relationship between Conservative MPs and candidates and their constituency associations. Under the new rules a Conservative candidate is precluded from making any contribution whatever towards the election expenses, other than his personal expenses. The maximum contribution which he may make to his association is £25 a year as a candidate, and £50 a year as an MP. In no circumstances, state the Party rules, may the payment of a subscription be made a condition of adoption.

There can be no doubt that the new rules are substantially adhered to, and the result has been that a large number of Conservative candidates without private means have been selected in the period since 1948. Whilst wealth is no handicap in the Conservative Party and rich men are often selected as candidates, money no longer plays a direct part in their selection.

The Labour Party's selection procedure is laid down in more detail in the party rules, and it is complicated by the existence of two classes of membership, individual and affiliated (principally trade unions). When a constituency party decides to select a candidate, its Executive Committee first consults with the regional organiser of the party to agree a timetable for the selection. The regional organiser is the representative of Transport House and it is his responsibility to ensure that the selection takes place according to the party rules. When the timetable has been approved by the General Management Committee of the constituency party, the secretary writes to each local or ward party or affiliated organisation inviting them to make a nomination before a certain date, normally a minimum period of one month being allowed for this.

No person may be considered for selection unless he or she has been nominated by a local party or affiliated organisation. There is no provision in the Labour Party for members to nominate themselves, though if a member has good personal contact with organisations with the right to nominate it is often not difficult for him to obtain a nomination.

Like the Conservative Central Office, Transport House maintains a list of possible Parliamentary candidates. It is in two parts: List A contains the names of individuals nominated by trade unions and in respect of whom the appropriate trade union is prepared to assume financial responsibility for the candidature. List B consists of persons nominated by constituency Labour parties and for whom no financial responsibility has been assumed.

The Executive Committee of a constituency party may ask for copies of either list for its own reference or to circulate to affiliated organisations, but there is no compulsion on them to do so, and frequently, particularly in the case of safe Labour seats, they make no effort to obtain the lists. There is little point in local parties in safe Conservative areas consulting list A, as trade unions are rarely willing to sponsor candidates who have no prospect of being elected. The more hopeless the seat, however, the more likely is a party to make use of list B and to write to perhaps a large number of the people included, asking them to accept nomination.

The number of nominations made varies enormously. In a 'hopeless' rural constituency many miles from a large centre of population there may be as few as two or three. In a safe Labour-held seat in a borough, with many affiliated organisations, there is likely to be anything from ten to twenty-five nominations, and even the latter figure is often exceeded. Trade Union branches in safe Labour seats, particularly those of the larger unions, are likely to be approached by their union headquarters and asked to nominate a member of the union's parliamentary panel. These nominations must be accompanied by a letter from the general secretary of the union confirming that it will assume financial responsibility for the candidature. Trade union branches are also able to nominate unsponsored members of their unions whose standing is the same as that of nominees of ward or local Labour parties.

When the period for nomination has passed it is the responsibility of the Executive Committee (which itself has the right to make one nomination) to consider all the nominations received and to draw up a short list. If there are fewer than half a dozen nominations this is normally unnecessary, but this is a rare event, except in strong Tory areas. The Executive Committee may decide to interview all the nominees before drawing up a short list, or it may send them questionnaires to fill in. Often, however, it does neither.

The Executive Committee usually recommends a short list with from four to six names and this is reported to the General Management Committee for its approval. It is open to any member of the GMC to move the addition, substitution, or deletion of names and this occurs with considerable frequency, though more often than not amendments are voted down.

People on the approved short list are then invited to a selection conference of the GMC whose procedure is not unlike that of the Executive Council of a Conservative association, though an exhaustive ballot is prescribed in the party rules. The choice of the GMC does not have to be confirmed by a general meeting of members, as in the case of the Conservative Party, but his candidature must be endorsed by the National Executive Committee of the party.

It is paradoxical that financial considerations now play a greater part in the selection of Labour candidates than of Conservatives. The restrictions on individuals are similar – no Labour candidate may subscribe more than £50 a year to his constituency party, and this rule is seldom transgressed. In fact the average Labour candidate or MP undoubtedly subscribes less to his constituency party than his Conservative counterpart.

The monetary element in the Labour |Party is represented by the system of trade union sponsorship of candidates, which goes back to the early days of the party when there was no individual membership and every candidature had to be sponsored by an official organisation. Under the so-called Hastings Agreement, dating from the Labour Party conference at Hastings in 1933, a trade union is permitted to contribute up to 80 per cent of the election expenses incurred on behalf of its nominee and a maximum of £420 a year, or 60 per cent of the agent's salary, to the constituency party.

There is thus a strong temptation for hard-up constituency parties to choose a sponsored candidate, and this applies especially in safe Labour seats in industrial areas. Many constituency parties take a pride in choosing the best nominee available irrespective of financial considerations and many sponsored nominees are able and public-spirited men. There have, however, certainly been cases where more competent nominees have been passed over in favour of a mediocrity whose principal recommendation has been the income which his selection would ensure.

Under the party rules no mention of financial matters

may be made at a selection conference and the regional
organiser, who attends on behalf of Transport House,
strictly enforces this rule. The significance of the distinction
between trade union and local party nominees is likely,
however, to be appreciated by at least the most alert of
GMC members. But it is at the short-listing stage that
sponsorship carries the greatest weight. For the Executive
Committee of a constituency party is acutely aware of the
difference that a sponsored candidate can make and, composed as it is of the dozen or so people with the greatest
responsibility for the party's affairs, financial worries are
likely to be very much on its mind. If an Executive Committee is determined to have a sponsored candidate it will
recommend a short list made up entirely of those with
financial backing, and there are fairly frequent examples of
this occurring in safe Labour seats.

It is a difficult problem, as it is probably only the sponsorship system which enables a fair number of people from
manual occupations to go straight from the workbench
to the House of Commons and thus enable Parliament to
contain a reasonable cross-section of the nation. If the
system were abandoned it might result in the long run in
the House being composed merely of people of the professional and middle classes, with a solid block of miners
remaining as the only representative of manual workers. It
is to be hoped, however, that one day the Labour Party
will devise some method of supplanting the sponsorship
system, without losing what has always been one of its
most attractive features – the very wide range of background and occupation from which its candidates are
drawn.

The proportion of candidates sponsored by trade unions
or by the Co-operative Party has gradually declined in the
years since 1945. Since the 1959 general election several
important unions have taken energetic steps to reverse this
trend. The 1964 general election will reveal whether they
have been successful.

The Liberal Party's selection procedure is virtually

identical to the Conservatives': the principal difference in practice is that there are nearly always far fewer nominees, and in many cases a Liberal Association has the claims of only one contender to consider. In the relatively small number of cases where a candidate has to be found for a Liberal-held seat or one where there is a good chance of a Liberal victory the competition is far stronger, and the method of selection is very similar to that of the Conservative Party.

Unlike in the Conservative and Labour parties, there is no limit to the amount of money which Liberal candidates or MPs are allowed to contribute to their election expenses or donate to their constituency party. It is unlikely that more than a handful contribute more than the maximum imposed by both the Conservative and Labour parties.

The methods of selection of minor parties differ considerably from that of the major parties, principally because they have so few members. Decisions, normally taken in the larger parties by constituency associations, are more likely to be taken by the national committees of the smaller parties. Selection conferences of the type described above are the exception rather than the rule.

A few general points may be made about selection procedures of all parties. One is the small number of people involved in making the choice. The drawing up of the short list – a vital stage – is the responsibility in the Conservative Party of less than a dozen people and in the Labour Party of less than 20. The final selection is seldom made by more than 200 people and most often by between 50 and 150. In the Liberal Party the numbers involved are much smaller.

The Selection Conference

The actual selection conference is the most dramatic stage in the selection process, and it is one that imposes considerable strain on the would-be candidates, as the author knows only too well from personal experience.

The nominees are asked to attend a conference lasting anything up to three or four hours, though most of the time they are cooped up in an ante-room with the other contenders while procedural matters are being discussed or one of their number is making his speech. There is a certain tactical advantage in being the last to speak (the order is normally decided by lot), but this is often offset by the tension of waiting until all your rivals have spoken. All one can hear of the proceedings are occasional muffled sounds of applause from which one imagines that one's rivals are making an extremely good impression. In fact the audience normally goes out of its way to encourage the nominees whose ordeal they can imagine, and are very free with their applause.

At last it is your turn. You are ushered into the conference, which as often as not is housed in a bleak Nonconformist church hall or school, but may occasionally be in the more regal surroundings of the council chamber of the Town Hall. Before you are perhaps 80 people, predominantly middle-aged, and you search eagerly for the encouragement of a familiar face, probably in vain.

You reach your seat on the platform, shake hands with the chairman, who announces that you are Mr X, whose biographical details have been circulated to all the delegates. You have 15 minutes to speak and another 15 minutes for questions. After 14 minutes the chairman will sound a warning bell and after 15 you will be stopped – if necessary in mid-sentence.

You stand up, try to show a confidence which you do not feel and launch into a well-prepared speech, which has been carefully timed in front of your bedroom mirror to last $14\frac{1}{2}$ minutes. In the event, you have either sat down after $9\frac{1}{2}$ minutes or are rudely cut short after 15 minutes – less than a third of the way through your oration. You then deal rather better than you had expected with three or four questions and are surprised to hear that another 15 minutes have gone by.

Back to the ante-room and the interminable wait while

a succession of ballots is taken. At last after two or three false alarms the regional organiser of the party will come into the room, look at you straight in the eye and announce that Mr Y has been selected. You shake hands with Mr Y and utter a few modest words of congratulation. Meanwhile that blithering idiot Mr Z, is slapping Mr Y on the back and saying he had always known that Y would be chosen.

Back to the conference chamber with the other nominees. Deafening applause. The chairman says that all the nominees were absolutely first class (even if this was patently not the case). They would have liked to have chosen all of them, nevertheless they had to make a choice, however difficult, and the mantle had fallen on Mr Y. He was quite sure that such excellent people as Messrs W, X and Z would have no difficulty in being chosen soon by another constituency, and the members of his constituency would follow their future careers with interest. Then votes of thanks all round, a few words from the selected candidate and a final rousing call from the chairman to rally round and ensure that Mr Y becomes the next member for the constituency.

It is not easy for nominees to decide what to talk about in their set speeches. Should they talk about party policy or their personal records of work for the party? There is no set formula for success. The speech which would be an utter failure in constituency A may turn out an un-qualified success in constituency B. All the nominee has to go on is his experience and the degree of his knowledge of local feeling. His main consolation is that all his rivals are confronted by the same dilemma.

WHO IS CHOSEN?

Looking at it from the other side, what are the members of the selection conference looking for in their candidate? This varies with the nature of the constituency, and especially according to the prospect of electoral success. If it is a marginal constituency the delegates are most likely to be impressed by the vote-winning prospects of their candidate and a pleasing personality would be the number one qualification. In a safe seat delegates are conscious of choosing the future Member rather than a candidate and are more concerned to choose a man with the requisite knowledge and experience to perform what they conceive to be the functions of an MP. In a hopeless constituency energy and enthusiasm count a great deal, and younger candidates are much more likely to be chosen.

Policy differences are relatively unimportant. It is commonly anticipated that left-wing constituency Labour parties are certain to select left-wing candidates and that right-wing Conservative associations, similarly, will pick extremist candidates. In fact, this happens much less frequently than is imagined. Selection conferences of all parties are more likely to pick the man or woman who 'looks the part' rather than to insist on the nominee whose political views most exactly coincide with their own.

Local interests undoubtedly often play a part. If one is nominated for a farming constituency it is prudent to show some knowledge of and interest in agriculture, similarly with industrial areas where one industry is predominant. But in mixed industrial areas and especially in suburban constituencies there is likely to be more interest in national than in purely local issues.

Age may play an important part in deciding between nominees, though this again will vary very much. There are a few parties which would regard a man of fifty as a 'young stripling', while others would regard a forty-year-old as a has-been. In general, the optimum age range is from thirty-five to forty-five, with a certain preference for younger candidates in hopeless and marginal seats and for older ones in safe constituencies.

Unlike in the United States and certain other countries, it is not customary for a candidate to be resident in the area which he seeks to represent. In fact the great majority of candidates in British Parliamentary elections are 'carpet baggers' with no personal stake in the community they seek to represent. At some selection conferences it is a major advantage to be a local man, but equally often it can be a handicap. To come in from outside with no previous connexions with local factions, can in many cases be a strong recommendation.

Regional prejudices seldom come into the picture in England, though in Scotland and Wales it is rare for a non-Scotsman or non-Welshman respectively to be chosen. Religion is not an important factor outside Northern Ireland, though Jews encounter strong prejudices in some local Conservative associations. In a few constituencies on Merseyside and in Glasgow Labour nominees who are Roman Catholics start with a distinct advantage.

A certain prejudice undoubtedly exists against women candidates, which is stronger in the Conservative Party than in the Labour Party and in rural areas than in towns. Many fewer women than men are selected and they tend to be chosen for the less hopeful seats.

In 1959 there were 28 Conservative women candidates out of 625, but of elected Conservative Members there were 12 out of 365. At the same election Labour fielded 36 women candidates out of 621 and 13 Labour women MPs were returned out of 258. There are undoubtedly many fewer women than men with Parliamentary ambitions but those who wish to be considered as candidates encounter stronger resistance than men. This, apparently, comes most often from their fellow women who are usually in a majority at Conservative selection conferences. A large number of these seem convinced that voters would be less likely to vote for a woman candidate than for a man.

The evidence for this belief is scanty. A Gallup poll taken in July 1952 revealed that 16 per cent of the voters thought that they would be less inclined to vote for a woman candidate, but this was partially offset by the 10 per cent who said they would be more inclined, 67 per cent saying that it would make no difference and 7 per cent expressing no opinion. On the basis of this poll it might be concluded that women candidates encountered a handicap of 6 per cent.

In practice it proves much less than this. The present author has made an exhaustive analysis of the results of the 1955 and 1959 elections, recording every constituency where a woman candidate in the 1955 election was replaced by a man of the same party in 1959 and vice versa, and comparing the results in these constituencies with the national trend.

The result of this analysis was that when a Conservative woman candidate had replaced a man, the pro-Conservative swing had averaged 0·4 per cent against a national average of 1·2 per cent.[1] Where a Conservative man had replaced a woman candidate, the pro-Conservative swing was 1·6 per cent. This means that in the average constituency a woman Conservative candidate might expect to receive about 300 votes less than a man. The same analysis revealed no difference at all in the case of Labour candidates, while for Liberals and minor party candidates and independents the numbers involved were too small to point to any reliable conclusion. The analysis does suggest that there is a small minority of normally Conservative voters who will not vote for a woman candidate.

It is not only women candidates who encounter difficulties in the Conservative Party. Despite frequent appeals from Central Office, culminating in a recommendation in the Selwyn Lloyd report of June 1963 that each selection conference should include one woman and one trade unionist among the nominees from which it makes its choice, it has proved virtually impossible to persuade Conservative constituency associations to select working-class candidates. Only one Conservative Member in the 1959 Parliament was a working trade unionist when selected, and there are unlikely to be many more in the 1964 Parliament.

The occupational backgrounds of candidates and elected members in the 1959 election are shown in Table 13 (taken from *The British General Election of 1959* by D. E. Butler and Richard Rose, Macmillan, 1960):

[1] For a definition of 'swing' see page 150 below.

Table 13—Occupational Backgrounds of candidates, 1959

	Conservative			Labour			Liberal Total %
	Elected %	De-feated %	Total %	Elected %	De-feated %	Total %	
Professions	46	40	43	38	42	40	47
Business	30	40	34	10	18	15	30
Miscellaneous	23	15	20	17	17	17	21
Workers	1	5	3	35	23	28	2
	100	100	100	100	100	100	100

In the Professions category the law, particularly the bar, is dominant in all three parties. There are a number of reasons for this. Traditionally the bar and politics have been associated professions. By virtue of their training and professional practice barristers are skilled at arguing a case and it may be expected that they would face a selection conference with more confidence than most. Barristers and solicitors also undoubtedly find it easier than most to organise their time in such a way that they can combine their profession with their parliamentary work.

There is a fair sprinkling from the other professions among the candidates of all parties, but it is only teaching – at both school and university level – which comes near to challenging the predominance of the law. In fact, teachers form the largest occupational group among Labour candidates and they are also well represented in the Liberal Party. Only a handful of Conservative candidates, however, are teachers – and those normally in unpromising constituencies.

It will come as a surprise to nobody to discover that business is largely represented in the Conservative Party and makes a good showing in the Liberal Party. The 15 per cent of Labour candidates with a business background are not really comparable, as a majority of these are small businessmen or employees of larger companies, often in junior positions, whereas a majority of the Conservatives in this category are company directors.

The largest groups in the miscellaneous category are farmers on the Conservative side and journalists in the Labour Party. Journalists, and especially public relations and advertising men are well represented in the Conservative and Liberal parties too. Amongst the workers, by far the largest group are the miners, who have practically a monopoly of Labour representation in coal-mining areas. Out of 36 miners who stood for Labour in 1959, no less than 34 were successful. A good proportion of the 'workers' who stood in 1959 were full-time trade union officials, but the majority were working at their trades when first elected and each general election brings to the Labour benches of the House of Commons reinforcements of members straight from the workbench. Most of these are sponsored candidates.

In all parties there is a recognised route which the majority of would-be MPs are expected to follow. They must first fight a hopeless seat and, fortified by this salutary experience they may then proceed to a marginal constituency and later, perhaps, to a safe one. A fair number of aspirants in both major parties, however, succeed in by-passing this route and secure election to the House of Commons at their first attempt.

How much influence have the party headquarters on the choice of candidates? It is clear that no HQ can force an individual on an unwilling constituency party. The most they can do is to try to persuade the constituency, through the regional organiser or agent, to include someone whom Transport House or the Central Office would like accommodated on the short list. Very often a constituency party is quite willing to accede to this, but it frequently happens, particularly in the Labour Party that the constituency party Executive Committee will have other ideas about whom to include on the short list, and it is their view which prevails. Even when someone recommended from headquarters is included it is by no means always an advantage for this fact to be known. The tag 'Transport House nominee' is the kiss of death in some constituency Labour parties. In the Conservative and Liberal parties there is a greater willingness to be guided by the higher levels of the party, but even here defiance is often practised. Once an officially recommended nominee is on the short list he takes his chance with everyone else.

The negative powers which the party headquarters possess to refuse endorsement to selected candidates are sparingly used. In the Labour Party, except in the rare case of someone who is clearly unsuited for personal reasons (such as the nominee for a Midlands constituency some years ago who, it later transpired, had recently been cashiered from the RAF for embezzling mess funds) it is in practice only used to exclude those with strong Communist or Trotskyist connexions. In the Conservative and Liberal parties it is even rarer for selected candidates to be blackballed for political heterodoxy.

How much security do prospective candidates enjoy? Not very much. Their relationship to their constituency parties is a delicate one. Disenchantment easily sets in on either side. This is not perhaps surprising, as candidate and constituency party have usually had only the most fleeting view of each other prior to selection.

Opportunities for disagreement abound. Parties and candidates often differ on how much work the candidate is expected to put in. It frequently happens that a prospective candidate visits the constituency less often than his party would like; less commonly parties may decide that they see altogether too much of their candidate. Changes in the personal position of the candidate may also occur. He may be offered a better job, or his employers may prove unexpectedly difficult about allowing time off. His health may suffer, or that of his family. He may take on other commitments which leave him less time for his candidature. Or he may wish to be considered for another, more promising constituency; so, for one reason or another, a sizeable number of prospective candidates withdraw 'for personal reasons' long before polling day, and the procedure for selecting a new candidate has to be gone through all over again.

On the other hand, once a candidate has been elected as a Member he normally has no difficulty in retaining the support of his own party, and unless his seat is a marginal one, he normally continues to represent it, if he wishes, until the end of his working life. It is extremely difficult for a constituency party to rid itself of an unwanted Member, the required procedure for doing this in both the Conservative and Labour parties being weighted heavily on the side of the Member. Surprisingly, in view of the fact that political differences are usually stronger in the Labour Party, it is constituency Conservative associations who more frequently attempt to unseat a Member with whom they disagree. Such efforts, however, are normally unsuccessful and it is rare for more than one or two Members to be forced out by their constituencies during the course of a Parliament.

An exception was the aftermath of the Suez operation, when feelings were running extremely high and four Conservatives and one Labour Member lost the support of their constituency parties. Two of these resigned their seats forthwith, the others were replaced by more orthodox party candidates at the subsequent general election.[1]

Many members of constituency parties would like their members to behave as delegates of the party rather than as representatives of the constituency, but they have little opportunity to enforce their will. Each of the three major parties sets its face firmly against such a conception of a Member's responsibilities, the Labour and Liberal parties implicitly, the Conservative Party explicitly. The Central Office pamphlet *Notes on Procedure for the Adoption of Conservative Candidates in England and Wales* quotes Burke, with approval: 'Your representative owes you not his industry only, but his judgment; and he betrays instead of serving

1. See Nigel Nicolson, *People and Parliament*, Weidenfeld and Nicolson, 1958, for a detailed account of these events by one of the Members involved.

you if he sacrifices it to your opinion . . . authoritative instructions, which the Member is bound blindly and implicitly to obey, though contrary to the dearest convictions of his judgment and conscience, are utterly unknown to the laws of the land, and against the tenor of our constitution.'

In practice, few Members encounter serious difficulties with their constituency parties over policy matters, though disagreements are frequent. It is rare for a Member who deviates towards an extreme position on the outside edge, as it were, of his party, to run into trouble with his constituency party. This is because constituency parties are normally more extreme than the party leadership. Members who deviate towards the centre may, however, find themselves in difficulty. It is not surprising that none of the Suez rebels on the right of the Conservative Party found themselves out of step with their constituency association, though four out of the five Conservative Members who most strongly opposed the original attack on Egypt were disowned by their associations. Conversely, in the Labour Party rightwing deviants are much more likely than left-wingers to meet trouble in their constituency parties. In general, however, the vast majority of constituency parties accept, however reluctantly, that they are unable to dictate the political line of their Members. It is a far more serious matter for a Member to be out of step with his party leadership in the House of Commons than to be in disagreement with the members of his constituency party.

CHAPTER EIGHT

THE CAMPAIGN – IN THE CONSTITUENCIES

THE ANNOUNCEMENT by the Prime Minister of an impending general election precipitates a flurry of activity in constituency and local party branches throughout the country. Emergency meetings are hastily convened to put the local party machines on a 'wartime footing' and to make arrangements for the formal adoption of Parliamentary candidates.

If, as happened in 1955, the dissolution is announced unexpectedly a fair number of constituency parties may find themselves without a prospective candidate, but even when the election is anticipated a handful of parties find themselves in the same position because of the recent resignation of their previously selected candidates. A few other prospective candidates are likely to find, when the dissolution is announced, that an election campaign at that particular time would be inconvenient and they therefore withdraw from the field. All in all, it is unlikely that fewer than half a dozen candidates have to be found at short notice at any general election by each of the Labour and Conservative parties, and in such circumstances the selection procedures outlined in Chapter VII are considerably telescoped.

The Liberal Party and each of the minor parties usually have to find a higher proportion of their candidates at this stage. In many constituencies a decision to fight has been left in abeyance and the first question to be resolved at their emergency meetings is whether a candidate is to be put into the field at all. (The Conservative and the Labour parties normally fight virtually every seat as a matter of principle. The only exceptions in recent times for the Labour Party are a few county constituencies in Northern Ireland where Labour is exceptionally weak and the constituency represented by the Speaker of the House of Commons.[1] Conservative candidates have occasionally stood down in a few constituencies to enable Liberals to have a straight fight with Labour.)

In deciding whether to put up a candidate, a constituency party will seriously consider not only its potential voting strength in the area and the availability of a suitable man or woman to stand, but its financial position. A deposit of £150 is required to be paid to the Returning Officer at the time of nomination, and this is returnable only if the candidate polls more than one-eighth of the total vote. In addition, a minimum of £250, and preferably at least £500, is needed if an adequate campaign is to be mounted.

As soon as the question of a candidate is resolved the election agent, who is the key figure in every campaign, is appointed. The position is a statutory one and every candidate is required to notify the name and address of the person appointed, in writing, to the Returning Officer. The election agent is legally responsible for authorising all expenditure on behalf of a candidature and his name must appear as the publisher on all printed material, including posters and window bills, issued in support of the candidate. His official duties do not end until he has sent in a return of election expenses to the Returning Officer after the result of the election has been declared.

A candidate may act as his own election agent, though this rarely happens except in the case of independents and minor party candidates. When a constituency party employs a full-time agent, he automatically takes on the job. Otherwise it is assumed by an experienced member of the local party. Most 'amateur' agents arrange to take at least three weeks off from their regular work to devote themselves to their electoral duties. The work of an election agent is extremely arduous, beginning early in the morning and continuing far into the night, at least during the three

[1] Though both the Labour and Liberal parties are to oppose the Speaker in the 1964 general election.

weeks prior to polling day. His wife and family can expect to see almost nothing of him during this time.

Once the question of a candidate and an agent have been settled, there is little more for a governing body of a constituency party to do. It is usual for a 'campaign committee', consisting of a handful of key workers prepared to devote virtually all their spare time to the election, to be appointed to supervise the details of the campaign, in conjunction with the agent and candidate. A financial appeal will be issued to members and known sympathisers and the agent will be authorised to spend up to a specified sum during the campaign. The party will then pass a resolution either formally dissolving itself or suspending all public propaganda activities for the duration of the election. The purpose of this is to emphasise that all activities on behalf of the candidature during the election period are the personal responsibility of the agent.

The first task of the agent is to obtain premises suitable for use as a campaign headquarters or central committee rooms, as they are called. When the party itself owns permanent premises which are suitable for this purpose there is no problem. Otherwise a frantic search is mounted for vacant shop or office premises, preferably in a prominent position in the main street of the principal town in the constituency. Labour candidates often experience great difficulties in obtaining premises of this kind because of the hostility of private commercial interests, but this is partly offset by the willingness of co-operative societies to make accommodation available. A high proportion of Labour committee rooms are housed above co-operative stores.

If commercial premises cannot be found or the party cannot afford to pay for them the committee rooms are likely to be established in the front room of a private house of a keen party member. The keenness of such a member will certainly be put to a severe test in such circumstances, for neither he nor his family is likely to be afforded much privacy in the succeeding weeks. Sub-committee rooms in each ward or polling district will also be set up; these will nearly always be in private houses.

Once established in his committee rooms, the agent is confronted with a bewildering multiplicity of duties. These come easily to the old hand, but to the inexperienced they can pose formidable problems. Fortunately, the party headquarters run excellent correspondence courses for those likely to be appointed as temporary agents and also publish handbooks setting out clearly the legal responsibilities of election agents and giving detailed guidance as to how their duties should be carried out. In case of difficulty a call to the party's regional organiser should elicit sound advice. The agent of an independent or minor party candidate is denied such help, and in practice it is he who is most likely to come unstuck. A prudent man in such a position would swallow his pride and equip himself with one of the agent's handbooks published by the major parties and freely on sale from their headquarters.

An election agent is unlikely to find himself short of willing helpers. The hard core of active party workers will devote the greater part of their spare time during evenings and weekends to the campaign, and they are likely to be supplemented by a larger number of normally inactive members who feel that they ought to rally round at election time. Many sympathetic members of the public, too, who are unwilling to become party members, will turn up at the committee rooms and offer to lend a hand. To keep this motley array of helpers happy and purposefully occupied requires high qualities of tact and diplomacy.

All the varied tasks undertaken by the election agent and his team of helpers are directed towards three objects: to familiarise the name of the candidate and underline his party affiliation, to identify the party's supporters within the constituency and to build up a machine capable of ensuring the maximum turn-out of these supporters on election day.

The first object would be less necessary if the existence of political parties was recognised more extensively in election law. In fact, no mention of a candidate's party affiliation is made on the ballot paper, so it is up to the parties to familiarise the electors with the names of their candidates. Hence, all election literature and posters and window bills give great prominence to linking the candidate's name with his party. JONES FOR LABOUR or VOTE SMITH, CONSERVATIVE X are slogans which become increasingly familiar to every voter, as polling day approaches.

The activities of the candidate during the election campaign are a continuation and intensification of the work which he has been doing in the constituency in the months and years leading up to the election. The main difference is that the word 'prospective' is at last dropped from his title and that the public can now be asked to 'Vote for Jones' instead of merely for the party. The transition is usually marked by an adoption meeting, held as soon as possible after the election is announced, at which the candidature is formally proclaimed. This is usually a public meeting, which every party member is strongly urged to attend, as a demonstration of enthusiasm and confidence. Speeches are made by the candidate and several other speakers, an appeal for financial support is made and a resolution formally adopting the candidate may be formally put to the meeting. It need hardly be added that such a resolution is invariably carried with acclamation. If the candidate is the retiring Member of Parliament for the constituency he will by this time have dropped the MP from his name, as he has ceased to be a Member since the dissolution of Parliament. During the election campaign he is merely a candidate and his status is no different from that of the other candidates in the constituency.

The adoption meeting has no legal standing and each candidate must be formally nominated in writing. Nominations may be made on any day after the publication by the Returning Officer of the date of the election but not later than the eighth day after the date of the Proclamation summoning the new Parliament. This gives, in practice, a period of five days in which nominations may be made, and the final day for nominations is also the final day on which a nomination may be withdrawn.

Table 14—General Election Calendar

Principal Events in the 1959 Election Campaign

September	7	Prime Minister announces election date from 10 Downing Street.
September	11	Conservative election manifesto published.
September	18	Parliament dissolved. Labour manifesto published.
September	19	First television election broadcast.
September	21	Liberal manifesto published.
September	22	Macmillan and Gaitskell begin election tours. Nominations open.
September	28	Nominations close.
October	5	Grimond makes one-day helicopter tour.
October	6	Final television broadcast.
October	7	Party leaders return to their constituencies.
October	8	Polling day.
N.B.		Appendix 6 contains an election timetable which can be applied to any general or by-election.

The nomination form must be signed by a proposer and seconder and by eight other people, all of whom must be electors for the constituency in which the candidate is to stand. The nomination form contains the candidate's full name, address and 'description' (or profession) and his proposers must sign their names in the same form in which they are listed in the election register and must also add their electoral numbers.

Only one nomination form is required but it is usual for an agent to arrange for several to be filled in by different electors, partly as an insurance against one form being invalid and partly as a demonstration of support for his candidate.

The nomination form or forms must be delivered in person to the Returning Officer by the candidate or his proposer or seconder between the hours of 10 am and 3 pm on one of the days when nominations may be made.

The nomination must be accompanied by the £150 deposit, and by the candidate's consent in writing to nomination, which must be attested by one witness.

Provided a nomination paper has been filled in and delivered exactly as described above it will be deemed valid by the Returning Officer. Representatives of candidates may inspect the nomination papers of their rivals and may lodge objections if they suspect them to be invalid. The Returning Officer must then give his decision as soon as possible and if he decides that a nomination paper is invalid he must endorse the paper as invalid and state on it the reasons for his decision. This does not happen at all frequently, and when it does there is normally time for the candidate to send in another nomination paper which is correctly filled in, as few candidates are so imprudent as to leave their nomination to the very last moment.

If by the time that nominations are closed only one valid nomination has been received, the Returning Officer declares that person elected and publishes notices to that effect throughout the constituency. Where there are at least two candidates, as happens in the vast majority of cases, the Returning Officer publishes a statement of persons nominated, together with the names of their proposers, seconders and assentors. This statement includes a notice of the poll, stating the date and time that the election is to be held, and gives particulars as to where people should go to vote. By this time things are hotting up; it is a mere nine days (excluding Sundays and Bank holidays) to polling day.

At least a fortnight before polling day, and probably a week or two earlier, the candidate will have moved into the constituency for the duration of the campaign. Unless he normally lives there, he will take a room at a hotel or lodge with one of his supporters. If he is married his wife will accompany him, family circumstances permitting, and she will be expected to take an active part in his campaign. Some idea of their daily life during the three weeks before polling day is given by the following imaginary timetable of a candidate in a county constituency.

7.30 am. Get up. Breakfast. Read all the papers – especially reports of the speeches of the party leaders and other election news.

8.30–9.30. Work in hotel bedroom on speeches to be delivered in the evening.

9.30. Meet reporter from local newspaper at hotel. Comment on speech given by rival candidate on previous day.

9.50. Arrive main committee rooms, in car driven by wife. Dictate replies to correspondence received from electors. Quick consultation with the agent on the day's programme.

10.30. Set off with woman councillor for door-to-door canvass of housewives on new housing estate.

12 noon. Visit hospital with wife to meet patients. Talk with matron to check that arrangements for postal votes for the patients have been made.

1 pm. Quick lunch in café.

1.30. Drive to town at other end of constituency.

2.15. Set off on loudspeaker tour – making short speeches and answering questions at street corners.

3.15. Wife leaves to have tea with the Townswomen's Guild.

4.30. Meet a deputation of Roman Catholics to hear their case for more public money to maintain Catholic schools.

5.30. Speak to factory gate meeting.

6.30. Return to main committee rooms, immediately set off with agent for quick tour of sub-committee rooms.

7.30. Supper at home of party chairman.

8.15. Leave for first of three village meetings.

9.45. Return to town hall for main evening meeting, which has already been addressed by a prominent visiting speaker.

10.15. Adjourn to pub with party supporters.

11.30. Return to hotel and to bed.

This cracking pace is sustained without much difficulty by nearly all candidates, though elderly men who are defending safe seats tend to take it a lot easier. The constant excitement and the enthusiastic encouragement of supporters go a long way to create fresh reserves of energy which the candidate would not previously have suspected himself of possessing. A major problem is to restrain the ardour of one's supporters who will quite happily keep one up talking all night. Here a firm intervention by the candidate's wife is indicated.

It is notable how little the campaigns of rival candidates impinge on each other. The candidates may meet once or twice on neutral ground – at a meeting for all candidates organised by the United Nations Association, perhaps, or at an inter-denominational service held for election workers. One candidate may take up some remarks of another, as reported in the local newspaper, and reply to them at one of his meetings or challenge the accuracy of his facts. Very occasionally a candidate may make a personal attack on his rival, but this is normally regarded as bad form and is likely to do the attacker more harm than good.

The great majority of candidates, however, totally ignore the existence of their rivals throughout the campaign. If they are government supporters they will doggedly defend the record of the government with an occasional side swipe at the irresponsibility of the opposition, but if any names are mentioned, it will be of well-known national leaders rather than the opposition's local standard bearer. The same is broadly true, in reverse, of opposition candidates, though a former Member defending his seat is more likely to be picked out by name than a newly arrived challenger.

Although they are rarely attended by more than 200–300 people, except when a party leader is one of the speakers, and in fact the *average* audience is probably not more than 10 per cent of this size, public meetings normally constitute by far the most interesting and colourful events in the candidate's timetable.

There are certain superficial differences between meetings held by the opposing parties. At Conservative meetings the platform is invariably draped with Union Jacks, for which the Labour Party substitutes banners advertising the *Daily Herald* and the *Sunday Citizen*. Tory meetings often conclude with the singing of 'God Save the Queen', a display of patriotism which is considered inappropriate by the other parties. A collection is invariably taken at Labour and Liberal meetings, less frequently at Conservative ones.

In other respects the pattern is fairly uniform. The speeches vary greatly in style and content, but more through differences in the background and experience of the speakers than because of political differences. The younger and less experienced they are, the more likely are they to keep pretty closely to their brief – which in most cases is based on speakers' notes distributed by the various party headquarters. Local issues are likely to be stressed by town councillors and others – particularly when the opposing candidate is a stranger to the district.

The arrival of the candidate is heralded by a round of applause from his own supporters and perhaps some good-humoured banter from the other side. If the opposition is well represented in the audience a more lively and interested meeting is likely to ensue. Hostile questions test the mettle of a candidate far more than the polite enquiries he receives from his own supporters, and at many meetings 'enemy intervention' extends to the interruption or 'heckling' of the speaker. A speaker who is quick and nimble-witted enough to score debating points against hecklers, without losing the thread of his speech, adds greatly to his stature. It is not common for heckling to get seriously out of hand but it occasionally does happen, especially in marginal constituencies where feeling is running high. In such cases it may be almost impossible for the speakers to make themselves heard and the chairman is forced to appeal for order. If he is wise he will do this in a good-humoured manner, appealing to the opponents' sportsmanship and belief in free speech and emphasising that questions will be welcomed at a later stage in the evening.

If such an appeal is ignored the chairman is placed in a tricky position. He can ask his stewards to eject people making a disturbance, but if the 'enemy' contingent is large this could prove a difficult job. He can swallow his

pride and ignore the continued disorder in the hope that
the speaker will eventually succeed in getting his message
across. Or he can solemnly remind the audience that any
person acting in a disorderly manner at a public meeting
for the purpose of preventing the transaction of business is
liable to a fine or imprisonment and announce that he is
sending for a police constable to ensure that the law is
enforced. This final course of action is virtually certain to
succeed in its purpose, at any rate when the constable has
arrived, but it is normally regarded as a moral defeat for the
platform and is rarely resorted to.

While the candidate is straining every effort to make
himself known to as many voters as possible, the agent is
equally busy ensuring that contact is established with every
potential supporter of the party in the constituency. If the
party organisation is good he will have started the campaign
with a marked-up register covering the greater part of the
constituency. In that case he will ask his team of canvassers
to call on all the 'F' (for) voters to confirm that they are
party supporters and on the 'D' or doubtful voters to see if
they have moved off the fence. Those voters marked 'A'
(against) are firmly left alone. Many agents find that no
reasonably up-to-date canvassing records are in existence
and they have to instruct their canvassers to call on every
voter. In either case canvassing is regarded as much the
most important activity which has to be undertaken during
elections, and every available person is pressed into service.
It is normal for canvassing teams to go out on every single
evening of the campaign and in the daytime during weekends. Theoretically, parties aim to make a 100 per cent
canvas of the constituency, but most agents are more than
pleased if their canvassers call on 80 per cent of the voters.
It is normal to begin with the most favourable parts of the
constituency and move on later to the less promising areas:
so if, as often happens, a party canvasses only 50 per cent
of the voters it may have called on 75 per cent of its supporters.

In a marginal constituency it is prudent to set a target

of 2,000 or 3,000 more favourable promises than would be necessary to win the seat. Most canvassers, particularly inexperienced ones who are much in evidence at election time, are incurably optimistic and are liable to read into a courteous reception a promise of support. It is this rather than deliberate deception which most often leads to voters being recorded in the 'F' column by canvassers representing opposing candidates. Whatever the reason, it is certain that nine candidates out of ten receive an inflated estimate of support from their canvassers.

Canvassers are asked to undertake a number of subsidiary jobs. They are liberally supplied with window bills to offer to supporters, and they are instructed to enquire about elderly or infirm voters who might require a lift to the poll or, if there is still time, to be assisted in applying for a postal vote. Canvassers also are often given leaflets to deliver 'on their rounds'. It is important for canvassers to ask to see every voter on the register at each house at which they call, and not to assume that the person who comes to the door speaks for the whole household. More families than most people imagine are divided in their voting habits, and households containing lodgers are unlikely to be politically homogeneous. A high proportion of canvassers, however, despite the instructions of their agents, take the easy way out and do not bother to interview all members of a household. This is a further source of gross inaccuracies in canvassing records.

After canvassing, the next biggest campaign chore is the addressing of envelopes for the candidate's election address. In most constituencies some 50,000–60,000 are required and this places a severe strain on the weaker constituency organisations. It is usual to ask each ward or local branch to be responsible for addressing the envelopes for its own area and each active member is given a quota of anything from 50 to 1,000 envelopes to address, together with the appropriate portion of the election register. Elderly and housebound people who are not available for canvassing and other outdoor work are often happy to volunteer to receive a large batch of envelopes. If the election occurs in the fifth year of the Parliament some parties will already have got their envelopes addressed before the campaign began, as they could be sure the election would be fought on the current register. Only a minority normally shows such foresight.

The election address is the traditional means by which the candidate introduces himself to the electorate. It normally contains a photograph of the candidate, and perhaps also of his wife and children, biographical details, a personal message in which he promises to devote himself to the service of the electors should he be elected and a summary of his party's programme. Often it will include a short message from the candidate's wife, addressed to women voters.

The post office is obliged at Parliamentary elections to make one free delivery to every elector on behalf of each candidate, and the great majority of candidates take advantage of this to send out their election address.

Serious doubt is often cast on whether the trouble and expenditure devoted by candidates to their election addresses is really worth while. Most candidates in fact spend between a quarter and half of their permitted expenditure on their election address. According to the Gallup Poll, however, more electors are reached by means of the election address than by any other *local* form of electioneering. In 1959 more than six voters out of ten claimed to have read at least one election address compared with five out of ten who had been canvassed and less than two out of ten who claimed to have attended election meetings.

An agent who has the assistance of an able and experienced election committee to which he is willing to delegate a great deal of responsibility, should find that, though he will work hard and for very long hours, his campaign will run fairly smoothly. One who is unable or unwilling to delegate is likely to find himself prey to constant crises. Ideally, each member of the election committee should be allocated responsibility for one specific field of duties, allowing the agent to free himself for the general oversight of the campaign. There should be a canvassing officer, another in charge of speakers, one responsible for the addressing of envelopes, one for dealing with the press, one in charge of leaflet distribution, one for organising cars for election day and one to organise the postal vote. The agent will probably reserve for himself the planning of the candidate's timetable and it is important that a fixed time be set aside each day for consultation between the candidate and the agent.

Planning the schedule of meetings is especially complicated in county constituencies where the candidate may easily be addressing six village meetings every evening, rounding them off with a larger meeting in one of the towns. Each meeting requires at least one or two supporting speakers, whose main qualification must be the ability to modify drastically the length of their speeches. It inevitably happens that on some evenings the candidate gets seriously held up at his earlier meetings and arrives at his final meeting anything up to an hour and a half late. A supporting speaker booked to speak for twenty minutes has consequently to spin out his speech or fill in the time answering questions. On another day, he will find that the candidate arrives at the meeting just as he has completed his introductory remarks and is about to embark on the main body of his speech. In that case he must cut himself short and make way for the candidate, with as little delay as possible.

Most agents are well conversant with electoral law and are aware of the things which may or may not be done during an election campaign. A much less detailed store of knowledge is normally possessed by voluntary workers, and care must be taken that through ignorance or misguided enthusiasm they do not transgress the law. If they do, they may lay themselves open, and possibly also the agent and the candidate, to heavy penalties and even to the invalidation of the election should their candidate be elected. A summary of election offences, with the penalties involved should be prominently displayed in all committee rooms.

In practice people involved in electioneering in Britain have proved extremely law abiding and after each general election there are never more than a handful of prosecutions for election offences.

The last time an election was invalidated because of an election offence was at Oxford in 1924. In Northern Ireland respect for the election laws is perhaps rather less strongly ingrained and attempts at personation (voting in the name of some other person) are not infrequent. Each party in Northern Ireland appoints special 'personation agents' who keep a close watch at each polling station to deter supporters of the other side from 'stealing' votes in this way. But even in Northern Ireland stories of attempted personation are probably greatly exaggerated. A summary of election offences and of the penalties involved is included in Appendix 7.

Especially in marginal constituencies, agents make daily reports by telephone to their regional organisers, who are also likely to make at least one personal visit. The regional officers of both the Labour and Conservative parties do their best to organise the transfer of workers from safe and hopeless into marginal constituencies so that the maximum effort can be mounted where it will have the greatest effect. As a much higher proportion of their active members are car owners and therefore more mobile, it is clear that the Conservatives have less trouble in organising such transfers and they are in fact able to effect them on a much larger scale.

As polling day draws near the tempo of the campaign appreciably quickens. More helpers turn up every day at the committee rooms and enthusiasm and confidence mounts. Almost all voluntary election workers and most professional ones become infected with over-optimism towards the end of the campaign, unless their own party is very obviously doing badly. It is normal to over-estimate the chances both of one's candidate in the constituency and of one's party throughout the country. It would indeed be strange if it were otherwise, for so much is seen of the results of one's own campaigning and so little of the other side's that it is all but impossible to form an objective view.

A week before polling day most agents make a rapid assessment of the progress already made in canvassing and other important activities and revise their plans accordingly.

Targets may be raised or lowered, or forces concentrated to recall at houses where the voters were 'out' or 'doubtful' on the first occasion that they were canvassed. All election workers are likely to be impressed at this stage by how much remains to be done and how little time is left in which to do it.

Meanwhile, the agent's attention will be more and more concentrated on preparations for polling day. The transporting of elderly and disabled voters to the polls (and of many others who are unlikely themselves to summon up enough energy to get themselves there unaided) can add several hundred votes to a candidate's poll. Every effort is therefore made to secure the services of the maximum number of cars and drivers on election day and, especially, in the evening. It is illegal to hire transport for this purpose and party members who are owner drivers are strongly encouraged to volunteer their services.

Between 1948 and 1958 there was a legal restriction on the number of cars which a candidate could use for this purpose and each car had to be registered with the Returning Officer in advance. The number of cars allowed was one per candidate for every 2,500 electors in boroughs and one for every 1,500 in counties. The purpose of the restriction was to prevent a party which had a preponderance of wealthy supporters from turning this fact to its advantage. It was repealed by a Conservative government in 1958, on the grounds that the increasing incidence of car ownership at once reduced the party advantage involved and made the law difficult to enforce. Although the Conservatives have undoubtedly benefited from the repeal of this restriction, the arguments which they advanced carry considerable weight and it is unlikely that a future Labour government would seek to reintroduce control in this field.

As well as compiling a roster of cars and drivers for election day, the agent will endeavour to persuade as many helpers as possible to take the day off work, so that a full-scale operation can be mounted to 'get out the vote'. Particularly in marginal constituencies, little difficulty is encountered in ensuring an adequate army of helpers on the big day.

Meanwhile, the Returning Officer will be busy with his own preparations. Soon after the nominations are closed he will send out, through the post office, to each elector, an official poll card. This will notify the voter of his electoral number and tell him how, where and when to vote. In the presence of the candidates, or more likely their representatives, he will also send out ballot papers to registered postal voters. In the average constituency there are about 1,000 of these (or roughly 2 per cent of the electorate), though the number varies widely. Each postal voter is sent, by post, four items, viz.:

(1) An ordinary ballot paper, duly marked or stamped.
(2) A form of declaration of identity.
(3) A small envelope for the ballot paper.
(4) A larger addressed return envelope.

The postal voter must sign the declaration of identity, and have his signature attested by one witness. He marks his X against the candidate of his choice, seals his ballot paper in the small envelope and returns it, together with the declaration of identity, in the larger envelope. The vote can be sent back to the Returning Officer at any time after it has been recorded, but it must reach him not later than 9 pm on polling day. On their receipt at the office of the Returning Officer the postal votes are dropped into a special ballot box.

The Returning Officer, like the agents, has to make arrangements to secure the services of a large number of assistants on polling day. Some of them will be polling clerks whose duty will consist of presiding over polling stations. Others will have the job of counting the votes. Unlike the parties' election workers, the Returning Officer's staff will be paid for their services. The greater number of them will be local government employees, transferred for the day from other work. They will be supplemented by others engaged specially for the day. School-teachers are a favourite source of labour for polling clerks, as most schools have a holiday on election day because their premises are used as polling stations. Bank clerks, for obvious reasons, are much in demand to assist in counting the votes.

CHAPTER NINE

THE NATIONAL CAMPAIGN

Fifty years ago election campaigns were conducted almost exclusively at a constituency level. Apart from organising speaking tours by the party leaders and other prominent personalities, the party headquarters played little direct part in the campaign. The newspapers were full of election news, but they were read only by a minority, and a far greater readership was claimed by regional and local papers than is the case today.

The irruption of mass readership national newspapers and, even more, the development of radio and television has changed all that. A general election was formerly a series of local contests to choose Members of Parliament, with the incidental effect of determining the political complexion of the next government. Now it is, in effect, a nationwide contest to choose a government and especially a prime minister. The fact that 630 individuals are in the same process elected to represent 630 different constituencies in Parliament has become a subordinate feature. This is the main reason why, as is shown in Chapter XI, there is so little variation in the results obtained in different constituencies – even in the case of those separated by hundreds of miles.

Unlike the majority of constituency parties, which are overwhelmingly dependent on voluntary labour, the party headquarters, staffed by full-time professionals, are not likely to be caught seriously unprepared by the announcement of a general election, even if it has come unexpectedly. Much of the work on which their employees have been engaged for several years past has been designed with this very moment in mind.

They are thus well prepared to produce within a few days speakers' handbooks, outlining the party policy on a wide range of issues and documenting the failures of the opposing parties, which are quickly despatched to all Parliamentary candidates and others who are to speak on behalf of the party. These handbooks are supplemented by daily briefings on specific issues which arise during the course of the campaign. A great mass of posters, leaflets, policy statements and other propaganda material is also produced for distribution through the constituency party organisations. Some of the money subscribed to the national election funds of the parties is also disbursed to constituency parties, at this stage, to ensure that even the poorest of these have some ready cash with which to finance their campaign. In recent elections the Liberals have not been able to extend such monetary help to their constituency branches. It is usual at the beginning of the campaign for the party leadership to depute two or three senior figures to remain in London to oversee the running of the party headquarters and to act as a campaign committee, co-ordinating the day-to-day running of the campaign and particularly to take charge of the party's television programmes and dealings with the press. It is usual to select MPs representing safe seats for this important assignment, as those with marginal constituencies could hardly be expected to leave them for the greater part of the campaign.

Within a few days of the announcement of the dissolution, each party publishes its election manifesto. This is a statement of the issues which the party considers of the greatest importance and an indication, in more or less precise terms, of the party's policies to meet them. The Labour Party, which is strongly wedded to the idea that a party winning an election receives a mandate from the people to carry out definite policies, is normally more specific in its proposals.

The manifestos, which run to about two to three thousand words, are given the widest possible distribution, the print orders running into millions. In addition to the large-scale distribution through constituency parties, they form the basis of the policy sections in candidates' election addresses and they are widely reported in the press and on radio and television.

Despite the prominence which they are accorded, the election manifestos are seldom notable for breaking new ground. Nearly all the major proposals contained in past manifestos had already been published as official party policy and the function of the manifestos was to bring them together in a sharp and challenging manner and perhaps to add a few minor twists to give them an air of originality. In 1959 none of the three manifestos – *The Next Five Years* (Conservative), *Britain Belongs To You* (Labour), and *People Count* (Liberal) – contained any substantial new policy proposal.

The major political exchanges during elections now take place on the television screen. The 1959 election was the first of which this was really true, as in previous elections only a minority of voters had access to a television set. But the trend had become increasingly apparent ever since the first television election broadcasts, watched by less than 10 per cent of the electorate, were screened in 1951. By 1959 75 per cent of households possessed television sets and in future elections the proportion will exceed 90 per cent.

Television election broadcasts consist of two kinds: those for which the parties are responsible and news and other broadcasts undertaken by the BBC and the various commercial companies. The party broadcasts have been transmitted at each election since 1951, but those for which the broadcasting companies were responsible date from the 1959 general election.

The allocation of time for party programmes on television is made at a meeting between the Chief Whips of the three main parties and representatives of the BBC and ITA. Such meetings take place annually to agree on the arrangements for broadcasts between elections, and it is usual for the general election schedule to be drawn up well in advance. At the 1959 election the Conservative and Labour parties were each allocated four broadcasts of twenty minutes and one of fifteen minutes. The Liberal Party was given one broadcast of fifteen minutes and one of ten minutes, but the minor parties were completely unrepresented.

The Liberal Party has consistently claimed parity with its two larger rivals, and when the party whips met the broadcasting authorities in July 1963 to make arrangements for the 1964 election they obtained a substantially larger share than before. In 1964 the Labour and Conservative Parties will receive a total of seventy-five minutes each, while the Liberals will have forty-five minutes.

Sound broadcasting time is allocated at the same meetings and it is divided up in similar proportions to that on television. Provision is made for minor parties putting up more than fifty candidates to have one sound broadcast, but none has qualified since 1950 when the Communist Party had one broadcast of five minutes. Plaid Cymru, which puts up candidates in a high proportion of Welsh seats (which total less than fifty in all) has strenuously demanded time on the Welsh services of the BBC, hitherto with no success. The minor parties are bitterly critical of their exclusion and a statement issued by the Communist Party in August 1963 denouncing the share-out as a 'fraud' and alleging that the Chief Whips of the three large parties 'have carved up the time among themselves' probably typifies the attitude of all the smaller parties.

The use which the parties have made of their television programmes has varied considerably, and none of them has stuck to a consistent style throughout the three general elections in which television broadcasts have taken place. A wide variety of techniques has been adopted – live talks delivered straight into the camera by party leaders, filmed interviews – sometimes conducted by hostile journalists, sometimes by friendly MPs, interviews with voters in the street, specially shot film sequences, newsreel material and a great many charts, graphs and animated cartoons. The parties have shown great hesitancy in deciding whether to build their programmes round the most senior party spokesmen or to make use of their more experienced television performers, most of whom are lower down in the party hierarchy. By 1959 all parties appeared to have come round to the view that the actual party leader, whose significance to the electorate as an actual or potential prime minister could scarcely be exaggerated, must have the lion's share of the available time. Apart from the straight talks by party leaders, at which Mr Macmillan, Hugh Gaitskell and Mr Grimond all showed themselves adept in 1959, the most effective formula for election broadcasts seems to have been that adopted by the Labour Party in 1959. This consisted of a magazine programme, based to a large extent on the BBC *Tonight* programme and produced in the same studios, in which an election 'operations room' was simulated. Though the broadcasts were the fruit of months of careful planning, the actual material used was compiled at the last moment, and they had a spontaneity and immediacy hitherto not achieved in an election broadcast. The great majority of press and other observers agreed that the Labour broadcasts in 1959 were the best yet screened and it seems likely that they will be used by all three parties as the model for their next exercises in this medium, though it is probable that not quite so much nor so diverse material will again be squeezed into each programme. With their great professionalism and technical resources, the Conservatives are unlikely to find themselves with the shorter end of the stick for the second time running.

The election programmes staged by the BBC and the commercial television companies were hindered, on the one hand by an understandable desire to do nothing which would offend any of the party authorities, and on the other by serious doubts as to the legal standing of such broadcasts. The Representation of the People Act of 1949 had laid down that any operation 'presenting the candidate or his views' should be chargeable to election expenses. Newspapers were specifically excluded from this provision, but no mention was made of radio or television. The television companies were also bound by the Television Act of 1954 which prohibited political broadcasting, other than party political broadcasts, unless it was in the form of 'properly balanced discussion or debates'.

These legal barriers partly account for the extreme timidity shown by the broadcasting authorities in the period before 1959. At no previous general election had they screened any programmes with a political content and their handling of election news items had been extremely circumspect. The Rochdale by-election in 1958, when the Granada network screened a programme in which all three candidates appeared, marked a new departure. By 1959, fortified by legal advice, both television services had resolved to take the plunge and to embark on their own election programmes.

The most notable of these, in 1959, were the BBC's 'Hustings' and Granada's 'Election Marathon'. In the former series, two of which were produced in each of six of the BBC's seven regions, selected candidates from each of the three parties answered questions from an invited audience made up of supporters of each party. In the Welsh service programmes a candidate representing Plaid Cymru also took part.

'Election Marathon' was intended to consist of very short speeches, presented at off-peak viewing hours, by all the candidates in the area covered by the Granada network. In fact, of the 348 candidates eligible to take part only 231 appeared, as a number refused and Granada took the view that if one candidate in a constituency declined to take part his opponents also must be barred from the screen.

More important than the election programmes sponsored by the television authorities, was the fact that for the first time full news coverage was given to the election. Several times every day newsreel extracts from the speeches of party leaders appeared on the screen and every effort was made to give a balanced and comprehensive account of the progress of the campaign.

The absence of accusations of partisanship and the high viewing figures obtained by political programmes in the 1959 election should ensure that the television authorities will give subsequent elections even more extensive coverage, though it may be some years before direct confrontations between the party leaders, on the lines of the Kennedy-Nixon debates in 1960, appear on British television screens. Some further clarification, possibly in the form of legislation, of the legal position of electoral broadcasting is highly desirable. In the absence of a test case, it is by no means clear that candidates who appear on television, without returning the cost of the broadcast in their election expenses, are not transgressing the law. It is also undesirable that, in programmes dealing with individual constituencies, the refusal of one candidate to appear can prevent any of his rivals from taking part. The most notable occasion when this occurred was in the Kinross and West Perthshire by-election in November 1963, when the refusal of the Liberal candidate to appear barred the Prime Minister from the nation's television screens.

There is much evidence that television enabled voters in the 1959 general election to be better informed on the issues and to be more familiar with the personalities of leading politicians concerned than ever before.[1] It has often been observed that television has enabled a modern political leader to speak to more people in one evening than the total number that Gladstone or Disraeli succeeded in addressing at all the meetings during their entire careers. In 1959 more than six voters out of ten heard one or more of the party political broadcasts and virtually 100 per cent must have heard some extracts from election speeches on television or radio news bulletins. This is a far higher proportion than has ever been reached through constituency campaigning.

Television has also had its effects on other aspects of electioneering. The reporting of speeches in news bulletins enables rival political leaders to reply to each others' charges several times during the course of a day and thus the whole tempo of campaigning has been speeded up. Television has greatly increased the exposure of partisans to the propa-

1. See *Television and the Political Image* by Joseph Trenaman and Denis McQuail, Methuen, 1961, for a detailed account of the effects of television in the 1959 election.

ganda of the other side and this has almost certainly led to greater sophistication in the propaganda of all parties. It has also resulted in less partisanship in the press, as radio and television programmes are widely and justifiably regarded as impartial, and are thus used as a yardstick against which newspaper reports may be measured.

The role of the press in general elections, while still important, is shrinking. Television and radio are regarded both as more impartial and more immediate sources of election news, while public opinion polls have largely robbed newspapers of their claim to represent public opinion. None the less, all newspapers continue to devote extensive space to covering elections and each in its own distinctive way attempts to persuade its readers to support the party of its choice.

The degree of partisanship displayed by newspapers and the consistency with which they support a political party varies considerably, but on the evidence of their current editorial policies and their record at recent general elections, the political affiliations of national daily newspapers can be spelled out with reasonable certainty. The present-line up, with the most recently available circulation figures (those for the period January–June 1963) is shown in Table 15.

Table 15—Circulations of National Newspapers, June 1963

Conservative		Labour	
Daily Express	4,224,148	Daily Mirror	4,630,964
Daily Mail	2,479,446	Daily Herald	1,301,631
Daily Telegraph	1,290,012	The Guardian	266,243
Daily Sketch	922,937		
The Times	254,754		
TOTAL	9,171,297		6,198,838

The Guardian is, traditionally, a Liberal newspaper and still gives a measure of support to that party, but in recent years it has moved rather nearer to the Labour Party. *The Times* has normally been pro-Government, but in recent years it has been sharply critical of the Conservatives and it is questionable whether it will support them in the 1964 election. The Conservative predominance in the national press has increased since the 1959 general election, through the disappearance in 1960 of the *News Chronicle*, which had consistently supported the Liberal Party. Its circulation at the time of the 1959 election was 1,125,000. Fears had been expressed that the *Daily Herald*, in which the Trades Union Congress has a minority shareholding and which is, in effect, an official Labour newspaper, might also cease publication, but it was announced at the TUC in September 1963 that Mr Cecil King, its principal proprietor, had agreed to continue to publish it at least until the next general election.

The various morning, daily and evening papers published outside London are much more uniformly pro-Conservative than is the national press. But, dependent as they are on sales to people of all political views within the area in which they are published, they tend to be less partisan in style. The majority of them give reasonably full coverage during and between elections to the activities and viewpoints of the anti-Conservative parties.

The influence which the press has on its readers' voting intentions is slight, and is probably stronger between elections than during the actual campaign. In fact the majority of voters read newspapers with which they are politically in agreement, so the scope for effecting conversions is limited. Among national newspapers, only the *Daily Express* and, to a lesser extent the *Daily Mirror*, enjoy a large readership amongst their political opponents.

It has been suggested by some authorities that the *Daily Mirror* alone of British newspapers had a significant influence on voting in recent years. Thus, the Labour victory in 1945 was partly attributed to a *Mirror* feature entitled 'Vote for them', in which wives, mothers and sweethearts of servicemen overseas were entreated to vote Labour for their absent loved ones. Again, in 1951, the *Daily Mirror* headline 'Whose finger on the trigger?' was supposed to have robbed the Conservatives of a more pronounced victory by suggesting, at the height of the Abadan crisis, that a Conservative Prime Minister was more likely to precipitate a war.

But the *Daily Mirror*'s reputation for influencing voters took a hard knock at the 1959 general election. Three days before polling day, when public opinion polls were showing the parties running neck and neck, it splashed a mammoth headline 'THE TIME HAS COME FOR THE TORIES TO GO' and it delivered a series of comparable hammer blows on the succeeding three mornings. Yet when the votes were counted, the Tories were returned with an increased majority. This did not prove that the *Daily Mirror* had no influence on its readers' voting habits, but since then much less has been heard of the unique role of this newspaper. Though newspapers remain a major source of election news and take a lively part in the campaign, all the evidence suggests their influence on the results is extremely limited.

The parties are nevertheless anxious to secure as much publicity in the press, as well as on television and radio, as possible. In the 1959 campaign the then General Secretary of the Labour Party, Morgan Phillips, held daily press conferences which proved so newsworthy that the Labour campaign threatened at one time almost to monopolise space in the most Conservative of newspapers. A week later the Conservatives retaliated and Lord Hailsham and Lord Poole, their then Chairman and Vice-Chairman, met the press each day at a similar function. It seems certain that this will set the pattern for future elections.

While their campaign committees are holding the fort in London and supervising in detail the arrangements for handling the press and television, the party leaders are roaming the country speaking to a large number of meetings, some of them in the open air, in support of their party's candidates. In 1959 Mr Macmillan in a 16-day tour made 74 speeches while Hugh Gaitskell made 53 speeches in 13 days. Both party leaders concentrated on marginal constituencies many of which received visits from both leaders though their paths never actually crossed. Mr Grimond, whose constituency in the remote Orkney and Shetland islands claimed much of his time, made a much more modest one-day tour by helicopter.

Apart from their publicity value, which is great, the tours by party leaders put great heart into their supporters wherever they go. Large crowds are almost invariably attracted, far larger than for other political gatherings. In 1959 the largest outdoor meetings attracted audiences of up to ten or twelve thousand; while the maximum indoor attendance was probably about 2,500. A visit by the party leader early in the campaign can give a tremendous fillip to a local party and help to attract a large number of volunteers to help in the campaign.

Travelling with each party leader, whose fatigue progressively increases as polling day draws near, is a large entourage of party officials, press men and radio and television interviewers and cameramen. The leaders are in constant telephonic communication with their party headquarters and their appearances in party election broadcasts are recorded, 'on the road' or in the BBC's regional television studios.

At the end of their election tour, the party leaders finally set off for their own constituencies with a sense of profound relief.

The extreme exertion of the preceding three weeks are over, and there is now no more that they can do to influence the result. Their absence from their constituencies during the greater part of the campaign is unlikely to have caused any undue concern, for party leaders normally represent safe seats. During the last one or two days before the votes are cast they occupy themselves in much the same way as other candidates, but with the knowledge that they will soon be set apart from them, either to taste the power and responsibility of the premiership or to assume the scarcely less onerous, but infinitely less rewarding, responsibility of leading their parties on the opposition benches of the House of Commons.

CHAPTER TEN

POLLING DAY

WHEN POLLING day finally arrives the limelight which has shone throughout the preceding weeks on the party leaders and the national campaigns of the parties swings decisively back to the constituencies. The morning papers carry final appeals to vote for one or other of the parties, but otherwise an uneasy quiet descends upon the national scene. The final shots have been fired on radio and television, the party headquarters have done their best or their worst, all now depends on the voter.

Polling day is a very long one for those most intimately concerned. The earliest risers are the presiding officers and poll clerks of the various polling stations. They have to be at their posts by 6.30 am, or thereabouts, in order to be ready to receive the first voters at seven o'clock.

Each polling station is in charge of a presiding officer, who has a number of poll clerks to help him. Most polling stations are housed in schools, but a wide variety of other premises are used in some constituencies. If no suitable building is available, a temporary prefabricated building may be erected for the occasion. On arrival at the polling station, the presiding officer has to satisfy himself that all the necessary equipment has been installed.

Inside the polling station will be a row of voting compartments, shaped like telephone kiosks, but with a sliding curtain covering the entrance to ensure privacy. Within the compartment will be a shelf, at waist height, on which voters can mark their ballot papers. A strong indelible pencil is attached by string to the shelf. A notice giving instructions how to vote is pinned up in each voting compartment, and is also displayed outside the polling station.

Opposite the voting compartments is a table or tables

behind which the presiding officer and his assistants sit. In between, in full view of the presiding officer, stand one or more ballot boxes. The presiding officer will have been supplied with a copy of the election register for his polling district, a list of proxy and postal voters, an adequate supply of ballot papers and equipment for marking the ballot papers with the official mark. The ballot papers are printed in books, with counterfoils, rather like cloakroom tickets. Serial numbers are printed on the back of each paper and each counterfoil.

The presiding officer is in sole charge of his polling station. He and his assistants have to swear a declaration of secrecy that they will not divulge, except for some purpose authorised by law, any information as to who has or has not voted or reveal to anyone before the close of the poll the nature of the official mark. A similar declaration has to be made by the candidate and his agent or representatives before they may be admitted to a polling station for any purpose except to cast their own votes.

It is the responsibility of the presiding officer to see that no unauthorised person is admitted to the polling station, that order is maintained and that the poll is conducted lawfully in every respect. At least one police constable will be on duty throughout the day at each polling station to assist the presiding officer to keep order.

Immediately before the poll opens at seven o'clock, the presiding officer must show the ballot box empty to whoever is in the polling station and then lock it and place his seal on the lock.

When the first voter arrives he will give his full name and address to a polling clerk who will tell him his number, put a tick against his name on the register, write his electoral number on the counterfoil of the ballot paper, emboss the ballot paper with the official mark and hand the ballot paper to the voter. The purpose of the official mark, the nature of which is kept secret, is to prevent the forgery of ballot papers. Poll clerks must take great care to remember to emboss each paper as it is issued, or the vote will later be invalidated through no fault of the voter.[1] It is improper to emboss ballot papers in advance, because of the risk of theft.

The voter takes his ballot paper into one of the voting compartments and marks an X against the candidate of his choice. There is no indication on the ballot paper of the party of the candidates, nor may the voter enquire this information of the presiding officer or poll clerks. Though the great majority of voters, will have learnt before reaching the polling station who represents whom, a handful of voters in each constituency are uncertain and confused and consequently find themselves voting by accident against the party of their choice.

All that the ballot papers do contain are the surnames of the candidates, in alphabetical order, and their full names and addresses and descriptions, which normally refers to their occupation. A sample ballot paper is shown in Figure 6.

When he has marked his ballot paper the voter must fold it, and, in the view of the presiding officer, drop it into the ballot box. By this elaborate procedure the secrecy of the ballot is at once protected and the possibility of forged papers being introduced into the ballot box virtually eliminated.

If a voter spoils his ballot paper he may obtain another one on application to the presiding officer, who will mark the spoiled paper 'cancelled' and put it on one side till the end of the day, when he has to account to the Returning Officer for all the ballot papers which he has issued.

Blind and incapacitated voters may ask the presiding officer to mark their ballot papers for them, or may bring a friend with them who will be permitted to mark their ballot papers for them.

If the election is on a Saturday, which does not normally happen in the case of Parliamentary elections though

1. In Derbyshire North-East, in 1922, the Labour candidate was elected by 5 votes, with a larger number of unmarked ballot papers in favour of his opponent. It is clear that he owed his victory to the failure of the poll clerks to mark some of the ballot papers.

many local government elections are held on that day, a Jewish voter who objects on religious grounds to voting in the prescribed manner may also request the presiding officer to mark his ballot paper for him.

By the time the first voters have cast their votes, the election agent and his helpers will already be in action.

Figure 6—Sample Ballot Paper

SMITH (James Henry Smith of 27 Roundchurch Mansions, London, S.E.22, Plumber.)	
TAYLOR (William Thomas Percy Taylor of 'Little-hammer', Abinger, Surrey, Company Director.)	
YOUNG (Mary Jane Young of 14 Argyll Road, Oldham, Lancashire, Housewife.)	

Outside each polling station will be 'tellers', each proudly sporting his party colours, who will ask voters for their electoral numbers as they leave the polling stations. There is no obligation on voters to reveal this information but the great majority of them are normally willing to do so, at least to the tellers representing their own party. Many of the tellers are school-children who are on holiday for the day and have been recruited for the job by parents who are staunch party members. Sometimes they may be paid by the party or their parents, but most of them are willing to help out for nothing. An excess of zeal may occasionally be revealed in a frosty unwillingness to co-operate with the tellers from 'the other side', but more frequently a feeling of *camaraderie* prevails and numbers are willingly swopped.

Tellers also represent the last resource of parties to remind voters of the names of their candidates, and it is fairly common for an absent-minded voter to check with his party's teller on his way into the polling station the name of the person for whom he should vote.

Each party will have established a sub-committee room near to the polling station which will contain a copy of the register on which will be marked all the voters who have promised to support the party's candidate. At hourly intervals, or possibly more frequently, throughout the day messengers will bring back from the tellers lists of the electoral numbers of those who have already voted so that they can be crossed off the register. An army of 'knockers up' will have been recruited to call later in the day on those who have not already voted.

Soon after breakfast the candidate, wearing an outsize rosette, will be ceremoniously introduced – probably by his agent – to the presiding officer, with whom he will exchange a few light-hearted remarks. The ostensible reason for the visit is to satisfy himself that everything is in order, though there is virtually never any question of this not being the case. During his tour the candidate will also drop into all his sub-committee rooms to give a word of encouragement to his supporters.

Throughout the day his party is likely to have one or more loudspeaker cars touring areas where its support is concentrated, urging voters to record their votes as early as possible in the day, thus reducing the pressure on the party machine during the evening. For much of the day the candidate himself is likely to be in charge of the loudspeaker, making a personal appeal to the voters to support him.

By 9 am perhaps one elector in ten may have voted.

The majority of these would be men, casting their votes on their way to work. During the daytime a steady trickle of housewives make their way to the polling stations, but a surprisingly high proportion prefer to wait until the evening and to go along with their husbands.

The result is that many party workers find themselves less than fully occupied until at least five or six o'clock in the evening. In the morning and afternoon sick and elderly voters are called on and offered lifts to the poll. Knockers up will be kept busy throughout the afternoon, but will find many houses empty and at others will be told to come back in the evening.

By six o'clock it is unusual for more than 50 per cent of the electors to have cast their votes and about that time begins an increasingly frantic effort by each party machine to get its supporters to the poll in the three hours remaining. This is especially important for the Labour Party, as working-class wives are much less likely to vote earlier in the day than their middle-class counterparts. A much higher proportion of Labour votes than of Conservative ones are cast in the evening, and non-political factors such as the weather and the appeal of the evening's television programmes can have an important effect on the result in closely contested constituencies.

In the evening every available helper is mobilised to knock up voters and, wherever possible, a car is provided for every group of knockers up, so that lifts to the poll may be offered to reluctant voters. Parties with a good and well-manned organisation may well be able to knock up all their supporters who have not voted earlier, as many as six times during the course of the evening. Despite this encouragement some voters remain obdurate and refuse to turn out, others delay so long that in the end it is too late to go, a few arrive at the polling station after nine o'clock and find it closed.

But allowing for inaccuracies in the election register, for removals and for people who are sick or away from their homes on election day, without having arranged to vote by post, the proportion of electors who actually vote in parliamentary elections is rather high. Since 1950 it has ranged from 76·7 per cent to 84 per cent, which suggests that the proportion of avoidable abstentions is probably no more than 10 per cent.

Promptly at 9 pm, the presiding officer must close his polling station, even if there are electors waiting to cast their votes. He must then seal the ballot boxes, so that no more ballot papers may be inserted. He then makes out his ballot paper account. On this he must state the number of ballot papers with which he had been issued at the beginning of the day, the number of papers in the ballot box and the number of unused and spoilt papers. He must then make up packages containing the marked registers, the counterfoils and the unused ballot papers and deliver these to the Returning Officer. The police, under the direction of the Returning Officer, will collect the ballot boxes and take them straight to the place where the votes are to be counted.

The count is usually held in the Town Hall or other large public hall in the constituency. In most borough constituencies it is held on the evening of polling day; in most counties it is postponed until the following morning. It is a crowded and lively occasion. The hall is furnished with long trestle tables at either side of which are seated the Returning Officer's assistants who are to count the votes. There is an air of expectancy as the room gradually fills up with candidates, their wives, agents and leading supporters, whose function is to act as 'counting agents' or scrutineers of the actual counting of the votes. The number of counting agents permitted to each candidate is decided by the Returning Officer, but the total should not be less than the number of counting assistants and each candidate must be allowed the same number. All attending the count must sign a declaration of secrecy, promising not to attempt to discover how any individual has voted or to reveal such information to any other person. The press may be admitted, at the discretion of the Returning Officer, and a public gallery may also be provided.

By about 9.15 in most boroughs the first ballot boxes will arrive from the polling stations. The ballot box containing the postal votes will be among the first to arrive.

Each box is emptied of its contents, which are immediately counted to make sure that they tally with the number given in the presiding officer's ballot paper account. When every box has been emptied and its contents counted the ballot papers are mixed together in one large pile, so that it is impossible to tell accurately how the voters of each polling district have recorded their votes.

The ballot papers are now sorted out into piles representing votes polled for each individual candidate. They are then counted into bundles of 100. All the time the counting agents, who will be standing behind the counting assistants, will be keeping an eagle eye on their activities – making sure that none of their candidate's papers have inadvertently been included amongst those of their opponents.

In a safe or hopeless constituency there is little tension, and the candidates and their supporters are much more concerned with whispered reports that may be coming in about the results in other constituencies, and the national trend to which they point. Some thoughtful Returning Officers go to the trouble of installing a television set in an anteroom and many scrutineers spend a lot of their time popping in and out to acquaint themselves with the latest position.

In a marginal constituency, however, attention is firmly fixed on the counting, and as the rival piles of votes mount so do the hopes and fears of the candidates and their supporters.

In the process of sorting the votes the counting assistants come across a number of ballot papers whose validity is doubtful. They place these on one side and when all the other votes have been counted the Returning Officer adjudicates them in the presence of the candidates and their agents, giving his reasons for accepting, or rejecting, them in each case.

There are four categories of ballot paper which must be declared void – those which do not bear the official mark, those on which votes are given for more than one candidate, those on which anything is written by which the voter can be identified and those which are unmarked.

Other papers in which the intention of the voter is unclear should be declared invalid by the Returning Officer, but where the intention is clear, but the mark has been incorrectly made he should accept their validity. Examples of incorrectly marked papers which are nevertheless valid are those where the X is placed otherwise than in the proper place, but still leaving no doubt which candidate the voter prefers; those where a tick or similar mark has been used instead of a cross and those where 'Yes' and 'No', or '1' and '2' or '1' and '0' have been written to express a preference between candidates.

When the Returning Officer has given his adjudication of the doubtful votes they should be added to their appropriate pile and the total of each candidate's votes will be recorded by the chief counting assistant who will give it to the Returning Officer. The Returning Officer will then privately inform the candidates and their agents of the result of the count. If the result is close the Returning Officer may order a recount, and any candidate may claim a recount which the Returning Officer may not reasonably refuse. If the first count shows a majority of less than 500 a demand for a recount is likely, and where the majority is less than a hundred several recounts may be held. It is also permissible for a recount to be demanded by a candidate in danger of losing his deposit where the number of his votes is close to the minimum required, even though the majority of the leading candidate may be numbered in tens of thousands.

If after several recounts, there is an equality of votes between the two leading candidates, the Returning Officer draws a lot to decide which is elected. Prior to 1948 the rule was that the Returning Officer should have a casting vote. The last occasion on which this invidious situation arose in Parliamentary elections was at Ashton-under-Lyne in 1886, but there have been a number of more recent examples in local government elections.

As soon as the result of the poll has been ascertained, the Returning Officer makes a public announcement of the votes obtained by the various candidates and declares the new Member elected. It is then usual for the winning candidate to propose a vote of thanks to the Returning Officer and his staff for their conduct of the election, during which he takes the opportunity also of thanking his own supporters and declaring that the result is a triumph for his party and the cause which it represents. The vote of thanks is seconded by the runner-up, who also gives his own partisan interpretation of the result, as do other candidates (if any) who are also expected to have their say. Great demonstrations of enthusiasm are made by their supporters, especially by the winning party when the seat has changed hands.

As soon as possible after the result has been declared, the Returning Officer must publish it in writing. He must also attach, to the writ which he has received from the Clerk of the Crown authorising him to conduct the election, a certificate naming the newly elected Member. The writ is then returned, post free, to the Clerk of the Crown.

The Returning Officer must also collect up all the documents concerned with the election – the ballot papers used and unused, the ballot paper accounts and rejected ballot papers, the marked copies of the election registers and lists of proxies and the counterfoils of all ballot papers – and send these to the Clerk of the Crown. All these documents will be retained for one year and then destroyed, unless an order to the contrary is made by the High Court or the House of Commons.

The validity of an election may be challenged by a petition to the High Court, which may be presented by an elector for the constituency concerned or by one of the candidates. The Court, in considering the petition, may order a scrutiny of the ballot papers and other relevant documents listed above. The High Court must report its findings to the Speaker of the House of Commons and if it has found the election invalid the House will proceed to authorise the issue of a writ for a new election.

Election petitions are rare, partly no doubt because of the great expense involved to the petitioner and partly because a Member is unlikely to be unseated if only minor irregularities are proved.[1] The most recent election petition, by Sir Oswald Mosley following his defeat as a Union Movement candidate at North Kensington in 1959, was unsuccessful as was that concerning the Drake division of Plymouth in 1929, the only other petition to be made, since 1924, except those concerning Mr Wedgwood Benn and the two Sinn Fein Members in Northern Ireland, discussed on page 84. In each of these three cases the issue was the qualification of the candidates not the conduct of the election. But the main reason why election petitions are seldom resorted to is the undoubted fact that major irregularities are almost unknown in modern British elections.

On election night special programmes relaying the constituency results as they become known are broadcast on sound radio and both television channels. Expert commentators interpret the results and, on the basis of the trend revealed by the first contests to be counted, attempt, usually with a large measure of success, to predict what the final result will be. Electronic computers, which have been used for the same purpose, have not noticeably improved on the accuracy of their predictions.[2]

There is lively competition to be the first constituency

1. Butler and Rose, op. cit., p. 280, quote a senior party organiser on this point: 'If we lost a seat by one vote and I could clearly prove illegal practices by the other side I wouldn't try. It would cost perhaps £5,000 and they might be able to show that our man had slipped up in some way. But worse than that, it might start tit-for-tat petitions and no party could afford a lot of them. On the whole, we are both law-abiding and it's as well to leave each other alone.'

2. It is the high degree of homogeneity of the British electorate which enables such forecasts to be made on the basis of the first handful of results.

to declare a result. Traditionally, the city of Salford which contains two constituencies has claimed this honour, but in 1959 it was pipped at the post by Billericay. Other constituencies which usually succeed in being amongst the first to declare their results are Watford and Cheltenham. But any constituency which consists of a highly concentrated urban area stands a good chance of being first, so long as its Returning Officer is prepared to spend extra money on employing more numerous and better skilled counting assistants – and unless, of course, there is a recount.

Normally, the first result is available by ten o'clock and by 2.30 am when the broadcasting programmes close down for the night almost 400 constituencies will have been counted. By this time the result of the election should be clear, unless it is extremely close. As it is the urban seats which are counted overnight, Labour needs to establish a considerable lead among these if it is to emerge as the final victor. A Labour lead of less than 50 overnight points to a Conservative victory while if the figures show Labour between 50 and 65 seats ahead it is certain that the result will be close.

At about ten o'clock the following day the count is begun in the other constituencies and from eleven o'clock onwards the results are broadcast, as they come in, to about 6 pm, by which time all but a handful of remote Scottish constituencies have declared their results. Long before this one of the party leaders will normally have conceded defeat, and it will be clear who is to govern the country for the next four or five years.

CHAPTER ELEVEN

PREDICTING THE RESULT

THE BRITISH voter is subjected to a heavy barrage of propaganda from all three major parties, and to occasional salvoes from minor groups and independents, during election campaigns and, to a lesser degree, at other times. Earlier chapters of this book have sought to describe the various ways in which the parties seek to influence public opinion. This chapter will attempt to discern whether all this activity makes much difference to the way that people vote.

The short answer is 'not much'. The majority of voters form their voting habits during their youth and do not deviate thereafter. The allegiance of a large, but decreasing, proportion of voters is determined predominately by social class. It is known that in every post-war election at least three-quarters of middle-class voters supported the Conservative Party and almost two-thirds of manual workers voted for the Labour Party. It is possible to draw up, with reasonable assurance of accuracy, an occupational scale, with mineworkers at one end and stockbrokers at the other, to show the degree of support commanded by each of the two parties.

With rising standards of living and a gradual blurring of class divisions, non-class factors are beginning to determine the electoral choice of an increasing number of voters. But it seems likely that for many years to come social class will remain the largest single factor influencing voters.

The first impression which British elections make on the observer is one of overwhelming solidity in the support of each party. In the 1959 election, for instance, the net result was that over the previous four years one person in every hundred had switched his vote from the Labour Party to the Conservatives. Evidence from the Gallup Poll suggests, however, that no less than one voter in six acted differently in 1959 than in 1955.[1] It was because changes between the parties took place in both directions and largely cancelled each other out that they appeared to have so little effect. From time to time a general election occurs in which the changes are predominately in one direction and then the net effect is much more dramatic. Such was the case in the elections of 1906, 1931 and 1945. In each of these the winning party – Liberal, Conservative and Labour respectively – made a net gain of over 200 seats, against an average gain of considerably less than 100 seats in all other general elections of the present century.

In a situation where support for the two main parties has been almost evenly balanced, as has been the case since 1950, the outcome of an election may be determined by the success of the parties in actually getting their supporters to the poll. If the number of abstainers who normally support one party is only marginally larger this may in itself make all the difference between victory and defeat. It appears to be established that middle-class electors are more likely to cast their vote in general elections (though not always in by-elections), and that abstainers are mostly found amongst working-class voters. It seems probable therefore that a high level of political interest, resulting in a poll of more than 80 per cent, is advantageous to the Labour Party. Where there is less interest and the total poll is lower, it may be expected to favour the Conservatives.

Despite the increasing interest which sociologists have, since 1945, shown in elections and in voting habits, little is known about what actually causes people to change their voting allegiances. There is evidence[2] that many more people switch over between elections rather than during

1. See Butler and Rose, op. cit., p. 196, 'the Conservative, Liberal and Labour parties each gained votes from the others and from abstainers – and each lost them'.

2. See Trenaman and McQuail, op. cit.

election campaigns. This has led the parties to begin their active campaigning at a much earlier stage than in the past. Hence the Conservatives' highly successful poster campaign (on the theme of 'Life is better with the Conservatives – don't let Labour ruin it') in 1958–9 and the extensive press advertising which both the major parties began in May 1963 in preparation for the general election of 1964.

But the majority of voters seem to be immune to direct influence by the political parties. The different items in a party's programme and the promises which it makes seem to make little difference to people's voting intentions. A glance at the charts produced by the Gallup Poll showing the fluctuations in the level of support of the different parties in the period since 1945 shows less correlation than one might expect with major political events and with the triumphs and disasters of ministers and opposition leaders. A closer examination reveals a high correlation with the general level of economic activity in the country. In a period of expansion, the Government, whatever its political complexion, tends to prosper – a rise in the bank rate a damper on wage claims, a restriction of credit facilities a rise in unemployment, and its support almost invariably slumps.

Support for the parties seems sometimes to be governed more by the activities of their natural allies than by what they do themselves. If businessmen are seen to be behaving in an abnormally rapacious manner, or a takeover battle is fought with obvious disregard to the public interest, it is the Conservative Party which suffers. Similarly, if trade unions appear to be behaving irresponsibly and, especially if strikes occur which inconvenience the public without at the same time strongly convincing them of the justice of the strikers' case, the Labour Party takes a hard knock. This is rough justice, perhaps, but each party gains considerably in financial and other ways from its alliances so they hardly complain too loudly at the compensating disadvantages.

The very small effect which the national campaigns of

the parties appear to have on the voters does not by any means prove that they have been misdirected. It is probable that each party's efforts largely cancel out those of its opponents, but if either were unilaterally to desist it would mean a walk-over for the other side. And it is the very volume and intensity of the campaigns of the two larger parties which guarantee for them a monopoly of the votes of some 90 per cent of the electorate. Any reduction of their efforts would open the way to one or other of them being supplanted by the Liberals or some other smaller party.

In one respect, television has proved a far more effective means of campaigning than any previously known. It has been established[1] that in 1959, as a result of the television election programmes, the majority of voters were substantially better informed than in any previous election about the issues of the election and the policies of the various parties. The fact that few voters actually changed their intentions as a result of these programmes, in 1959, does not necessarily mean that this would be the case in future elections. It is much too soon fully to gauge the effect that television will have on British elections, but it is likely to be far-reaching.

If the national campaigns of the parties appear to have had little effect on people's voting, what of the campaigns in the constituencies? In the period before the First World War many voters were probably directly influenced by these campaigns. But, as we have seen, the growth of the mass media has shifted attention overwhelmingly away from the individual candidates towards the party leaders. The result has been that neither the personality of the candidate nor the quality of his campaign has much effect on the average voter.

Nearly all authorities agree that virtually no candidate, however outstanding, is worth more than 500 extra votes to his party, and the great majority of candidates are clearly worth much less. This is not true of by-elections,

1. See particularly, Trenaman and McQuail, op. cit. Chapter X.

where voters are relieved of the responsibility of helping to choose a government and more of them feel freer to give weight to personality factors. It is also less true of Liberal candidates than of those representing the two larger parties. But it remains true that in the great majority of constituencies, the most distinguished of statesmen can hope to win very few extra votes than would the most mediocre of party hacks. If there are constituencies where the personality of the candidate and even more important, the trouble which he is prepared to take to serve his constituents, are still significant factors they are those in the most remote parts of Scotland and Wales. But there are probably less than a dozen of these remaining.

Nor does the efficiency of the party machine in the constituencies appear to have much influence on the result. Every party worker is vividly aware of specific voters who were got to the poll *only* because of his powers of persuasion or because he gave them a lift to the poll at the last possible hour. But the sum total of these achievements does not amount to a great deal. The number of people voting in constituencies in which each party has a high level of organisation is only fractionally higher than the turn-out in those constituencies where party organisation is most rudimentary.[1]

One field in which organisation does make a measurable contribution is postal voting. There is no doubt that the Conservatives have been much more successful in registering postal voters than their opponents. As over 2 per cent of votes cast in recent general elections have been postal votes, it is clear that, in closely contested constituencies postal voters can spell the difference between victory and defeat. It seems highly probable that the Conservatives have gained between 5 and 15 extra seats at each election since 1950 because of their greater success in this sphere. This may be a small number, but in 1950, when Labour was returned by a majority of seven and, according to Mr H. G. Nicholas, 'It seems hard not to believe that the

1. Butler and Rose, op. cit., pp. 194–5.

Conservatives owe at least 10 seats to the postal vote',[1] it was enough to make the difference between a small but viable majority and one which placed enormous strains on Labour MPs and led to a dissolution within two years.

In 1959 there were 24 seats in which the Conservative majority exceeded the total number of postal votes (see Appendix 5). It seems probable that in about half of these this factor alone accounted for their victory.

It is probably inevitable that the Conservatives should gain some advantage from the postal vote. Middle-class voters generally are more aware of their civic rights and more ready to claim them than are manual workers and their families. But the decisive edge which the Conservatives have achieved, which ensures them more than 75 per cent of the postal votes in most constituencies, is a direct result of their more professional organisation. It is here that their ability to employ more than twice as many agents as the Labour Party, and to provide them more often with clerical assistance has paid dividends. Although Labour certainly now shows more awareness of the importance of the postal vote than it did in 1950, it has only very partially succeeded in closing the gap. It is probably true that a big majority of Labour voters who move house or are taken seriously ill in the months preceding a general election do not record their votes. The number of lost Conservative votes is substantially less.

A striking fact about the British electorate is its homogeneity. There are virtually no important regional issues in British politics, except in Wales, Scotland and Northern Ireland, and in the first two of these they have remarkably little effect upon the voting. It is remarkable that in every general election the swing of opinion is almost uniform throughout the country and operating in the same direction. The 1959 general election was, to some extent, an exception, as it showed pro-Labour swings in South Lancashire and Scotland, whereas in the rest of the country the swing was to the Conservatives. This could be accounted for by

1. *The British General Election of 1950*, Macmillan, 1951, p. 9.

regional pockets of unemployment, and it was the first time in over thirty years that there had been region-wide variations from the national trend.

The degree of homogeneity is sufficient for highly accurate deductions to be made as to the composition of the House of Commons from any given percentage swing of opinion from one party to another. The term 'swing' was first applied to elections by Mr David Butler. It is defined as the average of one party's gain and another's loss. Thus, if at one election the Conservatives poll 50 per cent of the votes and Labour 45 per cent and at the next election the figures are reversed, there has been a swing to Labour of 5 per cent. (If both parties lose to a third it is calculated by taking half the difference between the two parties' losses, e.g. If at one election the Conservatives poll 60 per cent and Labour 40 per cent and at the next the Conservatives poll 50 per cent, Labour 38 per cent and the Liberals 12 per cent, the net swing from Conservative to Labour is 4 per cent.) On the basis of recent general elections, it can be assumed, provided there is no large variation in the proportion of the vote going to the Liberals and other smaller parties, that each swing of 1 per cent between the Labour and Conservative parties will lead to between 15 and 18 seats changing hands. Table 16 shows the probable division of seats in the House of Commons given any likely swing in the 1964 election.

Is it possible to forecast what the swing will be? News-papers and party organisations have never been shy of attempting to do so, but their predictions have often proved wide of the mark. There are, however, three rather more objective yardsticks which can be applied – by-elections, local elections and public opinion polls.

By-elections have been used as a rough and ready measure of the Government's standing for well over a hundred years. They are still regarded as important political indicators. To read too much into them may, however, have unfortunate consequences, for there are many reasons why the result of any particular by-election may be widely

Table 16—Swing from 1959 Result, and Change in Seats

% of votes*			Seats		
Swing from 1959	Con.	Lab.	Con.	Lab.	Con. maj.
Con. to Lab.					
10	39·4	53·8	194	429	−235
9	40·4	52·8	215	408	−193
8	41·4	51·8	234	389	−155
7	42·4	50·8	256	367	−111
6	43·4	49·8	276	347	− 71
5	44·4	48·8	284	339	− 55
4½	44·9	48·3	291	332	− 41
4	45·4	47·8	300	323	− 23
3½	45·9	47·3	311	312	− 1
3	46·4	46·8	323	300	23
2½	46·9	46·3	328	295	33
2	47·4	45·8	340	283	57
1½	47·9	45·3	345	278	67
1	48·4	44·8	351	272	79
½	48·9	44·3	357	266	91
Actual result:	49·4	43·8	365	258	107
Lab. to Con.					
½	49·9	43·3	374	249	125
1	50·4	42·8	388	235	153
1½	50·9	42·3	394	229	165
2	51·4	41·8	402	221	181
2½	51·9	41·3	409	214	195
3	52·4	40·8	420	203	217
3½	52·9	40·3	429	194	235
4	52·4	39·8	443	180	263
4½	53·9	39·3	448	175	273
5	54·4	38·8	462	161	301
6	55·4	37·8	471	152	319
7	56·4	36·8	482	141	341
8	57·4	35·8	496	127	369
9	58·4	34·8	504	119	385
10	59·4	33·8	509	114	395

* Based on percentage of total votes cast in whole country.

(The above table was first published in Butler and Rose, op. cit.)

misleading as a reflection of the national strength of the parties. Regional and local issues which tend to cancel out in a general election, may assume disproportionate importance; the turn-out, which at a general election is normally between 75 and 85 per cent, fluctuates widely (in the 1955–9 Parliament from 24·9 to 90 per cent); the personal qualities of candidates have a greater effect than in a general election; and minor party and independent candidates are more likely to intervene and their influence, though marginal, is difficult to interpret.

The trend revealed by a succession of by-elections does appear, however, from past experience to offer a fairly reliable guide to the movement of political opinion. But there is a marked tendency to exaggerate the trend against the existing Government. Governments invariably do a little better in general elections than preceding by-elections would have led one to expect. The greatest drawback about by-elections as political indicators, however, is that they take place only spasmodically and a by-election held in May often proves a poor guide to political feeling in November.

This is even more true of the second of our three yardsticks – local elections. These take place only once a year – in May – except every third year when county council elections are also held in March or April. As Mr Hugh Berrington[1] has shown, local elections – particularly those for borough councils – are a remarkably accurate political barometer at the time they are held, notwithstanding the considerably lower turn-out of voters at local as compared with general elections. A further disadvantage is that rather elaborate calculations have to be made before the results of local elections, which are held on the basis of different electoral areas, can be applied to general election trends.

None of these objections apply to opinion polls which are the newest and much the most reliable of election indicators.

Two polling organisations – the Gallup Poll whose

1. See articles in *Aspect*, May 1963 and January 1964.

results are published in the *Daily Telegraph* and the National Opinion Poll reported in the *Daily Mail* – take regular monthly, and sometimes weekly, soundings of the electorate. Appendix 4 contains a record of their findings for the period since the 1959 general election. The *Daily Express* Poll, whose methods are shrouded in some secrecy, publishes its findings more spasmodically.

Although the first two polls interview a sample of less than 2,000 electors, their predictions of general election results have been well within the range of the 4 per cent sampling error within which they work. Table 17 shows the record of the various polls in the general elections since the war:

Table 17—General Election Forecasts

Percentage gap between major parties:

		Forecast	Error
1945	Gallup	6·0	3·4
	Actual gap	9·4	
1950	Gallup	1·5	1·1
	Daily Express	0·5	2·1
	Actual gap	2·6	
1951	Gallup	−2·5	3·3
	Daily Express	−4·0	4·8
	Daily Sketch	−7·0	7·8
	Actual gap	0·8	
1955	Gallup	3·5	0·2
	Daily Express	2·7	0·6
	Actual gap	3·3	
1959	Gallup	2·0	2·2
	Daily Express	3·7	0·5
	NOP	3·9	0·3
	Actual gap	4·2	

In 1951 all the polls predicted a greater poll for the Conservatives, though in the event Labour gained more votes. But as the Conservatives won more seats in the

House of Commons, they could still claim to have picked the winner, as they have succeeded in doing at each post-war general election.

Their record in by-election predictions has proved rather less accurate.[1] Opinion polls are far from perfect, but they do give much the most accurate guide to the movement of political opinion and their forecasts immediately before a general election can be relied upon, with reasonable confidence, to pick the winner, unless the gap between the two leading parties is an extremely narrow one.

1. For a detailed description of public opinion polls and their record in predicting elections, see an article by the present author in *Aspect*, March 1963.

CHAPTER TWELVE

HOW MUCH DOES IT COST?

IT IS probable that the cost of elections is less in the United Kingdom than in most democratic countries, and in particular, substantially less than in the United States. But total election expenses do amount to a considerable sum, both those chargeable to the Exchequer and to local authorities and those for which the candidates and the political parties are responsible.

There are three categories of expenditure chargeable to public funds – the cost of printing and compiling the register, the Returning Officers' expenses and the cost to the post office of the free delivery of electoral communications.

Under the 1948 Representation of the People Act provision was made for the compilation of two election registers each year. In 1949 as an economy cut the number was reduced to one, thereby effecting a saving of about £650,000 per year. At present prices it would probably cost about a million pounds to reintroduce a second register and thus ensure that it was kept more up-to-date.

The cost of the election register is borne equally by the Treasury and the local authorities. It is of course an annual charge and the cost in 1961–2 was £2,360,000. As the register is used annually for borough council and other local government elections and every three years for county council elections, it would be unrealistic to count the whole cost of maintaining the register as part of the expense of a general election.

Other costs charged to the public are the Returning Officers' expenses. These include the cost of publishing the notice of the election, and receiving and publicising the nominations and of sending out poll cards to all electors. Much the largest expense, however, is the employing of polling-station clerks on election day and of people to count the votes after the poll has closed.

The total amount of Returning Officers' expenses in recent general elections is shown in Table 18.

Table 18—Returning Officers' Expenses

1945	£677,999	1951	£1,015,357
1950	£806,974	1955	£1,106,631
		1959	£1,303,694

This worked out in 1959 at an average of just over £2,000 per constituency, and it is chargeable to the Consolidated Fund. It is certainly an underestimate of the expense involved as no adequate provision is made for the temporary diversion from other work during elections of full-time local government employees.

The Treasury derive one small but regular source of income from elections – the forfeiture of deposits. This has brought in the following sums in post-war general elections:

Table 19—Lost Deposits

Year	Number of lost deposits	Total sum
1945	163	£24,450
1950	461	£69,150
1951	96	£14,400
1955	100	£15,000
1959	116	£17,400

No estimates are published of the cost to the post office of the free delivery of election literature, but as it must involve a considerable number of man hours it is by no means inconsiderable.

When every allowance is made, however, for indirect expenses it seems improbable that a general election costs the public purse more than about £2,000,000 plus a proportion of the *annual* cost of maintaining the election register. This is surely a small price to pay for the privilege of electing our own leaders.

The cost to candidates and their parties of fighting elections is substantially greater than the cost to the public. The amount of money which may be spent on behalf of a candidate during the actual election campaign is strictly limited by law. The campaign is usually regarded as dating from the announcement of a dissolution in the case of a general election or the date that the vacancy occurs in the case of a by-election, though the law is woolly on this point. It may be that only the shorter period following the actual dissolution (or issue of a writ) is in fact covered by the law. On the other hand, the campaign might be held to date from the announcement of a candidature and this is why all parties are careful to describe their standard bearers as *prospective* candidates until the announcement of the dissolution. The point has never been contested in the courts and, in practice, all candidates play safe and return their expenses for the longer period.

Until 1918 the whole of the Returning Officers' expenses in each constituency was chargeable to the candidates, and this constituted a considerable extra burden, especially for poorer candidates and parties. Since 1883 there has been a restriction on the amount which can be spent on behalf of each candidate, and though the electorate has greatly increased and the value of money depreciated, the level of permitted expenditure has been lowered both in 1918 and in 1948. The effect of this has been that the actual money expended was lower in the 1959 general election than in 1906.

Since 1948 the maximum expenditure permitted in Great Britain has been:

In county constituencies: £450 plus 2d. per elector.

In borough constituencies: £450 plus 1½d. per elector. In Northern Ireland the limits are 2d. per elector plus an allowance for agents' fee not exceeding £75 in a county election or £50 in a borough election. This amounts in practice to about two-thirds of the allowance in Great Britain.

Candidates' personal expenses, not exceeding £100, are excluded from the limitation. The effect of this restriction is that in the average constituency the maximum expenditure permitted is about £900 per candidate. The average maximum for county constituencies is about £950 and that for boroughs about £850, but as the former often contain widely scattered areas of population difficult to organise, the differential can easily be justified.

Within 35 days after the declaration of the result the agent of each candidate has to submit to the Returning Officer a complete statement of expenses incurred, together with the relevant bills and receipts. Within the following 10 days the Returning Officer is required to publish in at least two local newspapers a summary (under seven heads) of the expenses of all candidates concerned. Within a year of the election a summary of all the accounts, together with other relevant information, is published as a Parliamentary Paper, under the title, *Return of Election Expenses*.

The amounts expended by all candidates and by those of the three main parties in general elections since 1945 were as follows:

Table 20—Expenditure by Parliamentary candidates

Year	Candidates	Total expenditure	Average per candidate	Con.	Lab.	Lib.
		£	£	£	£	£
1945	1,468	1,073,216	645	780	595	532
1950	1,868	1,170,114	728	777	694	459
1951	1,376	946,013	688	773	658	488
1955	1,409	904,677	641	692	599	531
1959	1,536	1,051,217	684	761	705	532

In 1959 Conservative candidates spent on average 89 per cent of the permitted maximum, Labour candidates 83 per cent and Liberals 62 per cent. Minor party and independent candidates spent on average 36 per cent. The average for all candidates was 80 per cent.

Table 21 shows the returns made by the three candidates

in a London Borough constituency, South Kensington, in 1959 where the maximum permitted expenditure (excluding personal expenses) was £813.

All parties consistently spend more money in respect of their successful candidates than on behalf of their unsuccessful nominees, but it is in the highly marginal seats that candidates of all parties tend to spend very near the maximum permitted. Evasion of the law is apparently now fairly widespread in marginal constituencies, according to Mr David Butler who wrote after the 1959 election:

> Agents quite often admitted to subterfuges, some plainly legal, some more dubious, by which they kept their official expenses down. Sympathetic printers could undercharge, knowing that no objection would be raised to a compensating overcharge outside election time. Equipment needed solely for the campaign could be bought in advance and then hired to the agent at a very low notional figure. Although the likelihood of either side scrutinising its rivals' accounts or launching a petition is very small, it is unfortunate that the law should be so much circumvented.[1]

Table 21—*Election Expenses in South Kensington, 1959*

Nature of expenditure	W. L. Roots (Con.)	G. C. H. Millar (Lib.)	I. S. Richard (Lab.)
	£	£	£
Agents	30	0	0
Clerks, etc	30	9	44
Printing, stationery, etc	641	376	571
Public meetings	8	8	12
Committee rooms	59	18	15
Miscellaneous matters	33	4	77
Net total	811	415	719
Personal expenses	96	14	0
Grand total	897	429	719

Restriction of expenditure is highly desirable if money is not to talk at election time, but in view of the virtual

[1] Butler and Rose, op. cit., pages 144–5.

halving of the value of money since the end of the last war some upward revision of the permitted limits is probably now overdue. A far more serious problem, however, is the lack of any limitation on amounts which can be spent nationally and in the period between elections.

These amounts have now begun to dwarf the total sums spent on behalf of all candidates. In the period leading up to the 1959 election it has been estimated that the Conservative Party spent £468,000 on advertising alone, while over three times this amount was spent by business firms supporting the Conservative cause.

Neither the Labour nor the Liberal Party, or interests supporting them, made any attempt to match the scale of this expenditure. Since then, however, both parties have become seriously alarmed lest their case should go by default and both are aiming to spend considerably larger sums than ever before in the period leading up to the 1964 election. The Labour Party, fortified by large donations to its election fund from the trade union movement, announced in April 1963 that it would spend between £150,000 and £200,000 on advertising in the summer and autumn of 1963 and that the campaign would be continued through the winter and spring of 1964 if the election was not held during 1963. In August 1963 Mr Grimond launched an appeal for £500,000 to enable the Liberal Party to wage a similar campaign.

National expenditure on this scale goes a long way to thwart the intention of Parliament in restricting the level of expenditure in the constituencies. This has led to a growing demand for an enquiry into the whole subject of election expenditure, which so far has not been acceded to.

CHAPTER THIRTEEN

THE 1964 GENERAL ELECTION

THE PARLIAMENT elected in 1959 must be dissolved no later than 19 October 1964, which means that a general election must be held on or before 7 November 1964. This, however, is a Saturday, and as general elections are normally held on a Thursday, it would seem that the latest practical date is 5 November.

Should the election be held as late as this, or indeed at any time later than mid April 1964, the present Parliament will easily exceed the record duration for a peace-time Parliament since the five-year limit was set in 1911.

Had the outlook for the Government seemed brighter at the time, either May or October 1963 would have appeared likely times to choose for the election. But the collapse of the Common Market negotiations in January 1963 had removed what was intended to be the principal plank in the Conservatives' election platform and public opinion polls and by-election results, throughout the year, clearly indicated the likelihood of a heavy Conservative defeat in any early general election. The Profumo affair and the uncertainty over the future Conservative leadership which persisted throughout the summer of 1963, also militated against an early election.

So the Parliament entered its fifth year in October 1963, leaving the new Prime Minister less room to manoeuvre in the choice of election dates than, it may be supposed, he would have liked.

In the light of past precedents and of the considerations discussed in Chapter II, it would seem that there are three short periods in one of which the 1964 general election is most likely to take place. The first is early March, when a glance at the calendar suggests 19 March as the most probable date. A rather longer period is immediately after

Whitsun, when 28 May, 4 and 11 June would all be possibilities. The third period is in October, when any Thursday in the month could be chosen.

Past precedents points rather strongly to the second period – late May and early June – as the most likely to be selected, but the deciding factor will be the Prime Minister's estimate of the relative advantage to his party in choosing between the various alternatives. The decision to hold the Stratford-upon-Avon by-election in August 1963, the first by-election to be held in high summer for many years, may just possibly indicate a willingness to consider holding a general election in a period always hitherto regarded as a 'closed season'.

Whenever the 1964 election is held, it will be closely contested, and whatever its result it will be a remarkable one. The Conservatives will be defending the majority of 100 seats which they won in 1959. If they again emerge as victors they will have won four successive general elections, an entirely unprecedented achievement in modern British politics. A Labour victory, on the other hand, would be scarcely less notable as it would mean the recovery at one go of all the losses sustained in three consecutive general elections. But the only other possible result – a deadlock in which the Liberal Party held the balance of power – is, as will appear from the figures discussed below, highly improbable.

The aims of the three parties in the election may be simply stated. *The Conservative Party* can have few hopes of increasing its present majority of 100,[1] but will seek to minimise the inroads which the Labour and Liberal parties can make into it. If Conservative losses amount to fewer than 49 seats, they will still be in a majority in the House of Commons. To have a reasonably comfortable majority, however, they would need to lose no more than forty seats. A swing against the Government of more than $3\frac{1}{2}$ per cent, therefore, would almost certainly result in their defeat,

1. Appendix 2, on pp. 187–9, lists the Labour seats most vulnerable to Conservative attack.

while one of more than $2\frac{1}{2}$ per cent would leave them with a precarious majority.

The Labour Party needs to gain 58 seats to secure a majority in the House of Commons and at least 65 seats to form a reasonably secure government. A swing of 3·6 per cent is the minimum which it needs to win power. A swing of 4 per cent or more is needed to give Labour a working majority. The list of Conservative-held marginal seats is shown in Appendix 2, on page 184. Labour needs to win more than half of the constituencies in this list to form a government. The biggest concentrations of vulnerable Conservative-held seats are in the Greater London area, the Midlands, Lancashire and the West Riding.

The Liberal Party, though it is putting up at least 420 candidates – the largest number since 1950 – has no hope of winning a majority, or even of winning a substantial number of seats. To succeed in doubling their representation of seven would appear to be the limit of their practical hopes. At by-elections since 1959 there has been an average swing of 12·5 per cent from the Conservatives to the Liberals and such a swing at the general election would enable the Liberals to win 12 Conservative seats. All past experience suggests, however, that governments do better at general elections than at by-elections[1] and it seems unlikely that any more than the five Conservative-held seats listed in Appendix 2 on page 186 are seriously threatened by the Liberals. Appendix 2 shows also that a maximum of three Labour-held seats are vulnerable to Liberal attack and that four of the seven Liberal-held seats must be regarded as marginal. Even if the Liberal Party succeeds in doubling its 1959 aggregate vote of 1,641,000, it is unlikely to have more than a dozen Members in the new House of Commons.

The probable small number of Liberal MPs is the main reason why a deadlocked House of Commons is unlikely. To bring this about would need a swing from Conservative

1. See articles by the present author in *The Guardian*, 17 and 18 June 1963, for a detailed analysis of by-election trends.

to Labour of between about 3·4 and 3·7 per cent. A smaller pro-Labour swing or a swing to the Conservatives would ensure a Conservative Government, whereas a larger pro-Labour swing would bring a Labour victory. A swing of the above dimensions is, of course, quite possible but the statistical chances of this happening are rather small.

Writing several months before the election it would be foolhardy to hazard a prediction of the result. Working purely on the evidence of past trends, the most likely eventuality would appear to be that the Government would suffer some losses, but not necessarily on a sufficient scale to bring about its defeat. By election results and opinion poll trends throughout 1963[1] suggest, on the other hand, that Labour is well placed to win a decisive majority.

The election manifestos will not be published until a few weeks before the poll. The major issues on which the election will be fought can be deduced, in the meantime, with reasonable certainty, from the speeches of the party leaders and the various party publications which have appeared in recent years.

The Conservatives clearly intend to make 'modernisation' the key-note of their campaign. They will point to the Beeching Plan, the provision of Colleges of Advanced Technology and to their record and published plans in education, hospital building, housing, etc., to underline the theme. The head of Messrs Colman, Prentis and Varley, who handle political advertising for the Conservative Party was reported in *The Sunday Times* on 22 September 1963 as saying: 'In the 1959 election our advertising emphasis was on individual affluence. This time the emphasis is on institutionalised affluence.'

The Labour Party's key-note will be 'expansion', which the Party will stress as the only means of achieving the major extension of social services to which it is committed. It became clear at the Labour Party conference at Scarborough in 1963 that a major effort will also be made to attract the support of the growing numbers of scientists,

1. See Appendices 3 and 4.

technologists and technicians.

The Liberal Party's social policies are scarcely less ambitious than those of the Labour Party, but their emphasis is placed on the need to reform the structure of government, both at national and at local levels, so that Parliament is strengthened in relationship to the Government and considerable powers are devolved to new regional forms of local government. The table on the following pages briefly summarises the main policy differences between the three parties.

Table 22—Summary of Party Policies

Conservative

Economic Policy

The NEDC target of a 4 per cent growth rate accepted, but expansion to be achieved by the free co-operation of management and trade unions, rather than through 'an overall, rigid and centrally imposed plan'. Essential to achieve growth without risking inflation or balance of payments crises. The NIC to be the instrument for achieving wage restraint through influencing public opinion.

Taxation

Simplification, partly through reducing the number of different purchase-tax rates or by the substitution of an added value tax.

Pensions

Flat-rate national insurance benefits (at present 67s. 6d. for a single person, 109s. for married couple) to be retained, plus graduated benefit yielding 6d. per week for every £15 of contributions.

Housing

Aim to build 350,000 houses a year by 1965, target then to be raised to 400,000. Abolition of Schedule A tax, easier mortgages. £100 million allocated to help housing associations. Housing subsidies to be concentrated on those with greatest need, through differential and rent rebate schemes. Free market to be retained in land; all rent control eventually to be removed.

Table 22—Summary of Party Policies—continued

Labour	Liberal
End the 'stop-go' cycle and reach at least a 4 per cent growth rate. A national plan to be drawn up for the whole economy with targets for individual industries. This would 'direct the industrial expansion to areas where labour is available and where new work is needed'. 'Planned growth of incomes' to be achieved with the co-operation of the unions and by preventing other sources of income rising more steeply than wages.	A 5-year plan, with 1-year plans to implement it, to achieve a long-term growth rate of 5 per cent. National and regional planning bodies to be established and a strengthened 'Nicky' to be responsible for an incomes policy which would embrace working hours and social benefits as well as wages and salaries.
Higher unearned incomes to bear greater share of burden. Wealth tax suggested for large fortunes and tax on gifts to replace death duties. Stiffer capital gains tax.	Simplification of income tax and of profits tax. Extension of capital gains tax, and a gifts tax and legacy duty to replace death duties. Payroll tax on employers to finance social security. Abolition of tax on heavy oils.
Flat-rate system to be replaced by wage-related benefits giving half-pay in sickness, unemployment and retirement.	Flat-rate benefits to be increased over seven years to half average national earnings for married couples, less for single persons.
Aim to build 400,000 houses a year. Lower interest rates on mortgages and on loans to local authorities. Leasehold reform to enable those with long leases to buy their freeholds. Rent Act to be repealed and rent control restored. Local Authorities to be empowered to compulsorily purchase old rented housing. Land Commission to acquire freeholds of urban development land so that community benefits from future rises in values.	Aim to build 375,000 houses a year. Rent tribunals to fix rents of decontrolled property, which Local Authorities may compulsorily purchase if requested to do so by tenants. Abolition of stamp duty on mortgages, which will be made easier. New taxation to discourage land speculation.

Table 22—Summary of Party Policies—continued

Conservative

Education	Selection for secondary education to be retained, but to be more flexible. Public schools to be left alone. Priority to be given to reducing size of classes. Increased school building programme. Seven new universities being established and Colleges of Advanced Technology rapidly expanded. Robbins Report proposals on higher education accepted in principle.
Health	£600 million to be spent on hospitals in 10 years. Large hospitals to replace smaller units. GPs to have better access to hospital services.
Public Ownership	No more nationalisation. Remainder of publicly owned steel industry to be sold to private buyers when these come forward. Private air lines to be encouraged.
Transport	Railways to be pruned as recommended by Beeching Plan, while £600 million to be spent on new road-building programme during next five years. Aim to achieve co-ordinated inland transport system 'on a competitive basis and without extravagant use of national resources'.

*Table 22—Summary of Party Policies—*continued

Labour	Liberal
Abolish 11-plus examination. Secondary education to be comprehensive. Public schools to be integrated within state system. Size of classes to be reduced, school-leaving age raised to 16. Abolition of all fees and means tests for higher education, which is to be greatly expanded. University of the Air to be created.	Non-selective secondary education to be encouraged. Public schools to be integrated within state system. Reduce size of classes and introduce compulsory part-time education up to 18. Double number of students in higher education in 10 years.
Charges on teeth, spectacles, prescriptions and surgical appliances to be abolished. GPs to be encouraged to set up group practices and to run appointments systems.	Abolition of prescription and appliance charges. NHS contributions to be made on sliding scale according to income. Smaller hospitals to be retained as GP hospitals or as maternity or geriatric units.
Renationalise steel, expand British Road Services. Publicly owned factories to be set up in development areas. Remaining sections of water supply to be brought under public ownership. Private air lines lines to be discouraged.	No more nationalisation. Co-partnership schemes to be encouraged through private industry.
Rail closures to be deferred pending a national road survey. A national transport plan then to be prepared. British Road Services to be expanded and an integrated transport system built up which would take note of plans for future economic growth as well as of present demand.	Aim is to achieve the cheapest possible transport. Competition to be encouraged between different forms of transport and between public and private enterprise. Specific subsidies may be needed to maintain certain services for social reasons.

Table 22—Summary of Party Policies—continued

Conservative

Defence

Independent nuclear deterrent to be maintained through purchase of American Polaris missiles. V-bomber force to be assigned to NATO. Possibility of joining mixed-manned NATO nuclear force being considered.

Foreign

Strong British voice to be maintained in world affairs through membership of Western alliance, the Commonwealth and the maintenance of a British deterrent. United Nations to be supported, but not uncritically. Membership of Common Market still regarded as desirable if opportunity recurs. Partial Test Ban Treaty seen as first step towards disarmament.

Table 22—Summary of Party Policies—continued

Labour	*Liberal*
Independent deterrent to be given up. Greater conventional contribution to be made to NATO to help halt local conflicts with conventional weapons alone. Collective political control of Western nuclear weapons and military strategy to be sought.	As for Labour.
Eventual aim – World Government, to be achieved through steady increase in the authority and scope of the United Nations. Support for Western alliance, but multilateral disarmament under international control to be sought, and strong efforts made to prevent the spread of nuclear weapons and to agree on zones of disengagement, especially in Central Europe. China to be admitted to U.N. Arms boycott of South Africa.	Regional groupings to be fostered as stage towards World Government. Strong support for British membership of the Common Market. Otherwise – as for Labour.

The Rival Teams

A choice must be made in the 1964 general election not only between different policies but between rival teams of leaders. With the formation, in October 1963, of the government of Sir Alec Douglas-Home, uncertainty over the Conservative leadership was removed. In November 1963, the Conservative Cabinet was composed of the following members.

PRIME MINISTER AND FIRST LORD OF THE TREASURY – Rt Hon. Sir Alec Douglas-Home, KT, MP.

SECRETARY OF STATE FOR FOREIGN AFFAIRS – Rt Hon. R. A. Butler, CH, MP.

LORD PRESIDENT OF THE COUNCIL AND MINISTER FOR SCIENCE – Rt Hon. Quintin Hogg, QC.

LORD CHANCELLOR – Rt Hon. Lord Dilhorne.

CHANCELLOR OF THE EXCHEQUER – Rt Hon. Reginald Maudling, MP.

SECRETARY OF STATE FOR THE HOME DEPARTMENT – Rt Hon. Henry Brooke, MP.

SECRETARY OF STATE FOR COMMONWEALTH RELATIONS AND SECRETARY OF STATE FOR THE COLONIES – Rt Hon. Duncan Sandys, MP.

CHANCELLOR OF THE DUCHY OF LANCASTER – Rt Hon. Lord Blakenham, OBE.

MINISTER OF DEFENCE – Rt Hon. Peter Thorneycroft, MP.

MINISTER OF LABOUR – Rt Hon. Joseph Godber, MP.

LORD PRIVY SEAL – Rt Hon. Selwyn Lloyd, MP.

MINISTER OF TRANSPORT – Rt Hon. Ernest Marples, MP.

MINISTER OF AGRICULTURE, FISHERIES AND FOOD – Rt Hon. Christopher Soames, CBE, MP.

SECRETARY FOR INDUSTRY, TRADE, REGIONAL DEVELOPMENT AND PRESIDENT OF THE BOARD OF TRADE – Rt Hon. Edward Heath, MBE, MP.

CHIEF SECRETARY TO THE TREASURY AND PAYMASTER-GENERAL – Rt Hon. John Boyd-Carpenter, MP.

SECRETARY OF STATE FOR SCOTLAND – Rt Hon. Michael Noble, MP.

MINISTER OF HEALTH – Rt Hon. Anthony Barber, MP.

MINISTER OF EDUCATION – Rt Hon. Sir Edward Boyle, Bt, MP.

MINISTER OF HOUSING AND LOCAL GOVERNMENT AND MINISTER FOR WELSH AFFAIRS – Rt Hon. Sir Keith Joseph, Bt, MP.

MINISTERS WITHOUT PORTFOLIO – Rt Hon. W. F. Deedes, MC, MP. and Rt Hon. Lord Carrington.

Ranged against them will be the Labour Party's 'Shadow Cabinet' which consisted in November 1963 of the following members:

Leader of the Opposition: Rt Hon. Harold Wilson, OBE, MP.
Deputy Leader: Rt Hon. George Brown, MP.
Treasury spokesmen: James Callaghan, MP.
⠀⠀⠀⠀⠀⠀⠀⠀⠀⠀⠀⠀Douglas Houghton, MP.
Foreign Affairs: Rt Hon. Patrick Gordon Walker, MP.
Legal Affairs: Rt Hon. Sir Frank Soskice, QC, MP.
Defence: Denis Healey, MBE, MP.
Housing and Local Government: Michael Stewart, MP.
Transport: Ray Gunter, MP.
Pensions: G. R. Mitchison, CBE, QC, MP.
Power: Thomas Fraser, MP.
Education: Frederick Willey, MP.
Labour: Frederick Lee, MP.
Board of Trade: Rt Hon. Douglas Jay, MP.
Chief Whip: Herbert Bowden, MP.
Leader of Labour Peers: Rt Hon. Earl Alexander of Hillsborough, CH.

The Liberal Party has no shadow cabinet, as such, but it has appointed official spokesmen in the principal policy fields to reinforce the officers of the parliamentary Liberal Party. The Liberal team in November 1963 was:

Leader: Rt Hon. Jo Grimond, MP.
Deputy Leader: Donald Wade, MP.

Chief Whip: Eric Lubbock, MP.
Foreign Affairs: Mark Bonham Carter.
Commonwealth and Colonial Affairs: Rt Hon Lord Ogmore, TD, JP.
Social Security: Desmond Banks.
Economic Affairs: Christopher Layton.
Industrial Relations: Peter McGregor.
Agriculture: Richard Lamb.
Education: A. D. C. Peterson.
Leader of Liberal Peers: Lord Rea, OBE.

Brief notes follow on the careers to date of the leading figures in each of the three parties.

Conservative

SIR ALEC DOUGLAS-HOME, formerly 14th Earl of Home, Prime Minister since 19 October 1963. Born 2 July 1903, educated at Eton (for whom he scored 66 on a sticky wicket in a famous cricket match against Harrow), and Christ Church, Oxford. Was MP for South Lanark, 1931–45, and for Lanark 1950–51, when he vacated his seat on inheriting his earldom. Disclaimed his peerage in October 1963 and was elected for Kinross and West Perthshire in November 1963.

Was Parliamentary Private Secretary to the Prime Minister, Neville Chamberlain, from 1937–39, and accompanied him to Munich in September 1938. Joint Parliamentary Under-Secretary to the Foreign Office, May–July 1945, Minister of State, Scottish Office, 1951–55, Secretary of State for Commonwealth Relations, 1955–60. In 1960 was appointed Foreign Secretary in the Macmillan government, the first from the House of Lords for nearly 40 years. A supposedly reluctant candidate for the premiership, the personal support of Harold Macmillan seems to have been the decisive factor in his being chosen in preference to R. A. Butler, Quintin Hogg and Reginald Maudling. Since his appointment, has shown unsuspected talent as a television performer and his spirited by-election campaign at Kinross suggests that he will prove an effective election leader for the Conservatives.

R. A. BUTLER, Foreign Secretary since October 1963, formerly First Secretary of State and Deputy Prime Minister, Born 9 December 1902 in India, the son of a distinguished member of the Indian Civil Service. Educated at Marlborough and Pembroke College, Cambridge, where he won a 'double first'. He married a Courtauld heiress in 1926 and became MP for Saffron Walden three years later, a seat which he has held ever since. Became Under-Secretary of State in the India Office in 1932 and has since held ministerial office continuously, except during the Labour government of 1945–51. Was Under-Secretary of Foreign Affairs at the time of Munich (which may have cost him the premiership nineteen years later), Minister of Education from 1941 to 1945 during which period he introduced the Education Act of 1944, Chancellor of the Exchequer from 1951 to 1955, Leader of the House of Commons 1955–61, and Home Secretary from 1957 to 1959. He was Chairman of the Conservative Party 1959–61. Widowed in 1954, he married again (his first wife's cousin by marriage) in 1959. Did more than any other man to modernise the Conservative Party after 1945 and was unexpectedly passed over for the premiership both in 1957 and 1963.

REGINALD MAUDLING, Chancellor of the Exchequer since July 1962, was born on 7 March 1917. Educated at Merchant Taylors' School and Merton College, Oxford (1st Class Hons, Greats). MP for Barnet since 1950. Was in charge of abortive negotiations for a European Free Trade Area, as Paymaster-General in 1957. Became President of the Board of Trade in 1959, Colonial Secretary in 1961, succeeding Selwyn Lloyd as Chancellor the following year. A large jovial man, married to an ex-actress whose daughter is following in her mother's footsteps, he was the first choice of many Conservative back benchers as successor to Macmillan in 1963.

QUINTIN HOGG, formerly 2nd Viscount Hailsham, Lord President of the Council and Minister for Science. Born

9 October 1907, the son of an American mother, though he is by no means the most pro-American of British politicians. Educated at Eton and Christ Church, Oxford (Double 1st Class Hons), he practised as a barrister before his election for Oxford as a pro-Munich Tory in a famous by-election in 1938. Strongly objected to his elevation to the peerage on the death of his father in 1950, and in a dramatic bid for the Tory leadership announced his intention to disclaim his title in October 1963. Was Chairman of the Conservative Party from September 1957–October 1959 and remains immensely popular among the rank-and-file whose first choice as the Conservative leader he would undoubtedly have been.

EDWARD HEATH, Secretary for Industry and President of the Board of Trade, formerly Lord Privy Seal and principal foreign affairs spokesman in the House of Commons. A bachelor, born 9 July 1916, he was educated at Chatham House School, Ramsgate, and Balliol College, Oxford. MP for Bexley since 1950, he showed a remarkable blend of toughness and skill as Chief Whip from 1955 to 1959. His reputation soared when he was in charge of the negotiations for British membership of the European Economic Community in 1961 and 1962, but his hopes of the premiership faded in the spring of 1963 when Macmillan declined to promote him to one of the principal offices of state. His favourite recreation is organ-playing.

Labour

HAROLD WILSON, Leader of the Opposition since February 1963. Born 11 March 1916, son of a chemist. Educated at Wirral Grammar School and Jesus College, Oxford (1st Class Hons). Lecturer in economics, and then a temporary civil servant during World War II. MP for Ormskirk 1945–50 and for Huyton since 1950. Became the youngest Cabinet Minister since Pitt in 1947 on his appointment as President of the Board of Trade. Resigned in April 1955 with late Aneurin Bevan in protest against the level of arms expenditure. Unsuccessfully opposed Hugh Gaitskell for the leadership of the Labour Party in November 1960 and George Brown for the deputy leadership in November 1962. Defeated the latter for the leadership three months later. Wilson is known for his retentive memory and feared for his witty and telling performances in Parliamentary debates. Has rapidly established himself as a popular and effective leader of the Labour Party, which under his leadership appears more united than for many years past.

GEORGE BROWN, Deputy Leader of the Opposition since 1960. Born 2 September 1914, the son of a London lorry driver. Active in the trade union movement since his early teens, he was elected for Belper in 1945 as a sponsored candidate of the Transport and General Workers Union. A junior Minister in the Labour government from October 1947, he took an active part in an unsuccessful move to replace Attlee as Premier by Ernest Bevin, for whom he had a profound admiration. Bevin disapproved of his initiative, but Attlee later promoted him Minister of Works. Caused a sensation in 1956 by rowing with Khrushchev at a Labour Party dinner when he objected to the Soviet leader's attempted rewriting of history. A staunch supporter of Hugh Gaitskell throughout his leadership, he is widely admired for his courage, but his equally famous impetuosity was the probable cause of his defeat by Harold Wilson in the contest for the leadership of the Labour Party in February 1963.

JAMES CALLAGHAN, 'Shadow Chancellor of the Exchequer' since 1961. Born 27 March 1912, the son of a sailor, he served in the Royal Navy in World War II. Left school at 17 to work in a tax office, he later became Assistant Secretary of the Inland Revenue Staff Association. MP for Cardiff, South, 1945–50 and for Cardiff, South-east, since 1950. Was Parliamentary Secretary to the Ministry of Transport 1947–50 and to the Admiralty 1950–1. Has been Consultant to the Police Federation since 1955, with responsibility for negotiating police pay. Since becoming 'Shadow Chancellor' has spent much time at Nuffield College, Oxford picking the brains of distinguished economists. A quiet family man in private, he is an exceedingly combative Parliamentary performer.

PATRICK GORDON WALKER, 'Shadow Foreign Secretary' since February 1963. Born 7 April 1907, educated at Wellington School and Christ Church, Oxford (1st Class Hons, History). A history don for 9 years, his wartime role was to run a broadcasting service to German workers for the BBC. MP for Smethwick since October 1945, he was Commonwealth Relations Secretary in 1950–1, and, apart from Wilson, is the only member of the 'Shadow Cabinet' with Cabinet experience. A strong supporter of Gaitskell, Gordon Walker is a dull speaker, but his experience and widely respected judgment assure him a leading role should Labour win the 1964 election.

DENIS HEALEY, 'Shadow Minister of Defence'. Born 30 August 1917, educated at Bradford Grammar School and Balliol College, Oxford (Double 1st Class Hons). A major in World War II, he ran the Labour Party's international department from 1945–52. Elected for Leeds, South-east, in 1952, has represented Leeds, East, since 1955. Was a Communist for a short time as an undergraduate, but has been one of the staunchest supporters of the Western alliance throughout the post-war period. Immensely tough-minded and one of the handful of Britons who can hold their own in discussions on defence and disarmament with the leading American experts, he should reach very high office if Labour prospers.

Liberal

JO GRIMOND, Leader of the Liberal Party since 1956. Born July 1913, educated at Eton and Balliol College, Oxford (1st Class Hons.). Married in 1938, Laura Bonham Carter, grand-daughter of Asquith. Served with Fife and Forfar Yeomanry 1939–45, subsequently worked with UNRRA and as secretary of the Scottish National Trust. MP for Orkney and Zetland since 1960. An appealing television performer, the fortunes of the Liberal Party have somewhat revived under his leadership, but it has yet to achieve any mark improvement in its Parliamentary representation.

MARK BONHAM CARTER, Liberal spokesman on foreign affairs. Born February 1911, educated at Winchester School, Balliol College, Oxford, and Chicago University. A grandson of Asquith and brother-in-law of Jo Grimond. A publisher, who won a sensational by-election at Torrington in 1958, only to lose the seat the following year. Is now prospective candidate for Torrington and will play a leading part in the Parliamentary Liberal Party should he regain his seat.

ELECTION NIGHT GUIDE

On the evening of polling day the constituency results will be broadcast on radio and television from about ten o'clock onwards. Experts will attempt to predict the final trends on the basis of the first constituencies to declare their results. With the aid of the information given in this section, and in Appendix 2 on pages 184–90, any reader should be able to make his own predictions with a reasonable hope of success.

SWING – The swing revealed by the earliest results should point to the following probable outcomes:

Pro-Conservative swing = An increased Conservative majority.

Pro-Labour swing of less than 3 per cent = A reduced Conservative majority.

Pro-Labour swing of between 3 and 5 per cent = A close result: a small majority for either side or a deadlock.

Pro-Labour swing of more than 5 per cent = A Labour victory.

Pro-Labour swing of more than 7 per cent = A Labour majority of more than 100.

SEATS (mark results as they come in).

Conservative victories in these seats point to an IN-CREASED CONSERVATIVE MAJORITY: Eton and Slough . . .

Grimsby . . . Edinburgh, East . . . Accrington . . . North Kensington . . .

Conservative victories in these seats suggests a CONSERVATIVE VICTORY, possibly with a reduced majority: Uxbridge . . . Glasgow, Kelvingrove . . . Bristol, North-east . . . Wandsworth, Central . . . Birmingham, Yardley . . .

Mixed Labour and Conservative victories in these seats suggest a CLOSE RESULT: Watford . . . York . . . Doncaster . . . Preston, South . . . Battersea, South . . . Billericay . . .

Labour victories in these seats suggest a LABOUR MAJORITY: Ealing, North . . . Liverpool, Walton . . . Darlington . . . Reading . . . Manchester, Blackley . . . Hornchurch . . . Luton . . .

Labour victories here point to a LARGE LABOUR MAJORITY: Banbury . . . Bradford, West . . . Bath . . . Hendon, North . . . Exeter . . . Liverpool, Toxteth . . .

APPENDICES

APPENDIX 1

GENERAL ELECTION RESULTS

Table 23

Year	Parties	Candidates	MPs elected
1945	Conservative	624	213
	Labour	604	393
	Liberal	306	12
	Others	148	22
Turn-out:	72·7%	1,682	640
1950	Conservative	620	298
	Labour	617	315
	Liberal	475	9
	Others	156	3
Turn-out:	84·0%	1,868	625
1951	**Conservative**	617	321
	Labour	617	295
	Liberal	109	6
	Others	23	3
Turn-out:	82·5%	1,376	625
1955	**Conservative**	623	344
	Labour	620	277
	Liberal	110	6
	Others	56	3
Turn-out:	76·7%	1,409	630
1959	**Conservative**	625	365
	Labour	621	258
	Liberal	216	6
	Others	74	1
Turn-out:	78·8%	1,536	630

* The published figures for aggregate votes differ marginally.
D. E. Butler and Jennie Freeman,

1945–1959

Unopposed returns	Lost deposits	Total votes*	Percentage votes*
2	6	9,988,306	39·8
1	2	11,995,152	47·8
—	64	2,248,226	9·0
—	91	854,294	2·8
3	163	25,085,978	100·0
2	5	12,502,567	43·5
—	—	13,266,592	46·1
—	319	2,621,548	9·1
—	137	381,964	1·3
2	461	28,772,671	100·0
4	3	13,717,538	48·0
—	1	13,948,605	48·8
—	66	730,556	2·5
—	26	198,969	0·7
4	96	28,595,668	100·0
—	3	13,286,569	49·7
—	1	12,404,970	46·4
—	60	722,405	2·7
—	36	346,554	1·2
—	100	26,760,493	100·0
—	2	13,749,830	49·4
—	1	12,215,538	43·8
—	55	1,638,571	5·9
—	58	255,302	0·9
—	116	27,859,241	100·0

Those in this table are based on information contained in
British Political Facts, Macmillan, 1963.

MARGINAL CONSTITUENCIES

Table 24—Conservative Held Marginal Seats
(Figures refer to the 1959 general election)

	Constituency	Votes	Majority Percentage
1.	Derbyshire, South-east	12	0·1
2.	Birmingham, All Saints	20	0·1
3.	Newcastle, East	98	0·2
4.	Nottingham, West	164	0·4
5.	Keighley	170	0·4
6.	Hartlepools	182	0·4
7.	Meriden	263	0·5
8.	Swansea, West	403	0·8
9.	Rugby	470	1·1
10.	Wellingborough	606	1·3
11.	Kingston-upon-Hull, North	702	1·3
12.	Sunderland, South	990	1·8
13.	Holborn and St Pancras, South	656	2·0
14.	Rochester and Chatham	1,023	2·0
15.	Manchester, Wythenshawe	1,309	2·3
16.	Barons Court	913	2·4
17.	Acton	920	2·4
18.	Birmingham, Sparkbrook	886	2·6
19.	Cleveland	1,655	2·8
20.	Uxbridge	1,390	2·9
21.	Birmingham, Yardley	1,385	3·0
22.	Lowestoft	1,489	3·2
23.	Coventry, South	1,830	3·3
24.	Buckingham	1,746	3·7
25.	Bristol, North-west	1,919	4·0
26.	Wandsworth, Central	1,972	4·0
27.	Rutherglen	1,522	4·1
28.	King's Lynn	1,765	4·2
29.	Gravesend	2,162	4·2
30.	Dulwich	2,251	4·2
31.	Clapham	1,876	4·4
32.	Heywood and Royton	2,154	4·4
33.	Glasgow, Kelvingrove	1,101	4·5
34.	Halifax	2,515	4·5
35.	Nottingham, Central	2,135	4·7
36.	Carlisle	1,998	4·8

Table 24—Conservative Held Marginal Seats—continued

	Constituency	Votes	Majority Percentage
37.	Maldon	2,240	5·0
38.	Willesden, East	2,210	5·1
39.	Eye	2,484	5·2
40.	Bristol, North-east	2,684	5·3
41.	Bolton, East*	2,732	5·6
42.	Battersea, South	1,752	6·0
43.	Glasgow, Woodside*	2,084	6·2
44.	Norwich, South	2,244	6·2
45.	Bradford, North	2,671	6·2
46.	Dover	3,241	6·2
47.	Epping	4,393	6·2
48.	Watford	2,901	6·4
49.	Liverpool, Kirkdale	2,747	6·5
50.	Stockport, South	2,540	6·6
51.	York	4,074	6·6
52.	Berwick and East Lothian	2,850	6·8
53.	Hitchin	4,375	6·8
54.	Renfrew, West	2,753	7·0
55.	Eastleigh	3,256	7·0
56.	Brierley Hill	4,133	7·1
57.	Doncaster	3,586	7·2
58.	The Wrekin	2,978	7·2
59.	Bury and Radcliffe	3,908	7·3
60.	Preston, South	3,019	7·4
61.	Stockport, North	3,222	7·4
62.	Norfolk, South	2,733	7·6
63.	Billericay	4,822	7·7
64.	Liverpool, West Derby	3,333	7·9
65.	Woolwich, West	3,659	8·0
66.	Reading	3,942	8·1
67.	Walthamstow, East	2,901	8·2
68.	Ealing, North	4,276	8·5
69.	Yarmouth	3,579	8·5
70.	Bedfordshire, South	4,759	8·7
71.	Darlington	4,417	8·8
72.	Rushcliffe	4,440	8·8
73.	Brentford and Chiswick	2,919	8·9
74.	Putney	5,121	8·9
75.	Liverpool, Walton	4,034	9·1
76.	Peterborough	4,584	9·1
77.	Manchester, Blackley	4,373	9·3
78.	Ayr	3,356	9·3
79.	Devizes	3,838	9·5

Table 24—Conservative Held Marginal Seats—continued

	Constituency	Votes	Majority Percentage
80.	Gloucestershire, South	4,601	9·6
81.	Hornchurch	7,322	10·0
82.	Truro	4,487	10·1
83.	Luton*	5,019	10·2
84.	Preston, North	4,461	10·3
85.	Stroud	5,112	10·5
86.	Lewisham, North	4,613	10·8
87.	Liverpool, Toxteth	3,915	11·1
88.	Mid-Bedfordshire*	5,174	11·4
89.	Plymouth, Sutton	6,761	11·5
90.	Conway	4,535	12·0
91.	High Peak*	4,911	12·1
92.	Yeovil	6,133	12·1
93.	Burton	5,894	12·3
94.	Hendon, North	5,332	12·4
95.	Somerset, North	6,783	12·5
96.	Bradford, West	5,106	12·5
97.	Southampton, Test	6,766	12·6
98.	Brighton, Kemptown	5,746	12·7
99.	Exeter	5,661	12·8
100.	Plymouth, Devonport	6,454	12·8
101.	Banbury	6,714	12·9
102.	Chislehurst	6,679	13·0
103.	Westbury	5,826	13·0
104.	Chigwell	5,562	13·5
105.	Hemel Hempstead	8,235	13·6
106.	Bath	6,533	13·6
107.	Grantham	6,615	13·7
108.	Shipley	5,511	13·9
109.	Monmouth	6,257	14·0
110.	Northants, South*	5,934	14·0
111.	Cornwall, North†	989	2·8
112.	Torrington†	2,265	6·0
113.	Bodmin†	2,801	7·6
114.	Denbigh†	4,625	10·8
115.	Inverness†	4,075	11·5

* Indicates constituencies in which a by-election has subsequently occurred.

† Indicates constituencies in which the Liberal candidate secured second place in 1959.

Table 25—Labour Held Marginal Seats

	Constituency	Votes	Majority Percentage
1.	Brighouse and Spenborough*	47	0·1
2.	Flintshire, East	75	0·2
3.	Norfolk, South-west	78	0·2
4.	Eton and Slough	88	0·2
5.	Grimsby	101	0·2
6.	Birmingham, Perry Bar	183	0·5
7.	Faversham	253	0·5
8.	Edinburgh, East	231	0·7
9.	Edmonton	461	0·9
10.	Romford	607	1·0
11.	Lanark	540	1·1
12.	Chorley	676	1·3
13.	Accrington	600	1·4
14.	Dundee, West*	714	1·4
15.	Glasgow, Craigton	602	1·6
16.	Birmingham, Northfield	940	1·6
17.	Cardiff, South-east	868	1·6
18.	Norfolk, North	658	1·7
19.	Liverpool, Edge Hill	699	1·8
20.	Coatbridge and Airdrie	794	1·8
21.	Manchester, Gorton	857	1·9
22.	Leek	1,149	1·9
23.	Edinburgh, Central	617	2·0
24.	Dartford	1,276	2·3
25.	Wood Green	1,134	2·5
26.	Kensington, North	877	2·5
27.	Bosworth	1,393	2·6
28.	Paddington, North	768	2·7
29.	Coventry, North	1,241	2·8
30.	Stalybridge and Hyde	1,423	3·1
31.	Nelson and Colne	1,264	3·1
32.	Leicester, North-east*	1,431	3·8
33.	Brigg	2,104	3·8
34.	Lichfield and Tamworth	1,550	3·8
35.	Widnes	1,598	4·0
36.	Eccles	1,986	4·0
37.	Ayrshire, Central	1,676	4·0
38.	Oldham, East	1,830	4·2
39.	Leicester, North-west	1,773	4·3
40.	Oldbury and Halesowen	2,383	4·3
41.	Sowerby	1,956	4·5
42.	Northampton	2,717	4·5

Table 25—Labour Held Marginal Seats—continued

	Constituency	Votes	Majority Percentage
43.	Sunderland, North	2,208	4·8
44.	Newark	1,772	4·9
45.	Kingston-upon-Hull, West	2,435	5·0
46.	Ipswich	3,235	5·1
47.	Dunbartonshire, West	2,141	5·1
48.	Feltham	2,250	5·2
49.	Southall	2,319	5·5
50.	Ashton-under-Lyne	2,752	5·6
51.	Derby, North*	2,407	5·6
52.	Kettering	3,485	5·6
53.	Blackburn	2,866	5·6
54.	Stirling and Falkirk	2,626	5·8
55.	Rossendale	2,591	5·9
56.	Dunbartonshire, East	3,349	6·1
57.	Brixton	2,112	6·2
58.	Newport	3,648	6·2
59.	Birmingham, Aston	2,534	6·3
60.	Gloucester	2,771	6·4
61.	Bradford, South	3,014	6·5
62.	Salford, West	2,861	6·6
63.	Cardiff, West	3,132	6·6
64.	Southampton, Itchen	3,733	6·8
65.	Bilston	3,545	7·0
66.	Birmingham, Stechford	2,923	7·1
67.	Western Isles	1,167	7·2
68.	Fulham	2,944	7·3
69.	Bootle	2,915	7·3
70.	Leicester, South-west	2,743	7·3
71.	Bristol, Central	2,696	7·3
72.	Stockton-on-Tees*	3,277	7·3
73.	Glasgow, Scotstoun	3,370	7·3
74.	Belper	4,337	7·4
75.	Huddersfield, East	3,085	7·4
76.	Leyton	3,919	7·4
77.	Birkenhead	3,629	7·7
78.	Derby, South	3,431	8·0
79.	Dewsbury	3,669	8·1
80.	Loughborough	3,747	8·2
81.	Dundee, East	4,181	8·7
82.	Swindon	3,909	8·8
83.	Crewe	3,781	9·0
84.	Leeds, East	4,785	9·1

Table 25—*Labour Held Marginal Seats*—continued

	Constituency	Votes	Majority Percentage
85.	Salford, East	3,486	9·2
86.	Barrow-in-Furness	3,974	9·4
87.	Smethwick	3,544	9·4
88.	Newcastle, West	5,023	9·5
89.	Bothwell	4,352	9·5
90.	Falmouth and Camborne	4,197	9·6
91.	Leith	3,074	9·7
92.	Leeds, West	4,593	9·8
93.	Huyton	5,927	9·8
94.	Nottingham, North	5,053	9·9
95.	Dudley	5,725	9·9
96.	Oldham, West	4,119	10·0
97.	Enfield, East	3,624	10·0
98.	Pembroke	5,322	10·2
99.	Wolverhampton, North-east	3,797	10·2
100.	Lincoln*	4,389	10·2
101.	Motherwell	4,396	10·7
102.	Hayes and Harlington	4,152	11·2
103.	Glasgow, Provan	4,367	11·2
104.	Newcastle-under-Lyme	6,002	11·2
105.	Islington, North	3,898	11·6
106.	Greenwich	5,525	12·3
107.	Gloucestershire, West	5,411	12·4
108.	Warrington*	5,099	12·5
109.	Sheffield, Hillsborough	5,043	13·0
110.	Wallsend	8,766	13·1
111.	Erith and Crayford	5,760	13·3
112.	Coventry, East	7,762	13·4
113.	East Ham, North	3,826	13·6
114.	Cannock	7,139	13·7
115.	Burnley	6,773	13·9
116.	Merioneth†	976	4·4
117.	Rochdale†	2,740	5·2
118.	Carmarthen†	6,633	13·6

* Indicates constituencies in which a by-election has subsequently occurred.

† Indicates constituencies in which the Liberal candidate secured second place in 1959.

Liberal held marginal seats

Of the seven seats at present held by Liberals four may be regarded as marginal – Devon, North, because of its very small majority, Orpington because until the Liberal by-election victory in 1962 it was regarded as a safe Conservative seat, and Bolton, West, and Huddersfield, West, because Conservative candidates will be contesting them in 1964, whereas the Liberals were allowed a straight fight with Labour in 1951, 1955 and 1959.

Table 26

Constituency	Majority over Conservative	
	Votes	*Percentage*
Devon, North	362	1·0
Orpington (by-election, 1962)	7,855	18·2

Constituency	Majority over Labour	
	Votes	*Percentage*
Bolton, West	3,988	9·3
Huddersfield, West	9,652	23·6

BY-ELECTIONS 1959–63

In the 1959 Parliament, up to mid November 1963, there were 52 by-elections, resulting in the following gains and losses:

Table 27

Party	Gains	Losses
Conservative	1	5
Labour	4	1
Liberal	1	0

As Table 28 shows, the Conservatives gained ground in the by-elections held in 1960, winning one seat from Labour, but in 1961 a sharp anti-Conservative swing set in which was accelerated in 1962 and continued throughout 1963.

A marked feature of the by-elections was the strong showing of Liberal candidates who, in addition to winning Orpington and retaining Montgomery, came second in 18 out of the other 42 seats which they contested. The peak Liberal performance occurred in the spring and summer of 1962 and thereafter there was a marked falling away, though Liberal candidates invariably polled larger votes than had been obtained by previous Liberal candidates in the same constituencies. Labour candidates seldom increased their votes, but their relative position improved considerably as the Labour vote remained steady while the Conservative poll consistently fell. The net swing from Conservative to Labour is shown in the graph in Figure 7, which in the by-election results are plotted at six-monthly intervals.

Here is a list of the by-elections in chronological order; showing the percentage vote gained by each party, with the 1959 results in brackets.

Table 28

1. Harrow, West   Con. 55·8 (70·9), Lib. 21·4 (—), Lab. 18·2 (29·1).
2. Brighouse and Spenborough   Con. 50·7 (49·9), Lab. 49·3 (50·1), *Con. gain from Lab.*
3. Edinburgh, North   Con. 54·2 (64), Lab. 30·3 (36), Lib. 15·5 (—).
4. Bolton, East   Con. 37·8 (52·8), Lab. 36·2 (47·2), Lib. 24·8 (—), Other 1·2 (—).
5. Carshalton   Con. 51·7 (54), Lib. 27·6 (15·5), Lab. 20·7 (30·5).
6. Ebbw Vale   Lab. 68·7 (81), Con. 12·7 (19), Lib. 11·6 (—), Other 7·0 (—).
7. Ludlow   Con. 46·4 (60·3), Lib. 27·3 (—), Lab. 26·3 (39·7).
8. Petersfield   Con. 54·4 (60·9), Lib. 29 (17·8), Lab. 16·6 (21·3).
9. Tiverton   Con. 45·7 (55·6), Lib. 36·7 (25·2), Lab. 17·6 (25·2).
10. Mid-Bedfordshire   Con. 45·4 (46·8), Lab. 29·2 (35·4), Lib. 24·8 (17·8), Other 0·6 (—).
11. Blyth   Lab. 68·9 (74·6), Con. 21·6 (25·4), Other 9·5 (—).
12. Cambridgeshire   Con. 45·9 (57·9), Lab. 30·1 (42·1), Lib. 24 (—).
13. Colchester   Con. 47·2 (51·6), Lab. 33·1 (35·9), Lib. 19·7 (12·5).
14. High Peak   Con. 37·4 (46), Lab. 32·1 (34), Lib. 30·5 (20).
15. Worcester   Con. 39·7 (57·7), Lab. 30·2 (42·3), Lib. 30·1 (—).
16. Birmingham, Small Heath   Lab. 59·2 (57·4), Con. 28·8 (42·6), Lib. 12 (—).
17. Paisley   Lab. 45·3 (57·3), Lib. 41·4 (—), Con. 13·1 (42·7).
18. Warrington   Lab. 55·8 (56·2), Con. 31·6 (43·8), Lib. 12·6 (—).
19. Bristol, South-east   Lab. 69·5 (56·2), Con. 30·5 (43·8).
20. Manchester, Moss Side   Con. 41·1 (62·3), Lib. 27·9 (—), Lab. 25·8 (37·7), Other 5·4 (—).
21. Fife, East   Con. 47·5 (69·9), Lab. 26·4 (30·1), Lib. 26·1 (—).
22. Oswestry   Con. 40·8 (55·9), Lib. 28·4 (16·1), Lab. 27·9 (28), Other 2·9 (—).
23. Bridgeton   Lab. 57·6 (63·4), Con. 20·7 (36·6), Others 18·6 and 3·1 (—).
24. Lincoln   Lab. 50·5 (55·1), Con. 30·2 (44·9), Lib. 18·2 (—).
25. Blackpool, North   Con. 38·3 (57·8), Lib. 35·3 (20·6), Lab. 26·4 (21·6).
26. Orpington   Lib. 52·9 (21·2), Con. 34·7 (56·6), Lab. 12·4 (22·2). *Lib. gain from Con.*
27. Middlesbrough, East   Lab. 60·9 (61·5), Lib. 22·9 (—), Con. 14·8 (38·5), Other 1·7 (—).
28. Pontefract   Lab. 77·3 (76·4), Con. 19·4 (23·6).
29. Stockton-on-Tees   Lab. 45·2 (53·7), Con. 27·8 (46·3), Lib. 27 (—).
30. Derby, North   Lab. 49·4 (52·8), Lib. 25·4 (—), Con. 22·5 (47·2), Other 2·7 (—).
31. Montgomery   Lib. 51·3 (42·1), Con. 21·9 (31·3), Lab. 20·6 (26·6), Other 6·2 (—).

32. Middlesbrough, West Lab. 39·7 (35·4), Con. 33·7 (54·9), Lib. 25·8 (9·7), Others 0·8 (—). *Lab. gain from Con.*

33. Derbyshire, West Con. 36 (61·3), Lib. 32·5 (—), Lab. 27·3 (38·7).

34. West Lothian Lab. 50·8 (60·3), Other 23·3 (—), Con. 11·4 (39·7), Lib. 10·8 (—), Other 3·6 (—).

35. Leicester, North-east Lab. 41·5 (51·9), Lib. 34·3 (—), Con. 24·2 (48·1).

36. Chippenham Con. 36·8 (52·1), Lib. 32·5 (16·9), Lab. 29·1 (31).

37. Glasgow, Woodside Lab. 36 (43·1), Con. 30 (49·3), Lib. 22 (7·6), Others 12 (—). *Lab. gain from Con.*

38. Dorset, South Lab. 33·5 (34·7), Con. 31·8 (49·8), Lib. 21·7 (15·5), Others 13 (—). *Lab. gain from Con.*

39. Northants, South Con. 41·2 (57), Lab. 38·6 (43), Lib. 19·3 (—), Others 0·9 (—).

40. Norfolk, Central Con. 37·7 (50·4), Lab. 37 (34·8), Lib. 22·5 (14·8), Others 2·8 (—).

41. Colne Valley Lab. 44·5 (44·3), Lib. 39·5 (25·8), Con. 15·5 (29·9), Other 0·6 (—).

42. Rotherham Lab. 69·3 (62·8), Con. 28·4 (37·2), Other 2·3 (—).

43. Swansea, East Lab. 61·2 (67·5), Lib. 15·8 (—), Other 8 (—), Con. 7·3 (22·0), Others 5·2 and 2·5 (—).

44. Leeds, South Lab. 62·9 (58·6), Con. 20·1 (31·0), Lib. 14·7 (10·4), Others 2·3 (—).

45. West Bromwich Lab. 58·7 (57·4), Con. 23·6 (42·6), Lib. 17·7 (—).

46. Deptford Lab. 58·2 (62·0), Lib. 22·6 (—), Con. 19·2 (38).

47. Stratford-upon-Avon Con. 43·6 (68·5), Lab. 34·1 (31·5), Lib. 21·0 (—), Others 1·4 (—).

48. Bristol, South-east Lab. 79·7 (56·2), Others 21·3 (—).

49. Belfast, South Con. 64·3 (69·9), Lab. 25·8 (21·6), Lib. 9·9 (7·5), Other — (1·0).

50. Luton Lab. 48·0 (44·9), Con. 39·5 (55·1), Lib. 11·4 (—), Other 1·1 (—). *Lab. gain from Con.*

51. Kinross and West Perthshire Con. 57·4 (68·2), Lib. 19·5 (—), Lab. 15·2 (16·8), Others 7·9 (15).

52. Dundee, West Lab. 50·6 (49·7), Con. 39·4 (48·2), Others 7·4 and 2·6 (2·1).

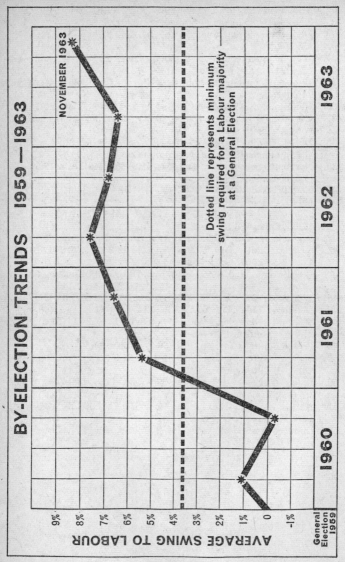

Figure 8

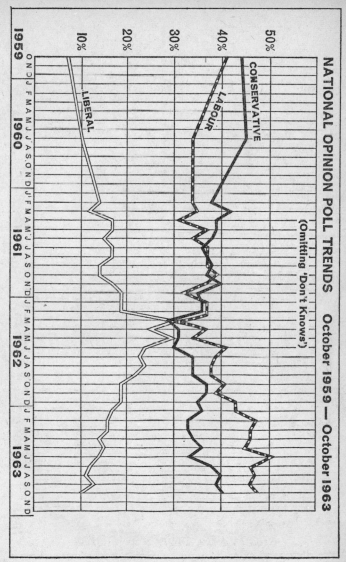

NATIONAL OPINION POLL TRENDS   October 1959 — October 1963
(Omitting 'Don't Knows')

Figure 9

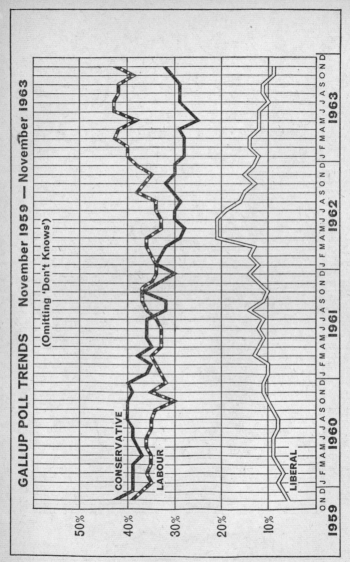

Figure 10

APPENDIX 5

POSTAL VOTES IN 1959 ELECTION

In the 1959 general election the postal vote exceeded the majority in 24 seats, won by the Conservatives. It seems probable that in about half of these constituencies this factor alone accounted for the Conservative victory. The constituencies were:

Table 29

	Constituency	Conservative majority	Number of postal votes
1.	Derbyshire, South-east	12	1,005
2.	Birmingham, All Saints	20	535
3.	Newcastle, East	98	976
4.	Nottingham, West	164	632
5.	Keighley	170	1,594
6.	Hartlepools	182	1,346
7.	Meriden	263	1,259
8.	Swansea, West	403	1,225
9.	Rugby	470	1,477
10.	Wellingborough	606	1,310
11.	Kingston-upon-Hull, North	702	1,072
12.	Sunderland, South	990	1,219
13.	Holborn and St Pancras, South	656	1,640
14.	Rochester and Chatham	1,023	2,023
15.	Manchester, Wythenshawe	1,309	1,431
16.	Barons Court	913	1,585
17.	Acton	920	1,816
18.	Cornwall, North	989	2,240
19.	Uxbridge	1,390	1,434
20.	Lowestoft	1,489	1,744
21.	Buckingham	1,746	2,201
22.	Wandsworth, Central	1,972	2,319
23.	Maldon	2,240	2,583
24.	Eye	2,484	3,233

APPENDIX 6

ELECTION TIMETABLE

The following chart lists the important days to remember during an election campaign. It is important to remember to exclude Sundays and bank holidays in the count of 17 days between the Proclamation and polling day.

Table 30

	General election	Chart days	Calendar dates		Example
Day					
0.	Proclamation	0	F	5	Proclamation
1.	Receipt of Writ	1	S	6	Receipt of Writ
2.		—	Su	7	
3.	Notice of Election				
4.	First day for Nomination	2	M	8	
5.	Last day to claim proxy or postal votes	3	T	9	Notice of Election
		4	W	10	First day for Nomination
6.		5	T	11	Last day to claim proxy or postal votes
7.					
8.	Last day for Nomination	6	F	12	
9.		7	S	13	
10.		—	Su	14	
11.		8	M	15	Last day for Nomination
12.					
13.		9	T	16	
14.		10	W	17	
15.		11	T	18	
16.		12	F	19	
17.	Polling day	13	S	20	
		—	Su	21	
		14	M	22	
		15	T	23	
		16	W	24	
		17	T	25	Polling day

In a by-election, the Returning Officer is allowed some discretion in his choice of polling day, as the following table shows.

Table 31

| | | By-election | |
County	Day	Borough	Day
Receipt of Writ	1	Receipt of Writ	1
	2		2
Notice of Election	3	Notice of Election	3
	4		4
	5		5
	6	Earliest final Nom.	6
Earliest final Nom.	7		7
	8	Latest final Nom.	8
	9		9
Latest final Nom.	10		10
	11		11
	12		12
	13	Earliest Poll	13
Earliest Poll	14		14
	15		15
	16		16
	17	Latest Poll	17
	18		
Latest Poll	19		

APPENDIX 7

CORRUPT AND ILLEGAL PRACTICES

Table 32

SUMMARY OF
CORRUPT

OFFENCES

BRIBERY.—No gift, loan, or promise of money or money's worth must be made to a voter to induce him either to vote or abstain from voting.

The offer or promise of a situation or employment to a voter or anyone connected with him, if made with the same object, is also bribery.

The consequences are the same whether bribery is committed before, during, or after an election.

Giving or paying money for the purpose of bribery is equivalent to the offence itself.

A gift or promise to a third person to procure a vote is bribery. Payment for loss of time, wages, or travelling expenses is equal to bribery.

Any person who receives a bribe, or bargains for employment or reward in consideration of his vote, is guilty of bribery.

TREATING.—No meat, drinks, entertainment or provisions can be paid for or provided for any person at any time, in order to induce him, or any other person, to vote or abstain from voting. The gift of tickets to be exchanged for refreshment is regarded as treating.

Treating the wives or relatives of voters is also forbidden.

The receiver of any meat, drink, etc., is equally guilty, and liable to the same consequences.*

UNDUE INFLUENCE.—No force, threat, restraint, or fraud may be used to compel an elector to vote or abstain.

Using or threatening any spiritual or temporal injury is undue influence.

The withdrawal of custom, or a threat to do so, comes under this prohibition. A threat to evict a tenant will also be undue influence.

UNAUTHORISED EXPENDITURE.—Incurring expenditure on account of holding public meetings or issuing advertisements, circulars or publications, by any person, other than the Election Agent, for the purpose of promoting or procuring the Election of any candidate at a parliamentary election, unless authorised in writing by such Election Agent and returned as an expense by the person incurring it.

PERSONATION.—Applying for a ballot paper in the name of another person, whether alive or dead.

Voting twice in the same Constituency at the same election.

Aiding or abetting the commission of the offence of personation.

Forging or counterfeiting a ballot paper.

ELECTION OFFENCES

PRACTICES

PENALTIES

Twelve months' imprisonment, or a fine of £200.

Deprivation of the right of voting for five years.

Removal from, and disqualification for, any public office.

Payment of costs of an election inquiry in certain cases.

If committed by the Candidate he also loses his seat, if elected, and is disqualified for ten years from representing the Constituency and is disqualified for five years from sitting for any other Constituency.

If committed by any Agent the election is void, and the Candidate is disqualified for five years.

NOTE.—Any recognized active worker may be held to be 'an Agent'.

Two years' imprisonment.

Five years' incapacity to vote, or hold any public office.

If committed by any Agent, the Candidate loses his seat.

Table 32—continued

ILLEGAL

OFFENCES

CONVEYANCE.—Paying or receiving money for conveyance of votes to or from the poll.

(Private conveyances lent gratuitously can alone be employed; hackney carriages are prohibited except when hired by voters for their own exclusive use.)

ADVERTISING.—Paying money to an elector for exhibiting bills, etc. The receiver is also guilty.

VOTING when prohibited, or inducing a prohibited elector to vote.

FALSE STATEMENT.—Publishing a false statement of the withdrawal of any Candidate or as to his character.

ILLEGAL PROXY VOTING.—Voting or attempting to vote in person after having appointed a proxy, and while such appointment is uncancelled.

Voting or attempting to vote as proxy on behalf of more than two absent voters at an election in any constituency, unless voting as the husband or wife, or the parent, brother or sister of the absent voter.

Voting or attempting to vote at any election under the authority of a proxy paper when the person knows or has reasonable grounds for supposing that the proxy paper has been cancelled, or that the elector on whose behalf it has been issued is dead or not entitled to vote at that election.

POLL CARDS.—Issuing at a Parliamentary Election any poll card or document resembling an official poll card.

PUBLISHING BILLS, placards, or posters, without the printer's name and address. (The Election Agent alone, or Sub-Agents in Counties, may issue any printed matter at the election.) Any process for multiplying copies of a document other than by copying it by hand is deemed to be printing.

ILLEGAL PAYMENT, EMPLOY-

PAYMENT FOR BANDS OF MUSIC, torches, flags, banners.

LENDING OR USING, for the conveyance of voters, **horses or vehicles usually kept for hire.**

EMPLOYMENT of any person as a canvasser.

USING A COMMITTEE ROOM in any licensed house, refreshment house, or public elementary school.

---

* NOTE

REFRESHMENT FOR WORKERS.—Whilst it is much better, and more prudent, to leave all workers, whether paid or unpaid, to find their own refreshments, the view has been expressed by some Judges that 'the

PRACTICES

PENALTIES

A fine of £100.
Incapacity to vote for five years.
If committed by a Candidate or an Agent, the election may be rendered void.

If the offender be the Candidate or his Agent, the full penalty attaching to an illegal practice as above.
If any other person, a fine not exceeding £100.

MENT, AND HIRING

A fine of £100.

---

giving of refreshments to persons employed at the Election, if bona fide and honestly done, **is not treating,** even though the workers be voters, if care be taken to confine it to persons actually engaged on the Election'.

BOOKLIST

ELECTION RESULTS. Full results of general elections, together with biographical details of Members and of defeated candidates are published shortly after each election in *The Times House of Commons*, published by *The Times*.

Less detailed results are also given in *Dod's Parliamentary Companion*, published annually, *Vacher's Parliamentary Guide*, quarterly and *Whitaker's Almanack*, annually.

Tabulated results over a 60-year period are included in *British Political Facts 1900–1960* by D. E. Butler and Jennie Freeman, Macmillan, 1963.

ACCOUNTS OF GENERAL ELECTIONS are provided by a series of books sponsored by Nuffield College, Oxford:

The British General Election of 1945 by R. B. McCallum and Alison Readman, Macmillan, 1947; *The British General Election of 1950* by H. G. Nicholas, Macmillan, 1951; *The British General Election of 1951* by D. E. Butler, Macmillan, 1952; *The British General Election of 1955* by D. E. Butler, Macmillan, 1955; *The British General Election of 1959* by D. E. Butler and Richard Rose, Macmillan, 1960.

Campaigns in individual constituencies are described in: *How People Vote* by M. Benney, A. P. Gray and R. H. Pear, Routledge and Kegan Paul, 1956 (Greenwich in 1950); *Straight Fight* by R. S. Milne and H. C. Mackenzie, Hansard Society, 1954. (Bristol, North-east in 1951); *Marginal Seat* by R. S. Milne and H. C. Mackenzie, Hansard Society, 1958. (Bristol, North-east in 1955).

THE ELECTORAL SYSTEM. The fullest account of its recent development is *The British Electoral System since 1918* by D. E. Butler, Oxford University Press, 1963 (second edition). A critical study, which includes much information about alternative systems of voting is *Elections and Electors* by J. F. S. Ross, Eyre and Spottiswoode, 1955. The impact of television on the 1959 general election is exhaustively examined in *Television and the Political Image* by Joseph Trenaman and Denis McQuail, Methuen, 1961.

POLITICAL PARTIES. The standard work is *British Political Parties* by R. T. McKenzie, Heinemann, 1963 (second edition). The best and almost the only source for information about local political parties is *Small Town Politics* by A. H. Birch, Oxford University Press, 1959 (a study of Glossop, Derbyshire). Details of the organisation of the three main parties are given in *The Party Organisation*, Conservative Party, 1961; *Party Organisation*, Labour Party, 1957, and *Effective Organising*, Liberal Party, 1963. See also *Voters, Parties and Leaders* by Jean Blondell, Penguin, 1963.

ELECTION LAW. The standard reference books are *Parliamentary Elections* by A. Norman Schofield, Shaw and Sons, 1959 (third edition); *Parker's Election Agent and Returning Officer*, Charles Knight and Co., 1959 (sixth edition) and *Sir T. Erskine May's Parliamentary Practice*, Butterworth, 1957 (sixteenth edition).

THE STATE OF THE PARTIES

In November 1963 the composition of the House of Commons was:

Conservatives	361
Labour	261
Liberal	7
Independent	1
	630

THE HOUSE OF COMMONS BY CONSTITUENCIES

Full election results, 1959 and subsequent by-elections

The figures following the name of the Constituency denote the total number of *Electors* in the Parliamentary Division at the General Election of 1959.

ABBREVIATIONS.—*C.* = Conservative; *Comm.* = Communists; *I.L.P.* = Independent Labour Party; *Ind.* = Independent; *L.* = Liberal; *Lab.* = Labour; *Nat. L.* = National Liberal; *Scot. Nat.* = Scottish Nationalist; *S.F.* = Sinn Fein; *U.U.* = Ulster Unionist; *Welsh Nat.* = Welsh Nationalist.

An asterisk * denotes membership of the last House for the same division; and obelisk †, for a different division.

Aberavon (Glamorgan)
E. 56,316

1 *J. Morris, Lab.*		30,397
R. E. G. Howe, *C.*		12,759
I. M. Lewis, *Welsh Nat.*		3,066
Lab. maj.		*17,638*
(1955 Lab. maj. 16,297)		

Aberdare (Welsh Borough)
E. 49,124

2 **A. R. Probert**, *Lab.*		30,889
B. McGlynn, *C.*		6,584
K. P. Thomas, *Welsh Nat.*		3,367
Lab. maj.		*24,305*
(1955 Lab. maj. 23,366)		

Aberdeen (2)
NORTH E. 66,351

3 **H. S. J. Hughes**, QC, *Lab.*		32,793
J. Stewart-Clark, *C.*		15,137
W. A. Milne, *Scot. Nat.*		2,964
Lab. maj.		*17,656*
(1955 Lab. maj. 16,796)		

SOUTH E. 58,086

4 **Lady Tweedsmuir**, *C.*		25,471
P. M. Doig, *Lab.*		17,349
Mrs E. T. Dangerfield, *L.*		4,558
C. maj.		*8,122*
(1955 C. maj. 7,190)		

Aberdeenshire (2)
EAST E. 44,628

5 **P. W. Wolrige-Gordon**, *C.*		18,982
J. B. Urquhart, *Lab.*		10,980
C. maj.		*8,002*
(Nov. 1958, by-election, C. maj. 6,328) (1955 C. maj. 10,057)		

WEST E. 46,429

6 *A. F. Hendry, C.*		22,937
W. Kemp, *Lab.*		10,542
C. maj.		*12,395*
(1955 C. maj. 10,928)		

Abertillery (Monmouthshire)
E. 38,674

7 **Rev. L. Williams**, *Lab.*		26,931
R. J. Maddocks, *C.*		4,740
Lab. maj.		*22,191*
(1955 Lab. maj. 21,518)		

Abingdon (Berkshire)
E. 63,844

8 **A. M. S. Neave**, DSO, OBE, MC, TD, *C.*		27,943
P. Picard, *Lab.*		16,971
Mrs V. I. Perl, *L.*		6,651
C. maj.		*10,972*
(1955 C. maj. 8,634)		

Accrington (English Borough)
E. 49,933

9*H. Hynd, Lab.		22,242
M. Henry, C.		21,642
Lab. maj.		*600*

(1955 Lab. maj. 1,345)

Acton (English Borough)
E. 46,835

10 P. W. Holland, C.		19,358
J. A. Sparks, Lab.		18,438
C. maj.		*920*

(1955 Lab. maj. 525)

Aldershot (Hampshire)
E. 56,820

11*Sir E. Errington, Bt, C.		25,161
R. E. Brooks, Lab.		12,270
Miss E. Lakeman, L.		5,679
C. maj.		*12,891*

(1955 C. maj. 9,572)

ALL SAINTS – *See* **Birmingham**

Altrincham and Sale
(English Borough)
E. 64,860

12*Rt Hon. F. J. Erroll, TD, C.		29,992
N. Atkinson, Lab		14,141
D. F. Burden, L.		9,415
C. maj.		*15,851*

(1955 C. maj. 18,412)

Anglesey
E. 36,281

13*C. Hughes, Lab.		13,249
O. M. Roberts, C.		7,005
Dr R. T. Jones, *Welsh Nat.*		4,121
R. G. Lloyd, L.		3,796
Lab. maj.		*6,244*

(1955 Lab. maj. 4,573)

Angus and Kincardine (2)
NORTH ANGUS AND MEARNS
E. 36,513

14*Sir C. N. Thornton-Kemsley, OBE, TD, L. & C.		17,536
R. Hughes, Lab.		8,486
L. & C. maj.		*9,050*

(1955 L. & C. maj. 10,193)

SOUTH E. 44,840

15*Capt. Sir J. A. L. Duncan, Bt, L. & C.		19,435
G. Y. Mackie, L.		8,139
J. L. Stewart, Lab.		6,477
L. & C. maj.		*11,296*

(1955 L. & C. maj. 14,971)

Antrim (2)
NORTH E. 69,880

16 H. Clark, U.U.		42,807
J. Dougan, S.F.		2,280
U.U. maj.		*40,527*

(1955 U.U. maj. 34,954)

SOUTH E. 93,634

17*S. K. Cunningham, QC, U.U.		52,786
M. Traynor, S.F.		2,745
U.U. maj.		*50,041*

(1955 U.U. maj. 45,192)

ARDWICK – *See* **Manchester**

Argyll
E. 40,015

18*Rt Hon. M. A. C. Noble, C.		16,599
D. Nisbet, Lab.		7,356
Hon G. E. W. Noel, L.		4,469
C. maj.		*9,243*

(June 1958, by-election, C. maj. 5,166) (1955 C. maj. 10,028)

Armagh
E. 73,416

19 J. E. Maginnis, U.U.		40,325
J. Lynch, S.F.		6,823
U.U. maj.		*33,502*

(1955 U.U. maj. 17,254)

Arundel and Shoreham
(West Sussex) E. 75,601

20*Capt. H. B. Kerby, C.		37,034
A. L. Bell, *Lab.*		12,745
A. L. Ford, L.		8,081
C. maj.		*24,289*

(1955 C. maj. 19,992)

Ashfield (Nottinghamshire)
E. 61,139

21*W. N. Warbey, Lab.		35,432
J. G. W. Sandys, C.		14,690
Lab. maj.		*20,742*

(1955 Lab. maj. 20,069)

Ashford (Kent)
E. 52,097

22*Rt Hon. W. F. Deedes, MC, C.		25,383
R. G. Ward, Lab.		14,983
C. maj.		*10,400*

(1955 C. maj. 8,307)

Ashton under Lyne
(English Borough)
E. 60,706

23*H. Rhodes, DFC, Lab.		25,991
R. Horrocks, C.		23,239
Lab. maj.		*2,752*

(1955 Lab. maj. 1,965)

ASTON — *See* **Birmingham**
ATTERCLIFFE — *See* **Sheffield**
Aylesbury (Buckinghamshire)
E. 54,089

24*Sir G. S. Summers, C.	22,504	
H. Gray, Lab.	13,549	
H. L. Fry, L.	7,897	
C. maj.		8,955

(1955   C. maj. 5,761)
Ayrshire and Bute (5)
AYR   E. 45,444

25*Sir T. C. R. Moore, Bt, CBE, C.	19,659	
A. Eadie, Lab.	16,303	
C. maj.		3,356

(1955   C. maj. 6,140)
BUTE AND NORTH AYRSHIRE
E. 44,291

26†Sir F. H. R. Maclean, Bt, CBE, MC, C.	20,270	
D. Lambie, Lab.	12,218	
C. maj.		8,052

(1955   C. maj. 9,155)
CENTRAL   E. 48,596

27 A. C. Manuel, Lab.	21,901	
*D. L. Spencer-Nairn, C.	20,225	
Lab. maj.		1,676

(1955   C. maj. 167)
SOUTH   E. 48,063

28*E. Hughes, Lab.	24,774	
W. H. Hunter, C.	14,105	
Lab. maj.		10,669

(1955   Lab. maj. 8,209)
See also **Kilmarnock**
Banbury (Oxfordshire)
E. 64,414

29 H. N. Marten, C.	26,413	
D. J. Buckle, Lab.	19,699	
K. Colman, L.	6,074	
C. maj.		6,714

(1955   C. maj. 4,125)
Banff
E. 32,129

30*Sir W. S. Duthie, OBE, C.	14,359	
R. W. Irvine, Lab.	5,992	
C. maj.		8,367

(1955   C. maj. 8,306)
Barking (English Borough)
E. 51,654

31 T. E. N. Driberg, Lab.	23,454	
K. F. Dibben, C.	11,454	
D. E. Evans, L.	5,648	
Lab. maj.		12,000

(1955   Lab. maj. 15,047)

Barkston Ash (Yorks, W.R.)
E. 54,448

32*Sir L. Ropner, Bt, MC, TD, C.	26,200	
R. W. Bowes, Lab.	18,647	
C. maj.		7,553

(1955   C. maj. 6,167)

Barnet (Hertfordshire)
E. 64,739

33*Rt Hon. R. Maudling, C.	33,136	
R. M. Prideaux, Lab.	19,737	
C. maj.		13,399

(1955   C. maj. 10,729)

Barnsley (English Borough)
E. 69,833

34*R. Mason, Lab.	42,565	
J. P. H. Bent, C.	15,189	
Lab. maj.		27,376

(1955   Lab. maj. 24,709)

Barons Court (London Borough)
E. 50,032

35 W. C. Carr, C.	18,658	
*W. T. Williams, Lab.	17,745	
S. H. J. A. Knott, Ind. L.	1,766	
C. maj.		913

(1955   Lab. maj. 125)

Barrow in Furness
(English Borough)   E. 51,904

36*W. Monslow, Lab.	23,194	
M. Metcalf, C.	19,220	
Lab. maj.		3,974

(1955   Lab. maj. 2,759)

Barry (Glamorgan)
E. 60,206

37*H. R. Gower, C.	30,313	
D. R. Evans, Lab.	20,790	
C. maj.		9,523

(1955   C. maj. 7,363)

Basingstoke (Hampshire)
E. 60,979

38*D. K. Freeth, C.	25,314	
S. G. Conbeer, Lab.	14,070	
Dr L. G. Housden, L.	9,126	
C. maj.		11,244

(1955   C. maj. 6,290)

Bassetlaw (Nottinghamshire)
E. 59,907

39*Rt Hon. F. J. Bellenger, Lab.	27,875	
M. J. Cowling, C.	20,162	
Lab. maj.		7,713

(1955   Lab. maj. 7,498)

Bath (English Borough)
E. 57,150

40*Sir I. J. Pitman, KBE, C.	24,048	
G. E. Mayer, Lab.	17,515	
G. R. Allen, L.	6,214	
C. maj.	6,533	

(1955   C. maj. 6,843)

Batley and Morley
(English Borough)   E. 56,031

41*A. D. D. Broughton, Lab.	26,781
Mrs B. M. Garden, C.	19,115
Lab. maj.	7,666

(1955   Lab. maj. 9,208)

Battersea (2)

NORTH   E. 40,937

42*Rt Hon. D. P. T. Jay, Lab.	19,593
R. G. Taylor, C.	9,289
Lab. maj.	10,306

(1955   Lab. maj. 12,922)

SOUTH   E. 37,320

43*E. Partridge, C.	14,203
G. W. Rhodes, Lab.	12,451
W. B. Mattinson, L.	2,774
C. maj.	1,752

(1955   C. maj. 679)

Bebington (English Borough)
E. 70,374

44*Sir H. D. Oakshott, Bt, MBE, C.	33,705
G. J. Oakes, Lab.	23,844
C. maj.	9,861

(1955   C. maj. 9,423)

Beckenham (English Borough)
E. 73,421

45*P. C. Goodhart, C.	36,528
H. Ferguson, Lab.	13,395
H. H. Monroe, L.	9,365
C. maj.	23,133

(March 1957, by-election, C. maj.
12,176) (1955 C. maj. 21,237)

Bedfordshire (3)

BEDFORD   E. 55,278

46*Rt Hon. A. C. J. Soames,	
CBE, C.	23,495
M. A. Foley, Lab.	16,728
M. L. Rowlandson, L.	5,966
C. maj.	6,767

(1955   C. maj. 4,941)

MID   E. 53,889

47*Rt Hon. A. T. Lennox-Boyd,	
CH, C.	21,301
B. E. Magee, Lab.	16,127
W. G. Matthews, L.	8,099
C. maj.	5,174

(By-election, 16 Nov. 1960)

S. L. E. Hastings, C.	17,503
B. E. Magee, Lab.	11,281
W. G. Matthews, L.	9,550
C. F. H. Gilliard, Ind.	235
C. maj.	6,222

(1955   C. maj. 3,964)

SOUTH   E. 65,416

48*N. J. Cole, VRD, L. & C.	25,861
W. H. Johnson, Lab.	21,102
Mrs R. R. Soskin, L.	7,912
L. & C. maj.	4,759

(1955   L. & C. maj. 2,468)

Bedwellty (Monmouthshire)
E. 44,890

49*H. J. Finch, Lab.	30,697
C. J. Cox, C.	6,817
Lab. maj.	23,880

(1955   Lab. maj. 23,692)

Belfast (4)

EAST   E. 58,663

50*S. R. McMaster, U.U.	26,510
J. S. Gardner, N.I. Lab.	16,412
B. Boswell, S.F.	1,204
U.U. maj.	10,098

(March 1959, by-election, U.U. maj.
5,260) (1955 U.U. maj. 13,897)

NORTH   E. 74,494

51 W. S. Mills, U.U.	32,173
J. W. McDowell, N.I. Lab.	18,640
F. McGlade, S.F.	2,156
U.U. maj.	13,533

(1955   U.U. maj. 18,680)

SOUTH   E. 59,861

52*Rt Hon. Sir D. C. Campbell,	
KBE, CMG, U.U.	30,164
N. Searight, N.I. Lab.	9,318
Miss S. M. Murnaghan, L.	3,253
B. O'Reilly, S.F.	434
U.U. maj.	20,846

(By-election, 22 October 1963)

R. Pounder, U.U.	17,989
N. Searight, N.I. Lab.	7,209
B. Hamilton, L.	2,774
U.U. maj.	10,780

(1955   U.U. maj. 25,884)

WEST   E. 73,405

53*Mrs F. P. A. McLaughlin,	
U.U.	28,898
J. Brennan, Ind. Lab.	20,062
T. A. Heenan, S.F.	4,416
U.U. maj.	8,836

(1955   U.U. maj. 18,141)

Belper (Derbyshire)
E. 69,336

54*Rt Hon. G. A. Brown, Lab.	31,344
Mrs J. Ratcliffe, C.	27,007
Lab. maj.	4,337

(1955   Lab. maj. 6,099)

Berkshire (4). *See* **Abingdon, Newbury, Windsor and Wokingham**

Bermondsey (London Borough)
E. 37,921

55*R. J. Mellish, Lab.	20,528
K. P. Payne, C.	6,107
Lab. maj.	14,341

(1955   Lab. maj. 17,400)

Berwick and East Lothian
E. 50,569

56*Maj. Rt Hon. Sir W. J. Anstruther-Gray, Bt, MC, C.	22,472
P. Jones, Lab.	19,622
C. maj.	2,850

(1955   C. maj. 2,710)

Berwick upon Tweed
(Northumberland)
E. 40,951

57*Viscount Lambton, C.	19,904
R. C. Jelley, Lab.	11,637
C. maj.	8,267

(1955   C. maj. 6,277)

Bethnal Green
(London Borough)
E. 57,617

58*P. Holman, Lab.	24,228
P. R. Roney, C.	7,412
J. Hart, L.	5,508
J. L. Read, Soc. Party of G.B.	899
Lab. maj.	16,816

(1955   Lab. maj. 20,701)

Bexley (English Borough)
E. 64,906

59*Rt Hon. E.R.G. Heath, MBE, C.	32,025
E. A. Bramall, Lab.	23,392
C. maj.	8,633

(1955   C. maj. 4,499)

Billericay (Essex)
E. 78,328

60 E. L. Gardner, QC, C.	29,224
Mrs R. A. Smythe, Lab.	24,402
P. M. T. Sheldon-Williams, L.	9,347
C. maj.	4,822

(1955   C. maj. 4,206)

Bilston (English Borough)
E. 65,861

61*R. J. Edwards, Lab.	27,068
F. J. Oxford, C.	23,523
Lab. maj.	3,545

(1955   Lab. maj. 7,008)

Birkenhead (English Borough)
E. 59,960

62*P. H. Collick, Lab.	22,990
K. G. Routledge, C.	19,361
G. F. Bilson, L.	4,658
Lab. maj.	3,629

(1955   Lab. maj. 3,174)

Birmingham (13)
ALL SAINTS   E. 48,611

63 J. H. Hollingworth, C.	17,235
*D. H. Howell, Lab.	17,215
C. maj.	20

(1955   Lab. maj. 1,307)

ASTON   E. 57,593

64*J. Silverman, Lab.	21,518
A. M. Beaumont-Dark, C.	18,984
Lab. maj.	2,534

(1955   Lab. maj. 8,262)

EDGBASTON   E. 55,719

65*Dame Edith Pitt, DBE, C.	26,401
Mrs N. F. Hinks, Lab.	11,473
C. maj.	14,928

(1955   C. maj. 14,094)

HALL GREEN   E. 61,066

66*Rt Hon. A. Jones, C.	29,148
D. H. V. Fereday, Lab.	15,431
H. W. Maynard, Ind. C.	1,955
C. maj.	13,717

(1955   C. maj. 10,697)

HANDSWORTH   E. 55,596

67*Rt Hon. Sir E. C. G. Boyle, Bt, C.	23,243
A. Murie, Lab.	13,116
S. W. Keatley, Ind.	1,867
C. maj.	10,127

(1955   C. maj. 10,285)

LADYWOOD   E. 39,131

68*V. F. Yates, Lab.	14,717
T. G. John, C.	8,393
Lab. maj.	6,324

(1955   Lab. maj. 8,811)

NORTHFIELD   E. 74,269

69*W. D. Chapman, Lab.	29,587
R. E. Eyre, C.	28,647
Lab. maj.	940

(1955   Lab. maj. 2,884)

PERRY BARR   E. 50,306

70*C. A. Howell, Lab.	16,811
S. C. Greatrix, C.	16,628
W. L. Lawler, L.	5,611
H. Pearce, Comm.	424
Lab. maj.	183
(1955 Lab. maj. 1,680)	

SELLY OAK   E. 58,017

71*H. E. Gurden, C.	24,950
J. O. Rhydderch, Lab.	16,594
C. maj.	8,356
(1955 C. maj. 6,720)	

SMALL HEATH   E. 51,004

72*W. E. Wheeldon, Lab.	19,213
B. C. Owens, C.	14,282
Lab. maj.	4,931
(By-election, 23 March 1961)	
†D. H. Howell, Lab.	12,182
B. C. Owens, C.	5,923
W. Kirk, L.	2,476
Lab. maj.	6,259
(1955 Lab. maj. 7,960)	

SPARKBROOK   E. 47,731

73 L. G. Seymour, C.	17,751
J. T. Webster, Lab.	16,865
C. maj.	886
(1955 Lab. maj. 3,211)	

STECHFORD   E. 55,674

74*R. H. Jenkins, Lab.	21,919
J. M. Bailey, C.	18,996
Lab. maj.	2,923
(1955 Lab. maj. 6,740)	

YARDLEY   E. 59,135

75 L. H. Cleaver, C.	23,482
*H. C. Usborne, Lab.	22,097
C. maj.	1,385
(1955 Lab. maj. 3,124)	

Bishop Auckland (Durham)
E. 48,865

76 H. J. Boyden, Lab.	21,706
N. W. Murray, C.	13,377
J. G. Pease, L.	4,377
Lab. maj.	8,329
(1955 Lab. maj. 5,845)	

Blackburn (English Borough)
E. 60,362

77*Mrs B. A. Castle, Lab.	27,356
J. M. A. Yerburgh, C.	24,490
Lab. maj.	2,866
(1955 Lab. maj. 489)	

BLACKLEY — See **Manchester**

Blackpool (2)

NORTH   E. 57,078

78*Rt Hon. Sir T. Low KCMG, CBE, DSO, TD, C.	25,297
W. H. Dugdale, Lab.	9,440
H. Hague, L.	8,909
C. maj.	15,857
(By-election, 13 March 1962)	
N. A. Miscampbell, C.	12,711
H. Hague, L.	11,738
Miss S. Summerskill, Lab.	8,776
C. maj.	973
(1955 C. maj. 16,030)	

SOUTH   E. 52,927

79*Rt Hon. Sir J. R. Robinson, C.	25,767
P. P. Hall, Lab.	13,337
C. maj.	12,430
(1955 C. maj. 12,225)	

Blaydon (Durham)
E. 47,854

80*R. E. Woof, Lab.	25,969
G. W. Iredell, C.	13,719
Lab. maj.	12,250
(Feb. 1956, by-election, Lab. maj. 10,714) (1955 Lab. maj. 12,523)	

Blyth (English Borough)
E. 62,599

81*Rt Hon. A. Robens, Lab.	38,616
D. M. Walters, C.	13,122
Lab. maj.	25,494
(By-election, 24 Nov. 1960)	
E. J. Milne, Lab.	23,438
D. M. Walters, C.	7,366
C. Pym, Ind.	3,223
Lab. maj.	16,072
(1955 Lab. maj. 23,093)	

Bodmin (Cornwall)
E. 45,000

82*Sir D. Marshall, C.	16,853
P. J. Bessell, L.	14,052
T. F. Mitchell, Lab.	5,769
C. maj.	2,801
(1955 C. maj. 7,659)	

Bolsover (Derbyshire)
E. 50,455

83*H. Neal, Lab.	32,536
R. G. Marlar, C.	9,076
Lab. maj.	23,460
(1955 Lab. maj. 22,019)	

Bolton (2)

EAST *E.* 60,580

84**P. I. Bell*, TD, QC, *C.*	25,885
R. Haines, *Lab.*	23,153
C. maj.	*2,732*

(By-election, 16 Nov. 1960)

E. Taylor, C.	15,499
R. L. Howarth, *Lab.*	14,858
C. F. Byers, OBE, *L.*	10,173
J. E. Dayton, *Ind.*	493
C. maj.	*641*
(1955 C. maj. 3,511)	

WEST *E.* 54,035

85**A. F. Holt, L.*	23,533
P. Cameron, *Lab.*	19,545
L. maj.	*3,988*
(1955 L. maj. 4,813)	

Bootle (English Borough)
E. 50,647

86**S. Mahon, Lab.*	21,294
H. O. Cullen, *C.*	18,379
Lab. maj.	*2,915*
(1955 Lab. maj. 1,438)	

Bosworth (Leicestershire)
E. 65,115

87 *W. L. Wyatt, Lab.*	27,734
P. L. Braithwaite, *C.*	26,341
Lab. maj.	*1,993*
(1955 Lab. maj. 4,100)	

Bothwell (Lanarkshire)
E. 55,845

88**J. Timmons, Lab.*	25,119
W. G. Greig, *C.*	20,767
Lab. maj.	*4,352*
(1955 Lab. maj. 3,610)	

Bournemouth (2)

EAST AND CHRISTCHURCH
E. 60,657

89 *J. H. Cordle, C.*	29,014
J. D. Rutland, *Lab.*	9,222
W. J. Wareham, *L.*	8,308
C. maj.	*19,792*
(1955 C. maj. 18,498)	

WEST *E.* 68,209

90**Sir J. B. Eden, Bt, C.*	33,575
W. Spicer, *Lab.*	15,957
C. maj.	*17,618*
(1955 C. maj. 16,784)	

Bradford (4)

EAST *E.* 47,514

91**F. McLeavy, Lab.*	20,056
D. A. Dalgleish, *C. &*	
Nat. L.	14,529
Lab. maj.	*5,527*
(1955 Lab. maj. 8,875)	

NORTH *E.* 51,957

92**Sir W. J. Taylor, Bt*, CBE,	
C. & Nat. L.	22,850
J. Marshall, MBE, *Lab.*	20,179
C. & Nat. L. maj.	*2,671*
(1955 C. & Nat. L. maj. 69)	

SOUTH *E.* 57,018

93**G. Craddock, Lab.*	21,172
R. Winston Jones, *C. &*	
Nat. L.	18,158
H. Womersley, *L.*	6,850
Lab. maj.	*3,014*
(1955 Lab. maj. 3,710)	

WEST *E.* 50,044

94**A Tiley, C. & Nat. L.*	23,012
S. Hyam, *Lab.*	17,906
C. & Nat. L. maj.	*5,106*
(1955 C. & Nat. L. maj. 3,159)	

Brecon and Radnor
E. 51,357

95**T. E. Watkins, Lab.*	25,411
J. H. Davies, *C.*	18,939
Lab. maj.	*6,472*
(1955 Lab. maj. 7,541)	

Brentford and Chiswick
(English Borough) *E.* 39,881

96 *D. G. Smith, C.*	17,869
Dr H. B. O. Cardew, *Lab*	14,950
C. maj.	*2,919*
(1955 C. maj. 2,105)	

Bridgwater (Somerset)
E. 55,770

97**Sir G. Wills*, MBE, *C.*	23,002
J. Finnigan, *Lab.*	14,706
P. G. Watkins, *L.*	7,893
C. maj.	*8,296*
(1955 C. maj. 7,717)	

Bridlington (Yorkshire E.R.)
E. 55,006

98**Rt Hon. R. F. Wood, C.*	27,438
H. Moor, *Lab.*	10,047
C. maj.	*17,391*
(1955 C. maj. 15,266)	

Brierley Hill (Staffordshire)
E. 71,161

99	*J. E. Talbot, C.*	31,202
	C. J. Simmons, Lab.	27,069
	C. maj.	4,133

(1955   Lab. maj. 949)

Brigg (Lincolnshire)
E. 71,138

100*	E. L. Mallalieu, QC, Lab.	28,997
	R. C. Baker, C.	26,893
	Lab. maj.	2,104

(1955   Lab. maj. 5,021)

Brighouse and Spenborough
(English Borough)   E. 54,422

101*	Rt Hon. L. J. Edwards, OBE, Lab.	23,290
	M. N. Shaw, L. & C.	23,243
	Lab. maj.	47

(By-election, 17 March 1960)

M. N. Shaw, L. & C.	22,472
G. C. Jackson, Lab.	21,806
L. & C. maj.	666

(1955   Lab. maj. 1,626)

Brighton (2)

KEMPTOWN   E. 61,119

102	D. P. James, C.	25,411
	L. C. Cohen, Lab.	19,665
	C. maj.	5,746

(1955   C. maj. 5,257)

PAVILION   E. 57,238

103*	Sir L. W. B. Teeling, C.	27,972
	R. G. White, Lab.	11,998
	C. maj.	15,974

(1955   C. maj. 14,386)

Bristol (6)

CENTRAL   E. 49,476

104*	S. S. Awbery, Lab.	19,905
	L. G. Pine, C.	17,209
	Lab. maj.	2,696

(1955   Lab. maj. 8,752)

NORTH EAST   E. 64,319

105	A. C. N. Hopkins, C. & Nat. L.	24,258
	W. Coldrick, Lab.	21,574
	Mrs A. M. Pearce, L.	5,030
	C. & Nat. L. maj.	2,684

(1955   Lab. maj. 876)

NORTH WEST   E. 57,831

106	M. McLaren, C.	24,938
	T. C. Boyd, Lab.	23,019
	C. maj.	1,919

(1955   Lab. maj. 1,655)

SOUTH   E. 58,671

107*	W. A. Wilkins, Lab.	27,010
	G. E. McWatters, C.	17,428
	Lab. maj.	9,582

(1955   Lab. maj. 10,976)

SOUTH EAST   E. 57,416

108*	Hon. A. N. W. Benn, Lab.	26,273
	M. A. J. St. Clair, C.	20,446
	Lab. maj.	5,827

(By-election, 4 May 1961) See p. 253

*Visct Stansgate (A. N. W. Benn), Lab.	23,275
M. A. J. St. Clair, C.	10,231
Lab. maj.	13,044

(On 28 July 1961, M. A. J. St. Clair,
C. was declared to have been elected).
(1955   Lab. maj. 8,047)

WEST   E. 56,080

109*	R. G. Cooke, C.	27,768
	M. Cocks, Lab.	7,651
	C. A. Hart-Leverton, L.	5,835
	C. maj.	20,117

(March 1957, by-election, C. maj.
14,162) (1955 C. maj. 22,001)

BRIXTON – See **Lambeth**

Bromley (English Borough)
E. 48,937

110*	Rt Hon. H. Macmillan, C.	27,055
	A. J. Murray, Lab.	11,603
	C. maj.	15,452

(1955   C. maj. 13,139)

Bromsgrove (Worcestershire)
E. 66,924

111*	J. C. G. Dance, ERD, C.	32,473
	C. B. B. Norwood, Lab.	23,433
	C. maj.	9,040

(1955   C. maj. 5,174)

Buckinghamshire (4)

BUCKINGHAM   E. 54,905

112*	Sir S. F. Markham, C.	22,304
	Capt. I. R. Maxwell, Lab.	20,558
	E. L. F. Richards, L.	4,577
	C. maj.	1,746

(1955   C. maj. 1,140)

SOUTH   E. 72,466

113*	R. M. Bell, C.	34,154
	Dr R. J. Sankey, Lab.	13,050
	R. K. Brown, OBE, TD, QC, L.	10,589
	C. maj.	21,104

(1955, C. maj. 17,981)

See also **Aylesbury** and **Wycombe**

Burnley (English Borough)
E. 57,990

114	D. Jones, Lab.	27,675
	E. Brooks, C.	20,902
	Lab. maj.	6,773
	(1955 Lab. maj. 5,636)	

Burton (Staffordshire)
E. 58,229

115*	J. C. Jennings, C.	26,926
	E. McGarry, Lab.	21,032
	C. maj.	5,894
	(1955 C. maj. 2,973)	

Bury and Radcliffe
(English Borough)　E. 64,897

116*	J. C. Bidgood, C.	28,623
	R. P. Walsh, Lab.	24,715
	C. maj.	3,908
	(1955 C. maj. 3,749)	

Bury St Edmunds (Suffolk)
E. 57,908

117*	Sir W. T. Aitken, KBE, C.	26,730
	Mrs A. M. A. Walter, Lab.	18,768
	C. maj.	7,962
	(1955 C. maj. 4,570)	

Bute and North Ayrshire—See
Ayrshire and Bute

Caernarvonshire (2)
CAERNARVON　E. 41,202

118*	G. O. Roberts, Lab.	17,506
	T. E. Hooson, C.	9,564
	D. O. Jones, Welsh, Nat.	7,293
	Lab. maj.	7,942
	(1955 Lab. maj. 9,221)	

See also **Conway**

Caerphilly (Glamorgan)
E. 46,671

119*	Rt Hon. N. Edwards, Lab.	28,154
	W. R. Lewis, C.	7,181
	J. D. A. Howell, Welsh Nat.	3,420
	Lab. maj.	20,973
	(1955 Lab. maj. 18,672)	

Caithness and Sutherland
E. 26,716

120*	Sir D. Robertson, Ind.	12,163
	R. K. Murray, Lab.	6,438
	Ind. maj.	5,725
	(1955 C. maj. 5,089)	

Camberwell (2)
DULWICH　E. 66,988

121*	R. C. D. Jenkins, C.	24,991
	A. L. Hill, Lab.	22,740
	W. J. Searle, L.	5,324
	C. maj.	2,251
	(1955 C. maj. 1,851)	

PECKHAM　E. 57,850

122*	Mrs F. K. Corbet, Lab.	24,389
	A. F. Lockwood, C.	13,007
	Lab. maj.	11,382
	(1955 Lab. maj. 13,768)	

Cambridge (English Borough)
E. 59,745

123*	Sir H. W. Kerr, Bt, C.	24,350
	R. M. D. Davies, Lab.	17,543
	A. G. de Montmorency, L.	5,792
	C. maj.	6,807
	(1955 C. maj. 7,127)	

Cambridgeshire
E. 60,698

124*	S. G. Howard, QC, C.	27,407
	W. Royle, Lab.	19,928
	C. maj.	7,479
(By-election, 16 March 1961)		
	F. L. Pym, C.	17,643
	R. M. D. Davies, Lab.	11,566
	R. Moore, L.	9,219
	C. maj.	6,077
	(1955 C. maj. 3,974)	

Cannock (Staffordshire)
E. 65,472

125*	Miss J. Lee, Lab.	29,624
	P. H. Lugg, C. & L.	22,485
	Lab. maj.	7,139
	(1955 Lab. maj. 8,298)	

Canterbury (Kent)
E. 62,011

126*	Sir L. M. Thomas, MBE, TD, C.	30,846
	G. E. Peters, Lab.	15,746
	C. maj.	15,100
	(1955 C. maj. 14,295)	

Cardiff (3)
NORTH　E. 59,986

127	D. S. Box, C.	28,737
	G. S. Viner, Lab.	18,054
	E. P. Roberts, Welsh Nat.	2,553
	S. G. Worth, Ind.	408
	C. maj.	10,683
	(1955 C. maj. 9,185)	

South East   E. 64,574
128*L. J. Callaghan, Lab.   26,915
     M. H. A. Roberts, C.   26,047
     Lab. maj.   868
     (1955 Lab. maj. 3,240)
West   E. 59,524
129*T. G. Thomas, Lab.   25,390
     A. L. Hallinan, C.   22,258
     Lab. maj.   3,132
     (1955 Lab. maj. 4,962)

Cardiganshire
E. 38,878
130*E. R. Bowen, QC, L.   17,868
     Mrs L. Rees Hughes,
       Lab.   8,559
     G. W. Evans, Welsh Nat.   3,880
     L. maj.   9,309
     (1955 L. maj. 8,817)

Carlisle (English Borough)
E. 49,519
131*Dr D. M. Johnson, C.   21,948
     A. Hargreaves, Lab.   19,950
     C. maj.   1,998
     (1955 C. maj. 370)

Carlton (Nottinghamshire)
E. 64,554
132*Sir K. W. M. Pickthorn,
       Bt, C.   30,722
     P. Myers, Lab.   22,645
     C. maj.   8,077
     (1955 C. maj. 6,857)

Carmarthenshire (2)
Carmarthen   E. 57,195
133*Lady Megan Lloyd-George,
       Lab.   23,399
     A. T. Davies, L.   16,766
     J. B. Evans, C.   6,147
     H. H. Roberts, Welsh
       Nat.   2,545
     Lab. maj.   6,633
(Feb. 1957, by-election, Lab. maj.
3,069) (1955 L. maj. 3,333)
See also **Llanelly**

Carshalton (Surrey)
E. 68,391
134*Rt Hon. A. H. Head, CBE,
       MC, C.   30,454
     J. H. Powell, Lab.   17,210
     J. H. G. Browne, L.   8,744
     C. maj.   13,244

(By-election, 16 Nov. 1960)
     Capt. W. Elliot, DSC, RN,
       C.   19,175
     J. H. G. Browne, L.   10,250
     B. Thomas, Lab.   7,696
     C. maj.   8,925
     (1955 C. maj. 11,505)
Cathcart — See **Glasgow**

Cheadle (Cheshire)
E. 71,205
135*W. S. Shepherd, C.   32,787
     R. N. Cuss, L.   15,469
     C. R. Morris, Lab.   11,373
     C. maj.   17,318
     (1955 C. maj. 19,974)
Cheetham — See **Manchester**

Chelmsford (Essex)
E. 61,630
136*Sir H. Ashton, KBE, MC,
       C.   29,992
     B. R. Clapham, Lab.   20,124
     C. maj.   9,868
     (1955 C. maj. 5,149)

Chelsea (London Borough)
E. 47,085
137 Capt. J. S. S. Litchfield,
       RN, C.   20,985
     L. Goldstone, Lab.   6,308
     K. G. Wellings, L.   3,662
     C. maj.   14,677
     (1955 C. maj. 15,052)

Cheltenham (English Borough)
E. 52,946
138*Maj. W. W. Hicks Beach,
       TD, C.   21,997
     Dr K. G. Pendse, Lab.   12,725
     G. G. Watson, L.   8,428
     C. maj.   9,272
     (1955 C. maj. 7,621)

Chertsey (Surrey)
E. 55,609
139*Rt Hon. Sir L. F. Heald,
       QC, C.   24,836
     J. S. Barr, Lab.   14,150
     A. R. Mayne, L.   5,146
     C. maj.   10,686
     (1955 C. maj. 8,365)

Cheshire (10). See **Cheadle, Chester
City of), Crewe, Knutsford,
Macclesfield, Nantwich, North-
wich, Runcorn, Stalybridge and
Hyde and Wirral**

Chester (City of) (Cheshire)
E. 57,617

140*J. M. Temple, C.	27,847
L. Carter-Jones, Lab.	17,492
C. maj.	10,355

(Nov. 1956, by-election, C. maj.
6,348) (1955 C. maj. 11,002)

Chester-le-Street (Durham)
E. 53,884

141*N. Pentland, Lab.	33,901
W. R. Rees-Mogg, C.	10,838
Lab. maj.	23,063

(Sept. 1956, by-election, Lab. maj.
21,287) (1955 Lab. maj. 22,276)

Chesterfield (English Borough)
E. 65,270

142*Sir G. Benson, Lab.	30,534
J. A. Lemkin, C. & Nat. L.	17,084
G. R. Smedley-Stevenson, L.	6,360
Lab. maj.	13,450

(1955 Lab. maj. 7,854)

Chichester (West Sussex)
E. 63,958

143*W. H. Loveys, C.	30,755
J. S. Spooner, Lab.	9 546
J. Newman, L.	6,913
C. maj.	21,209

(Nov. 1958, by-election, C. maj.
13,654) (1955 C. maj. 18,122)

Chigwell (Essex)
E. 50,213

144*J. A. Biggs-Davison, C.	23,422
A. S. Harman, Lab.	17,860
C. maj.	5,562

(1955 C. maj. 1,875)

Chippenham (Wiltshire)
E. 51,923

145*Rt Hon Sir D. M. Eccles, KCVO, C.	21,696
R. W. Portus, Lab.	12,911
J. C. Hall, L.	7,059
C. maj.	8,785

(By-election, 22 Nov. 1962)

D. E. Awdry, C.	13,439
Hon C. W. Layton, L.	11,851
R. W. Portus, Lab.	10,633
K. Jerrome, Ind.	260
J. P. Naylor, Ind.	237
M. J. A. Saint, Ind.	88
C. maj.	1,588

(1955 C. maj. 6,695)

Chislehurst (Kent)
E. 59,646

146*Rt Hon. Dame Patricia Hornsby-Smith, DBE, C.	25,748
Mrs M. Reid, Lab.	19,069
D. C. Blackburn, L.	6,366
C. maj.	6,679

(1955 C. maj. 3,870)

Chorley (Lancashire)
E. 59,086

147*C. Kenyon, Lab.	25,641
F. H. Taylor, C.	24,965
Lab. maj.	676

(1955 Lab. maj. 1,338)

Cirencester and Tewkesbury (Gloucestershire)
E. 58,099

148 Hon. N. Ridley, C.	28,169
J. M. Bowyer, Lab.	16,314
C. maj.	11,855

(1955 The Speaker's maj. 12,978)

Cities of London and Westminster
E. 68,896

149†Rt Hon. Sir H. B. H. Hylton-Foster, QC, C. (now The Speaker)	27,489
W. Howie, Lab.	10,301
D. Monsey, L.	4,409
C. maj.	17,188

(1955 C. maj. 18,044)

Clackmannan and East Sterling –
See **Stirling and Clackmannan**
CLAPHAM – See **Wandsworth**

Cleveland (Yorkshire, N.R.)
E. 71,281

150 G. W. Proudfoot, C.	30,445
*A. M. F. Palmer, Lab.	28,790
C. maj.	1,655

(1955 Lab. maj. 181)

Clitheroe (Lancashire)
E. 44,350

151 F. F. Pearson, C.	22,314
W. Rutter, Lab.	16,103
C. maj.	6,211

(1955 C. maj. 4,944)

Coatbridge and Airdrie (Scottish Burgh)
E. 53,223

152 J. Dempsey, Lab.	22,747
Mrs C. S. Morton, C.	21,953
Lab. maj.	794

(1955 Lab. maj. 4,664)

Colchester (Essex)
E. 57,776

153*Rt Hon. C. J. M. Alport, TD, C.	24,592
Mrs J. I. Edmondson, Lab.	17,096
P. M. Linfoot, L.	5,942
C. maj.	*7,496*

(By-election, 16 March 1961)

P. A. F. Buck, C.	17,891
J. W. Fear, Lab.	12,547
Capt. H. Fry, L.	7,487
C. maj.	*5,344*

(1955   C. maj. 4,898)

Colne Valley (Yorks, W.R.)
E. 51,777

154*Rt Hon. W. G. Hall, Lab.	19,284
C. J. Barr, C.	13,030
R. S. Wainwright, L.	11,254
Lab. maj.	*6,254*

(By-election, 21 March 1963)

A. E. P. Duffy, Lab.	18,033
R. S. Wainwright, L.	15,994
A. Alexander, C.	6,238
A. Fox, Ind.	266
Lab. maj.	*2,039*

(1955   Lab. maj. 3,596)

Consett (Durham)
E. 59,206

155*W. Stones, Lab.	32,307
D. A. Orde, C.	16,037
Lab. maj.	*16,270*

(1955   Lab. maj. 15,755)

Conway (Caernarvonshire)
E. 45,660

156*P. J. M. Thomas, C.	17,795
S. Jones, Lab.	13,260
J. H. Bellis, L.	3,845
I. B. Rees, Welsh Nat.	2,852
C. maj.	*4,535*

(1955   C. maj. 4,824)

Cornwall (5)

NORTH   E. 42,764

157 J. S. R. Scott-Hopkins, C.	16,701
E. T. Malindine, L.	15,712
W. C. Ferman, Lab.	3,389
C. maj.	*989*

(1955   C. maj. 1,604)

See also **Bodmin, Falmouth and Camborne, St. Ives and Truro**

Coventry (3)

EAST   E. 70,689

158*R. H. S. Crossman, OBE, Lab.	32,744
W. J. Biffen, C.	24,982
Lab. maj.	*7,762*

(1955   Lab. maj. 6,104)

NORTH   E. 53,598

159*M. Edelman, Lab.	23,035
F. C. Maynard, C.	21,794
Lab. maj.	*1,241*

(1955   Lab. maj. 3,173)

SOUTH   E. 67,394

160 P. N. Hocking, C.	28,584
*Miss E. F. Burton, Lab.	26,754
C. maj.	*1,830*

(1955   Lab. maj. 1,688)

CRAIGTON — *See* **Glasgow**

Crewe (Cheshire)
E. 50,971

161*S. S. Allen, QC, Lab.	22,811
G. L. Beaman, C.	19,030
Lab. maj.	*3,781*

(1955 Lab. maj. 6,356)

Crosby (English Borough)
E. 57,495

162*R. G. Page, MBE, C.	29,801
D. E. Brown, Lab.	14,745
C. maj.	*15,056*

(1955   C. maj. 15,436)

Croydon (3)

NORTH EAST   E. 57,174

163*Vice-Adm. J. Hughes-Hallett, CB, DSO, C.	24,345
W. J. Wolfgang, Lab.	15,440
Dr A. E. Bender, L.	6,109
C. maj.	*8,905*

(1955   C. maj. 8,481)

NORTH WEST   E. 58,177

164*F. W. Harris, C.	25,111
D. W. Chalkley, Lab.	14,658
Miss I. E. Thurston, L.	6,061
C. maj.	*10,453*

(1955   C. maj. 10,537)

SOUTH   E. 63,636

165*Sir R. H. M. Thompson, Bt, C.	29,284
F. A. Messer, Lab.	21,069
C. maj.	*8,215*

(1955   C. maj. 6,700)

Cumberland (3). *See* **Penrith and the Border, Whitehaven and Workington**

Dagenham (English Borough)
E. 73,968

166*J. Parker, Lab.	37,009	
A. F. Waley, C.	16,626	
Lab. maj.	*20,383*	

(1955   Lab. maj. 25,093)

Darlington (English Borough)
E. 59,342

167 A. T. Bourne-Arton, C.	24,318	
R. H. Lewis, Lab.	19,901	
J. P. McQuade, L.	5,863	
C. maj.	*4,417*	

(1955   C. maj. 2,581)

Dartford (Kent)
E. 66,599

168*S. Irving, Lab.	25,323	
P. E. Walker, C.	24,047	
B. C. Davis, L.	5,881	
Lab. maj.	*1,276*	

(1955   Lab. maj. 4,198)

Darwen (Lancashire)
E. 55,461

169*C. Fletcher-Cooke, QC, C.	27,483	
T. Park, Lab.	19,141	
C. maj.	*8,342*	

(1955   C. maj. 7,916)

Dearne Valley (Yorks, W.R.)
E. 59,444

170 E. Wainwright, BEM, Lab.	39,088	
D. S. W. Blacker, C.	11,205	
Lab. maj.	*27,883*	

(1955   Lab. maj. 26,316)

Denbighshire (2)

DENBIGH   E. 53,000

171 W. G. O. Morgan, C.	17,893	
Dr G. T. Hughes, L.	13,268	
S. Williams, Lab.	8,620	
Dr D. A. Jones, Welsh Nat.	3,077	
C. maj.	*4,625*	

(1955   Nat. L. maj. 4,641)

See also **Wrexham**

Deptford (London Borough)
E. 49,412

172*Sir L. A. Plummer, Lab.	21,226	
J. D. Brimacombe, C.	13,038	
Lab. maj.	*8,188*	

(By-election, 4 July 1963)

Hon. J. E. Silkin, Lab.	12,209	
D. J. Penwarden, L.	4,726	
J. D. Brimacombe, C.	4,023	
Lab. maj.	*7,483*	

(1955   Lab. maj. 11,453)

Derby (2)

NORTH   E. 55,976

173*Group-Capt. C. A. B. Wilcock, OBE, AFC, Lab.	22,673	
R. J. Maxwell-Hyslop, C.	20,266	
Lab. maj.	*2,407*	

(By-election, 17 April 1962)

†N. MacDermot, QC, Lab.	16,497	
L. Irving, L.	8,479	
T. M. Wray, C.	7,502	
T. Lynch, Ind.	886	
Lab. maj.	*8,018*	

(1955   Lab. maj. 5,006)

SOUTH   E. 54,131

174*Rt Hon. P. J. Noel-Baker, Lab.	20,776	
T. M. Wray, C.	17,345	
A. L. Smart, L.	4,746	
Lab. maj.	*3,431*	

(1955   Lab. maj. 6,509)

Derbyshire (7)

NORTH EAST   E. 73,678

175 T. Swain, Lab.	37,444	
R. A. Ward, C.	22,112	
Lab. maj.	*15,332*	

(1955   Lab. maj. 17,344)

SOUTH EAST   E. 65,457

176 F. L. J. Jackson, C.	25,374	
*A. J. Champion, Lab.	25,362	
T. Lynch, L.	4,980	
C. maj.	*12*	

(1955   Lab. maj. 1,581)

WEST   E. 43,881

177*E. B. Wakefield, CIE, C.	22,034	
A. E. Kitts, Lab.	13,925	
C. maj.	*8,109*	

(By-election, 6 June 1962)

A. M. Crawley, MBE, C.	12,455	
Lt-Col R. Gardner-Thorpe, L.	11,235	
J. Dilks, Lab.	9,431	
R. E. Gregory, Ind.	1,433	
C. maj.	*1,220*	

(1955   C. maj. 6,756)

See also **Belper, Bolsover, High Peak** and **Ilkeston**

Devizes (Wiltshire)
E. 50,779

178*H. P. Pott, C.	20,682	
W. E. Cave, Lab.	16,844	
J. Norton, Ind.	2,707	
C. maj.	*3,838*	

(1955   C. maj. 2,075)

DEVONPORT – *See* **Plymouth**

Devonshire (6)

NORTH   *E.* 43,486

179 *J. J. Thorpe, L.*	15,831	
Hon. J. L. Lindsay, C.	15,469	
G. W. Pitt, *Lab.*	5,567	
L. maj.		*362*

(1955   C. maj. 5,226)

See also **Honiton, Tavistock, Tiverton, Torrington** and **Totnes**

Dewsbury (English Borough)
E. 54,894

180 *D. Ginsburg, Lab.*	20,870	
J. M. Fox, *C.*	17,201	
J. M. McLusky, *L.*	7,321	
Lab. maj.		*3,669*

(1955   Lab. maj. 7,417)

Doncaster (English Borough)
E. 58,505

181**A. P. L. Barber*, TD, *C.*	26,521	
W. E. Garrett, *Lab.*	22,935	
C. maj.		*3,586*

(1955   C. maj. 1,660)

Don Valley (Yorks, W.R.)
E. 68,876

182 *R. Kelley, Lab.*	40,935	
G. H. Dodsworth, *C.*	16,787	
Lab. maj.		*24,148*

(1955   Lab. maj. 24,732)

Dorking (Surrey)
E. 51,092

183**Rt Hon. Sir G. C. Touche, Bt, C.*	24,564	
S. R. Mills, *Lab.*	9,605	
W. S. Watson, *L.*	6,582	
C. maj.		*14,959*

(1955   C. maj. 12,509)

Dorset (3)

NORTH   *E.* 46,844

184**Col. Sir R. H. Glyn, Bt, OBE, TD, C.*	20,255	
J. A. Emlyn-Jones, *L.*	11,604	
H. J. Dutfield, *Lab.*	6,548	
C. maj.		*8,651*

(June 1957, by-election, C. maj. 3,102)   (1955   C. maj. 7,159)

SOUTH   *E.* 56,196

185**Viscount Hinchingbrooke, C.*	22,050	
C. F. Ascher, *Lab.*	15,357	
L. I. Norbury-Williams, *L.*	6,887	
C. maj.		*6,693*

(By-election, 22 Nov. 1962)

N. G. Barnett, Lab.	13,783
A. E. U. Maude, TD, *C.*	13,079
L. I. Norbury-Williams, *L.*	8,910
Sir P. A. Debenham, Bt, *Ind.*	5,057
P. Burn, *Ind.*	181
M. Fudge, *Ind.*	82
J. C. O'Connor, *Ind.*	45
Lab. maj.	704

(1955   C. maj. 5,417)

WEST   *E.* 44,109

186**K. S. D. W. Digby*, TD, *C.*	19,747	
L. W. King, *Lab.*	11,536	
J. H. Goodden, *L.*	4,850	
C. maj.		*8,211*

(1955   C. maj. 6,763)

Dover (Kent)
E. 63,512

187**J. S. W. Arbuthnot*, MBE, TD, *C.*	27,939	
H. W. Lee, *Lab.*	24,698	
C. maj.		*3,241*

(1955   C. maj. 3,018)

Down (2)

NORTH   *E.* 89,686

188**G. B. H. Currie*, MBE, *U.U.*	51,773	
J. Campbell, *S.F.*	1,039	
U.U. maj.		*50,734*

(1955   U.U. maj. 48,678)

SOUTH   *E.* 77,628

189**Capt. L. P. S. Orr, U.U.*	36,875	
K. O'Rourke, *S.F.*	6,928	
U.U. maj.		*29,947*

(1955   U.U. maj. 18,297)

Dudley (English Borough)
E. 72,829

190**G. E. C. Wigg, Lab.*	31,826	
F. E. Spiller, *C.*	26,101	
Lab. maj.		*5,725*

(1955   Lab. maj. 11,051)

DULWICH – *See* **Camberwell**

Dumfries
E. 57,212

191**Rt Hon. N. M. S. Mac-pherson, Nat. L. & C.*	25,867	
G. C. Moodie, *Lab.*	18,437	
Nat. L. & C. maj.		*7,430*

(1955 Nat. L. & C. maj. 9,078)
(By-election pending.)

Dunbartonshire (2)

EAST *E.* 64,961

192*C. R. Bence, Lab.	27,942
D. C. Anderson, VRD, QC, C.	24,593
A. E. Henderson, Comm.	2,200
Lab. maj.	3,349
(1955 Lab. maj. 1,130)	

WEST *E.* 50,277

193*T. Steele, Lab.	22,105
N. M. Glen, C.	19,964
Lab. maj.	2,141
(1955 Lab. maj. 1,952)	

Dundee (2)

EAST *E.* 58,537

194*G. M. Thomson, Lab.	26,263
R. A. McCrindle, C. & Nat. L.	22,082
Lab. maj.	4,181
(1955 Lab. maj. 4,040)	

WEST *E.* 62,804

195*Rt Hon. E. J. St. L. Strachey, Lab.	25,857
Dr R. R. Taylor, C.	25,143
D. P. Bowman, Comm.	1,087
Lab. maj.	714
(1955 Lab. maj. 1,874)	
(By-election 21 Nov. 1963),	
P. M. Doig, Lab.	22,449
Dr. R. R. Taylor, C.	17,494
Dr. J. C. Lees, Scot. Nat.	3,285
D. P. Bowman, Comm.	1,170
Lab. maj.	4,955

Dunfermline (Scottish Burgh)

E. 47,737

196 Dr A. E. Thompson, Lab.	23,478
W. A. Elliott, Nat. L. & C.	14,744
Lab. maj.	8,734
(1955 Lab. maj. 7,976)	

Durham (9)

DURHAM *E.* 62,192

197*C. F. Grey, Lab.	33,795
C. P. MacCarthy, C.	17,106
Lab. maj.	16,689
(1955 Lab. maj. 15,772)	

NORTH WEST *E.* 50,629

198*J. W. Ainsley, Lab.	28,064
Mrs O. Sinclair, C.	13,172
Lab. maj.	14,892
(1955 Lab. maj. 14,006)	

See also **Bishop Auckland, Blaydon, Chester-le-Street, Consett, Easington, Houghton-le-Spring** and **Sedgefield**

Ealing (2)

NORTH *E.* 59,768

199*J. W. Barter, C.	27,312
W. S. Hilton, Lab.	23,036
C. maj.	4,276
(1955 C. maj. 240)	

SOUTH *E.* 53,296

200*B. C. C. Batsford, C.	24,761
H. G. Garside, Lab.	12,039
Sir J. J. A. Mostyn, Bt, L.	4,842
C. maj.	12,722
(June 1958, by-election, C. maj., 6,159)	
(1955 C. maj. 12,530)	

Easington (Durham)

E. 56,690

201*Rt Hon. E. Shinwell, Lab.	36,552
G. W. Rossiter, C.	9,259
Lab. maj.	27,293
(1955 Lab. maj. 25,257)	

Eastbourne (East Sussex)

E. 62,971

202*Sir C. S. Taylor, C.	27,874
A. A. Dumont, Lab.	11,837
Lt-Col R. L. Gardner-Thorpe, L.	8,955
C. maj.	16,037
(1955 C. maj. 14,218)	

East Grinstead (East Sussex)

E. 65,437

203*Mrs E. V. E. Emmet, C.	31,759
R. W. G. Humphreys, Lab.	10,104
P. A. T. Furnell, L.	9,100
C. maj.	21,655
(1955 C. maj. 16,700)	

East Ham (2)

NORTH *E.* 38,014

204*R. E. Prentice, Lab.	16,001
J. H. S. Bangay, C.	12,175
Lab. maj.	3,826
(May 1957, by-election, Lab. maj. 5,979)	
(1955 Lab. maj. 5,545)	

SOUTH *E.* 39,764

205*A. E. Oram, Lab.	18,230
R. J. Watts, C.	11,422
Lab. maj.	6,808
(1955 Lab. maj. 8,699)	

Eastleigh (Hampshire)
E. 55,215

206*D. E. C. Price, C.	24,949	
C. J. S. Rowland, Lab.	21,693	
C. maj.		3,256

(1955   C. maj. 545)

Ebbw Vale (Monmouthshire)
E. 39,299

207*Rt Hon. A. Bevan, Lab.	27,326	
A. G. Davies, C.	6,404	
Lab. maj.		20,922

(By-election, 17 Nov. 1960)

M. M. Foot, Lab.	20,528	
Sir B. M. Rhys-Williams, Bt, C.	3,799	
Lt-Col P. H. Lort-Phillips, L.	3,449	
E. Roberts, Welsh Nat.	2,091	
Lab. maj.		16,729

(1955   Lab. maj. 19,236)

Eccles (English Borough)
E. 59,315

208*W. T. Proctor, Lab.	25,566	
B. R. O. Bell, C.	23,580	
Lab. maj.		1,986

(1955   Lab. maj. 2,326)

EDGBASTON – See **Birmingham**
EDGE HILL – See **Liverpool**

Edinburgh (7)
CENTRAL   E. 42,781

209*T. Oswald, Lab.	15,849	
N. R. Wylie, C.	15,232	
Lab. maj.		617

(1955   Lab. maj. 939)
EAST   E. 54,756

210*E. G. Willis, Lab.	22,244	
Earl of Dalkeith, C.	21,932	
Lab. maj.		312

(1955   Lab. maj. 2,042)
LEITH   E. 39,750

211*J. H. Hoy, Lab.	15,092	
G. Stewart, Nat. L. & C.	12,018	
Sir A. H. A. Murray, OBE, L.	4,475	
Lab. maj.		3,074

(1955   Lab. maj. 5,644)
NORTH   E. 42,270

212*Rt Hon. W. R. Milligan, QC, C.	19,991	
G. G. Stott, QC, Lab.	11,235	
C. maj.		8,756

(By-election, 19 May 1960)

Earl of Dalkeith, C.	12,109	
R. King Murray, Lab.	6,775	
R. McPake, L.	3,458	
C. maj.		5,334

(1955   C. maj. 7,761)
PENTLANDS   E. 53,178

213*Rt Hon. Lord John Hope, C.	25,742	
J. P. Mackintosh, Lab.	16,950	
C. maj.		8,792

(1955   C. maj. 7,485)
SOUTH   E. 48,767

214*A. M. C. Hutchison, C.	22,799	
A. D. Reid, Lab.	11,285	
Hon. W. Douglas-Home, L.	5,505	
C. maj.		11,514

(May   1957,   by-election,   C.   maj. 4,640)

(1955   C. maj. 12,887)
WEST   E. 57,293

215 J. A. Stodart, C.	25,976	
J. K. Stocks, Lab.	14,044	
D. F. Leach, L.	5,962	
C. maj.		11,932

(1955   C. maj. 13,216)

Edmonton (English Borough)
E. 67,837

216*A. H. Albu, Lab.	25,958	
W. H. Bishop, C.	25,497	
Lab. maj.		461

(1955   Lab. maj. 7,038)

Enfield (2)
EAST   E. 47,183

217 J. Mackie, Lab.	20,101	
F. J. V. Brown, C.	16,477	
Lab. maj.		3,624

(1955   Lab. maj. 7,701)
WEST   E. 44,983

218*Rt Hon. I. N. Macleod, C.	24,861	
G. Hickman, Lab.	11,058	
C. maj.		13,803

(1955   C. maj. 11,518)

Epping (Essex)
E. 83,647

219*G. B. Finlay, C.	31,507	
D. F. W. Ford, Lab.	27,114	
L. T. J. Arlott, L.	11,913	
C. maj.		4,393

(1955   C. maj. 3,523)

Epsom (Surrey)
E. 69,592

220*Sir P. A. G. Rawlinson, QC, C.	35,484
D. E. Heather, Lab.	11,039
R. W. M. Walsh, L.	9,910
C. maj.	24,445
(1955 C. maj. 22,073)	

Erith and Crayford
(English Borough)
E. 53,057

221*N. N. Dodds, Lab.	24,523
J. J. Davis, C.	18,763
Lab. maj.	5,760
(1955 Lab. maj. 8,618)	

Esher (Surrey)
E. 72,183

222*Sir W. Robson-Brown, C.	37,155
P. E. Vanson, Lab.	12,934
G. E. Owen, L.	8,730
C. maj.	24,221
(1955 C. maj. 20,642)	

Essex (10)
SOUTH EAST   E. 60,316

223*B. R. Braine, C.	28,124
R. M. Fryer, Lab.	17,991
C. maj.	10,133
(1955 C. maj. 6,690)	

See also **Billericay, Chelmsford,
Chigwell, Colchester, Epping,
Harwich, Maldon, Saffron Walden**
and **Thurrock**

Eton and Slough
(English Borough)
E. 52,114

224*A. F. Brockway, Lab.	20,851
A. J. Page, C.	20,763
Lab. maj.	88
(1955 Lab. maj. 2,443)	

EXCHANGE — See **Liverpool and
Manchester**

Exeter (English Borough)
E. 54,084

225*R. D. Williams, C.	21,579
A. J. Rogers, Lab.	15,918
G. C. Taylor, L.	6,852
C. maj.	5,661
(1955 C. maj. 5,388)	

Eye (Suffolk)
E. 56,395

226*Col Sir J. H. Harrison, Bt,	
TD, C.	22,333
E. L. Granville, Lab.	19,849
Mrs. S. Robson, L.	5,215
C. maj.	2,484
(1955 C. maj. 889)	

Falmouth and Camborne
(Cornwall)
E. 53,763

227*F. H. Hayman, Lab.	20,083
Miss A. M. Tennant, C.	15,886
N. A. S. Gibson, L.	7,890
Lab. maj.	4,197
(1955 Lab. maj. 1,047)	

Farnham (Surrey)
E. 50,249

228*Sir G. Nicholson, Bt, C.	29,538
Dr J. G. Turner, Lab.	9,800
D. W. Saunders, L.	6,538
C. maj.	13,738
(1955 C. maj. 10,906)	

Farnworth (Lancashire)
E. 56,094

229*E. Thornton, MBE, Lab.	27,393
A. S. Royse, C.	19,356
Lab. maj.	8,037
(1955 Lab. maj. 6,598)	

Faversham (Kent)
E. 57,760

230*P. L. Wells, Lab.	24,327
Mrs E. M. S. Olsen, C.	24,074
Lab. maj.	253
(1955 Lab. maj. 59)	

Feltham (English Borough)
E. 53,417

231*A. E. Hunter, Lab.	20,320
J. B. W. Turner, C.	18,070
L. A. de Pinna, L.	4,533
Lab. maj.	2,250
(1955 Lab. maj. 3,350)	

Fermanagh and South Tyrone
E. 64,022

232*Lt-Col R. G. Grosvenor,	
TD, U.U.	32,080
J. H. Martin, S.F.	7,348
U.U. maj.	24,732
(Sept. 1955, U.U. declared elected)	
(1955 S.F. maj. 261)	

Fife (2)

East *E.* 50,537

233	*Sir J. Henderson-Stewart,*	
	Bt, L. & C.	26,585
	J. Nicol, *Lab.*	11,421
	L. & C. maj.	*15,164*

(By-election, 8 Nov. 1961)

	Sir J. E. Gilmour, Bt, DSO,	
	TD, *C.*	15,948
	J. Smith, *Lab.*	8,882
	D. Leach, *L.*	8,786
	C. maj.	*7,066*

(1955 L. & C. maj. 15,232)

West *E.* 55,992

234	*W. W. Hamilton, Lab.*	25,554
	A. L. Buchanan-Smith, *C.*	11,257
	L. Daly, *Ind.*	4,886
	W. Lauchlan, *Comm.*	3,828
	Lab. maj.	*14,297*

(1955 Lab. maj. 16,211)

Finchley (English Borough)
E. 69,123

235	*Mrs M. H. Thatcher, C.*	29,697
	E. P. Deakins, *Lab.*	13,437
	H. I. Spence, *L.*	12,701
	C. maj.	*16,260*

(1955 C. maj. 12,825)

Flintshire (2)

East *E.* 52,635

236	*Mrs E. L. White, Lab.*	22,776
	F. Hardman, *C.*	22,701
	Lab. maj.	*75*

(1955 Lab. maj. 2,274)

West *E.* 47,490

237	*Rt Hon. E. N. C. Birch,* OBE,	
	C.	20,446
	R. G. Waterhouse, *Lab.*	12,925
	L. E. Roberts, *L.*	4,319
	E. N. C. Williams, *Welsh*	
	Nat.	1,594
	C. maj.	*7,521*

(1955 C. maj. 8,352)

Folkestone and Hythe (Kent)
E. 50,825

238	A. P. Costain, *C.*	21,726
	W. E. Simpkins, *Lab.*	9,346
	R. D. Emerson, *L.*	7,351
	C. maj.	*12,380*

(1955 C. maj. 11,002)

Fulham (London Borough)
E. 52,088

239	*R. M. M. Stewart, Lab.*	21,525
	Mrs M. L. de la Motte, *C.*	18,581
	Lab. maj.	*2,944*

(1955 Lab. maj. 4,394)

Gainsborough (Lincolnshire)
E. 50,051

240	*M. R. Kimball, C.*	20,056
	H. D. L. G. Walston, *Lab.*	13,247
	Dr R. I. Douglas, *L.*	7,147
	C. maj.	*6,809*

(Feb. 1956, by-election, C. maj. 1,006)

(1955 C. maj. 4,469)

Galloway
E. 36,296

241	*H. J. Brewis, C.*	15,454
	S. B. Mackay, *L.*	6,412
	J. Pickett, *Lab.*	5,590
	C. maj.	*9,042*

(April 1959, by-election, C. maj. 6,403)

(1955 C. maj. 8,014)

Garston – *See* **Liverpool**

Gateshead (2)

East *E.* 52,662

242	*A. S. Moody, Lab.*	25,319
	G. Glover, *C.*	17,654
	Lab. maj.	*7,665*

(1955 Lab. maj. 4,947)

West *E.* 42,643

243	*H. E. Randall, Lab.*	21,277
	D. A. Wright, *C.*	11,509
	Lab. maj.	*9,768*

(Dec. 1955, by-election, Lab. maj. 6,535)

(1955 Lab. maj. 10,331)

Gillingham (English Borough)
E. 48,390

244	*F. F. A. Burden, C.*	23,142
	G. B. Kaufman, *Lab.*	15,863
	C. maj.	*7,279*

(1955 C. maj. 4,145)

Glamorganshire (7). *See* **Aberavon, Barry, Caerphilly, Gower, Neith, Ogmore** and **Pontypridd**

Glasgow (15)

Bridgeton *E.* 48,473

245	*J. Carmichael, Lab.*	21,048
	R. J. Docherty, *C.*	12,139
	Lab. maj.	*8,909*

(By-election, 16 Nov. 1961)

J. Bennett, Lab.	10,930
M. McNeill C.	3,935
I. Macdonald, Scot. Nat.	3,549
G. W. Stone, I.L.P.	586
Lab. maj.	6,995
(1955 Lab. maj. 8,101)	

CATHCART E. 64,703

246*J. Henderson, C.	30,743
J. Jarvie, Lab.	21,169
C. maj.	9,574
(1955 C. maj. 15,751)	

CENTRAL E. 36,540

247*J. McInnes, MBE, Lab.	15,918
I. D. Barber-Fleming, C.	8,712
Lab. maj.	7,206
(1955 Lab. maj. 6,367)	

CRAIGTON E. 46,768

248 B. Millan, Lab.	19,649
*J. N. Browne, C.	19,047
Lab. maj.	602
(1955 C. maj. 210)	

GORBALS E. 48,004

249*Mrs A. Cullen, Lab.	20,732
W. C. Hunter, C.	10,072
P. Kerrigan, Comm.	1,939
Lab. maj.	10,651
(1955 Lab. maj. 10,728)	

GOVAN E. 51,084

250*J. Rankin, Lab.	23,139
A. G. Hutton, C.	13,319
G. McLennan, Comm.	1,869
Lab. maj.	9,820
(1955 Lab. maj. 9,602)	

HILLHEAD E. 38,154

251*Hon. T. G. D. Galbraith, C.	20,094
T. B. Duncan, Lab.	9,317
C. maj.	10,777
(1955 C. maj. 10,458)	

KELVINGROVE E. 34,319

252 F. J. P. Lilley, C.	12,355
*Mrs M. A. McAlister, Lab.	11,254
W. C. Park, I.L.P.	740
C. maj.	1,101
(March 1958, by-election, Lab. maj. 1,360)	
(1955 C. maj. 2,888)	

MARYHILL E. 46,422

253*W. Hannan, Lab.	21,893
N. J. Adamson, C.	12,311
Lab. maj.	9,502
(1955 Lab. maj. 8,638)	

POLLOK E. 52,472

254*Sir J. C. George, KBE, C.	24,338
J. M. Smith, Lab.	17,072
C. maj.	7,266
(1955 C. maj. 8,845)	

PROVAN E. 49,284

255*W. Reid, Lab.	21,608
R. D. Kernohan, C.	17,241
Lab. maj.	4,367
(1955 Lab. maj. 180)	

SCOTSTOUN E. 56,278

256 W. W. Small, Lab.	24,690
J. Bias, C.	21,320
Lab. maj.	3,370
(1955 C. maj. 428)	

SHETTLESTON E. 49,987

257 Sir M. Galpern, Lab.	22,916
D. E. Donaldson, C.	14,743
Lab. maj.	8,173
(1955 Lab. maj. 5,819)	

SPRINGBURN E. 38,147

258*J. C. Forman, Lab.	16,297
E. M. Taylor, C.	10,167
F. Hart, Comm.	1,235
Lab. maj.	6,130
(1955 Lab. maj. 5,773)	

WOODSIDE E. 44,746

259*Rt Hon. W. Grant, TD, QC, C.	16,567
J. McGinley, Lab.	14,483
G. V. McLaughlin, L.	2,583
C. maj.	2,084
(By-election, 22 Nov. 1962)	
N. G. Carmichael, Lab.	8,303
N. M. Glen, C.	6,935
J. House, L.	5,000
A. Noven, Scot. Nat.	2,562
G. A. Alred, Ind. Soc.	134
R. Vallar, Soc. Party of G.B.	83
Lab. maj.	1,368
(1955 C. maj. 4,303)	

Gloucester (English Borough)
E. 52,836

260*J. Diamond, Lab.	19,450
H. D. K. Scott, C.	16,679
Lt-Col P. H. Lort-Phillips, L.	7,336
Lab. maj.	2,771
(Sept. 1957, by-election, Lab. maj. 8,374)	
(1955 Lab. maj. 748)	

Gloucestershire (4)

SOUTH   *E.* 57,026

261*Capt. F. V. Corfield, C.	26,168
J. Holland, Lab.	21,567
C. maj.	4,601
(1955 C. maj. 1,726)	

WEST   *E.* 54,202

262 C. W. Loughlin, Lab.	21,634
Miss O. K. L. Lloyd-Baker, CBE, C.	16,223
E. J. Radley, L.	5,921
Lab. maj.	5,411
(1955 Lab. maj. 4,020)	

See also **Cirencester and Tewkesbury** and **Stroud**

Goole (Yorks W.R.)

E. 53,191

263*G. Jeger, Lab.	26,352
D. Sisson, C. and L.	16,581
Lab. maj.	9,771
(1955 Lab. maj. 9,964)	

GORBALS – *See* **Glasgow**

GORTON – *See* **Manchester**

Gosport and Fareham

(English Borough)   *E.* 73,284

264*R. F. B. Bennett, VRD, C.	35,808
A. S. Pratley, Lab.	19,654
C. maj.	16,154
(1955 C. maj. 12,486)	

GOVAN – *See* **Glasgow**

Gower (Glamorgan)

E. 49,480

265 I. Davies, Lab.	27,441
M. R. D. Heseltine, Nat. L. & C.	9,837
Dr J. G. Griffiths, Welsh Nat.	3,744
Lab. maj.	17,604
(1955 Lab. maj. 18,169)	

Grantham (Lincolnshire)

E. 59,026

266*Rt Hon. J. B. Godber, C.	27,482
T. C. Skeffington-Lodge, Lab.	20,867
C. maj.	6,615
(1955 C. maj. 2,375)	

Gravesend (Kent)

E. 63,299

267*P. M. Kirk, C.	27,124
C. J. V. Mishcon, Lab.	24,962
C. maj.	2,162
(1955 C. maj. 2,909)	

Greenock (Scottish Burgh)

E. 48,366

268*Dr J. D. Mabon, Lab.	19,320
W. T. C. Riddell, L.	10,238
L. M. Turpie, C.	8,616
Lab. maj.	9,082
(Dec. 1955, by-election, Lab. maj. 2,694)	
(1955 Lab. maj. 1,033)	

Greenwich (London Borough)

E. 60,561

269 R. W. Marsh, Lab.	25,204
J. R. Holmes, C.	19,679
Lab. maj.	5,525
(1955 Lab. maj. 7,939)	

Grimsby (English Borough)

E. 64,350

270 C. A. R. Crosland, Lab.	24,729
W. Pearson, C.	24,628
Lab. maj.	101
(1955 Lab. maj. 3,522)	

Guildford (Surrey)

E. 58,963

271*Rt Hon. Sir G. R. H. Nugent, Bt, C.	27,198
G. R. Bellerby, Lab.	13,756
Maj A. R. Braybrooke, L.	6,318
C. maj.	13,442
(1955 C. maj. 11,328)	

Hackney, Central

(London Borough)

E. 62,561

272*H. W. Butler, Lab.	25,407
J. C. T. Waring, C.	15,905
Lab. maj.	9,502
(1955 Lab. maj. 11,800)	

Halifax (English Borough)

E. 67,149

273*M. V. Macmillan, C.	29,212
P. Shore, Lab.	26,697
C. maj.	2,515
(1955 C. maj. 1,535)	

HALL GREEN – *See* **Birmingham**

HALLAM – *See* **Sheffield**

Haltemprice (Yorkshire, E.R.)

E. 53,906

274*P. H. B. Wall, MC, VRD, C.	26,102
D. N. Bancroft, Lab.	9,750
W. I. Cooper, L.	7,562
C. maj.	16,352
(1955 C. maj. 14,342)	

Hamilton (Lanarkshire)
E. 51,995

275*T. Fraser, Lab.	27,423	
J. A. Davidson, C.	11,510	
D. R. Rollo, Scot. Nat.	2,586	
Lab. maj.	15,913	

(1955 Lab. maj. 13,526)

Hammersmith, North
(London Borough) E. 51,680

276*F. Tomney, Lab.	21,409	
W. D. A. Bagnell, C.	14,662	
Lab. maj.	6,747	

(1955 Lab. maj. 8,863)

Hampshire (6). See **Aldershot, Basingstoke, Eastleigh, New Forest, Petersfield** and **Winchester**

Hampstead (London Borough)
E. 69,438

277*Rt Hon. H. Brooke, C.	25,506	
Dr D. T. Pitt, Lab.	13,500	
H. C. Seigal, L.	8,759	
C. maj.	12,006	

(1955 C. maj. 12,186)

HANDSWORTH – See **Birmingham**

Harborough (Leicestershire)
E. 67,790

278 J. A. Farr, C.	29,281	
J. R. Mably, Lab.	16,767	
E. G. Rushworth, L.	11,333	
C. maj.	12,514	

(1955 C. maj. 10,184)

Harrogate (Yorks, W.R.)
E. 53,248

279*J. E. Ramsden, C.	29,466	
F. B. Singleton, Lab.	10,196	
C. maj.	19,270	

(1955 C. maj. 16,541)

Harrow (3)

CENTRAL E. 47,615

280*F. P. Bishop, MBE, C.	23,813	
F. W. Powe, Lab.	14,049	
C. maj.	9,764	

(1955 C. maj. 8,041)

EAST E. 49,273

281*Cmdr A. T. Courtney, OBE, C.	23,554	
M. Rees, Lab.	17,607	
C. maj.	5,947	

(March 1959, by-election. C. maj. 2,220)

(1955 C. maj. 3,622)

WEST E. 54,295

282*Sir A. N. Braithwaite, DSO, MC, C.	30,512	
P. J. Jenkins, Lab.	12,512	
C. maj.	18,000	

(By-election, 17 March 1960.)

A. J. Page, C.	18,526	
J. Wallbridge, L.	7,100	
P. J. Jenkins, Lab.	6,030	
J. E. Dayton, Ind.	1,560	
C. maj.	11,426	

(1955 C. maj. 17,297)

The Hartlepools
(English Borough)
E. 60,888

283 Cdr J. S. Kerans, C.	25,463	
*D. T. Jones, Lab.	25,281	
C. maj.	182	

(1955 Lab. maj. 1,585)

Harwich (Essex)
E. 58,194

284*J. E. Ridsdale, C. & Nat. L.	23,653	
W. O. J. Robinson, Lab.	11,588	
T. E. Dale, L.	5,507	
L. F. Rose, Ind.	3,744	
C. & Nat. L. maj.	12,065	

(1955 C & L. maj. 9,464)

Hastings (English Borough)
E. 48,569

285*Sir N. Cooper-Key, C.	22,458	
J. P. Bryant, Lab.	13,576	
C. maj.	8,882	

(1955 C. maj. 8,536)

Hayes and Harlington
(English Borough)
E. 46,244

286*A. M. Skeffington, Lab.	18,301	
J. A. Grant, C.	14,149	
S. Gay, L.	4,235	
F. Foster, Comm.	527	
Lab. maj.	4,152	

(1955 Lab. maj. 6,148)

HEELEY – See **Sheffield**

Hemel Hempstead
(Hertfordshire)
E. 70,962

287 J. H. Allason, OBE, C.	30,189	
B. F. C. Floud, Lab.	21,954	
Miss M. Neilson, L.	8,358	
C. maj.	8,235	

(1955 C. maj. 6,136)

Hemsworth (Yorks, W.R.)
E. 65,705

288	*A. Beaney, Lab.*	45,153
	W. H. Leay, *C.*	9,788
	Lab. maj.	*35,365*

(1955   Lab. maj. 34,042)

Hendon (2)

NORTH   *E.* 52,729

289*	*Sir C. I. Orr-Ewing, Bt,* OBE, *C.*	21,898
	C. H. Genese, *Lab.*	16,566
	Lady Hills, *L.*	4,598
	C. maj.	*5,332*

(1955   C. maj. 4,060)

SOUTH   *E.* 53,545

290*	*Sir H. Lucas-Tooth, Bt, C.*	22,971
	P. K. Archer, *Lab.*	11,016
	P. H. Billenness, *L.*	7,134
	C. maj.	*11,955*

(1955   C. maj, 10,436)

Henley (Oxon)   *E.* 58,319

291*	*J. A. Hay, C.*	24,417
	A. Ledger, *Lab.*	15,014
	C. Truman, *L.*	6,261
	(*C. maj.*	*9,403*

(1955   C. maj. 7,081)

Herefordshire (2)

HEREFORD   *E.* 45,340

292*	*J. D. Gibson-Watt,* MC, *C.*	17,763
	R. Day, *L.*	10,185
	J. W. Wardle, *Lab.*	8,097
	C. maj.	*7,578*

(Feb. 1956, by-election, C. maj. 2,150)

(1955   C. maj. 9,400)

See also **Leominster**

Hertfordshire (7)

EAST   *E.* 66,913

293*	*Rt Hon. Sir D. C. Walker-Smith, Bt,* TD, QC, *C.*	28,201
	S. J. Bidwell, *Lab.*	18,020
	K. J. W. Spargo, *L.*	8,656
	C. maj.	*10,181*

(1955   C. maj. 6,518)

HERTFORD   *E.* 64,106

294*	*Lord Balniel, C.*	31,418
	G. D. Southgate, *Lab.*	22,597
	C. maj.	*8,821*

(1955   C. maj. 5,984)

SOUTH WEST   *E.* 69,291

295*	*G. J. M. Longden,* MBE, *C.*	29,724
	A. J. Whiteside, *Lab.*	19,487
	D. A. H. Banks, *L.*	9,278
	C. maj.	*10,237*

(1955   C. maj. 6,969)

See also **Barnet, Hemel Hempstead** and **St Albans**

Heston and Isleworth
(English Borough)
E. 55,121

296*	*R. R. Harris, C.*	24,486
	T. Ponsonby, *Lab.*	15,636
	W. P. Letch, *L.*	4,867
	C. maj.	*8,850*

(1955   C. maj. 6,512)

Hexham (Northumberland)
E. 49,906

297*	*R. M. Speir, C.*	25,500
	W. H. W. Roberts, *Lab.*	14,980
	C. maj.	*10,520*

(1955   C. maj. 10,264)

Heywood and Royton
(Lancashire)
E. 57,868

298*	*J. A. Leavey, C.*	19,742
	H. Nevin, *Lab.*	17,588
	G. E. MacPherson, *L.*	11,713
	C. maj.	*2,154*

(1955   C. maj. 3,210)

High Peak (Derbyshire)
E. 49,196

299*	*Rt Hon. A. H. E. Molson, C.*	18,738
	B. Conlan, *Lab.*	13,827
	Hon. S. R. Cawley, *L.*	8,138
	C. maj.	*4,911*

(By-election, 16 March 1961)

	A. D. Walder, C.	13,069
	W. M. Halsall, *Lab.*	11,201
	D. Wrigley, *L.*	10,674
	C. maj.	*1,868*

(1955   C. maj. 5,442)

HILLHEAD – *See* **Glasgow**

HILLSBOROUGH – *See* **Sheffield**

Hitchin (Hertfordshire)
E. 75,493

300*	*M. F. M. Maddan, C.*	30,193
	P. J. H. Benenson, *Lab.*	25,818
	R. Glenton, *L.*	8,481
	C. maj.	*4,375*

(1955   C. maj. 965)

Holborn and St Pancras, South
(London Borough)
E. 48,504

301 G. Johnson Smith, C.	17,065	
*Mrs L. M. Jeger, Lab.	16,409	
C. maj.		656

(1955 Lab. maj. 931)

Holland with Boston
(Lincolnshire)
E. 70,588

302*Sir H. W. Butcher, Bt, Nat.		
L. & C.	29,013	
J. D. T. Williamson, Lab.	17,839	
C. Valentine, L.	7,334	
Nat. L. & C. maj.		11,174

(1955 Nat. L. & C. maj. 9,083)

Honiton (Devonshire)
E. 57,172

303*R. Mathew, TD, C.	25,959	
J. B. Halse, L.	12,906	
F. W. Morgan, Lab.	6,928	
C. maj.		13,053

(1955 C. maj. 14,741)

Horncastle (Lincolnshire)
E. 42,262

304*Comdr Sir J. F. W.		
Maitland, C.	19,799	
H. W. Peck, Lab.	9,928	
C. maj.		9,871

(1955 C. maj. 10,270)

Hornchurch (English Borough)
E. 87,544

305*G. W. Lagden, C.	34,852	
Miss J. Richardson, Lab.	27,530	
L. H. Jones, L.	11,056	
C. maj.		7,322

(1955 C. maj. 1,372)

Hornsey (English Borough)
E. 71,151

306*Lady Gammans, C.	30,048	
F. E. Mostyn, Lab.	17,710	
S. Solomon, L.	5,706	
G. J. Jones, Comm.	1,107	
C. maj.		12,338

(May 1957, by-election, C. maj.
3,131)
(1955 C. maj. 12,726)

Horsham (West Sussex)
E. 76,618

307*C. F. H. Gough, MC, TD, C.	37,275	
A. E. Pegler, Lab.	24,012	
C. maj.		13,263

(1955 C. maj. 11,510)

Houghton-le-Spring (Durham)
E. 56,780

308*W. R. Blyton, Lab.	35,960	
A. R. C. Arbuthnot, C.	11,398	
Lab. maj.		24,562

(1955 Lab. maj. 22,899)

Hove (English Borough)
E. 67,018

309*A. A. H. Marlowe, QC, C.	36,150	
T. J. Marsh, Lab.	12,206	
C. maj.		23,944

(1955 C. maj. 22,353)

Howden (Yorkshire, E.R.)
E. 47,310

310*P. E. O. Bryan, DSO, MC, C.	20,681	
J. Rhodes, Lab.	7,809	
R. H. Hargreaves, L.	7,384	
C. maj.		12,872

(1955 C. maj. 11,398)

Huddersfield (2)

EAST E. 52,729

311*J. P. W. Mallalieu, Lab.	22,474	
P. M. Beard, C.	19,389	
Lab. maj.		3,085

(1955 Lab. maj. 4,224)

WEST E. 51,284

312*D. W. Wade, L.	25,273	
J. Marsden, Lab.	15,621	
L. maj.		9,652

(1955 L. maj. 7,927)

Hull (3)

EAST E. 72,441

313*Cmdr H. Pursey, Lab.	30,667	
Mrs F. C. M. Heath,		
MBE, C.	17,648	
J. J. McCallum, L.	10,043	
Lab. maj.		13,019

(1955 Lab. maj. 12,706)

NORTH E. 63,918

314 J. M. Coulson, C.	23,612	
J. H. Foord, Lab.	22,910	
A. Butcher, L.	5,604	
C. maj.		702

(1955 C. maj. 590)

WEST E. 64,100

315*M. Hewitson, Lab.	25,446	
T. H. F. Farrell, C.	23,011	
Lab. maj.		2,435

(1955 Lab. maj. 5,523)

Huntingdonshire
E. 46,794

316*Rt Hon. D. L. M. Renton,
TD, QC, Nat. L. & C.   20,254
J. W. Fear, Lab.   11,983
R. E. W. Vanderplank, L. 5,389
Nat. L. & C. maj.   8,271
(1955 Nat. L. & C. maj. 5,939)

Huyton (Lancashire)
E. 77,371

317*Rt Hon. J. H. Wilson, OBE, 33,111
Lab.
G. B. Woolfenden, C.   27,184
Lab. maj.   5,927
(1955 Lab. maj. 2,558)

Ilford (2)

NORTH   E. 67,208

318*T. L. Iremonger, C.   29,609
C. F. H. Green, Lab.   15,962
D. K. Mills, L.   7,915
C. maj.   13,647
(1955 C. maj. 10,501)

SOUTH   E. 60,678

319*A. E. Cooper, MBE, C.   23,876
G. J. Borrie, Lab.   16,569
R. V. Netherclift, L.   6,832
C. maj.   7,307
(1955 C. maj. 6,478)

Ilkeston (Derbyshire)
E. 69,719

320*G. H. Oliver, QC, Lab.   39,930
G. I. Walters, C.   18,286
Lab. maj.   21,644
(1955 Lab. maj. 21,693)

Ince (Lancashire)
E. 51,273

321*T. J. Brown, Lab.   30,752
W. Clegg, C.   11,795
Lab. maj.   18,957
(1955 Lab. maj. 18,647)

**Inverness-shire and Ross
and Cromarty** (3)

INVERNESS   E. 49,546

322*N. L. D. McLean, DSO, C. 15,728
J. M. Bannerman, L.   11,653
J. F. Coulter, Lab.   8,073
C. maj.   4,075
(1955 C. maj. 966)

ROSS AND CROMARTY   E. 25,350

323*Sir J. Macleod, TD, Nat. L. 7,813
Mrs J. B. Saggar, Lab.   4,815
C. Murchison, L.   3,918

Nat. L. maj.   2,998
(1955 Nat. L. maj. 3,926)
See also **Western Isles**

Ipswich (English Borough)
E. 77,633

324*D. M. Foot, QC, Lab.   25,858
J. C. Cobbold, C.   22,623
Miss A. M. P. H. Sykes,
L.   14,359
Lab. maj.   3,235
(Oct. 1957, by-election, Lab. maj.
7,737)
(1955 Lab. maj. 3,582)

Isle of Ely
E. 61,387

325*Maj. Sir E. A. H. Legge-
Bourke, KBE, C.   26,173
J. D. Page, Lab.   19,705
C. maj.   6,468
(1955 C. maj. 6,446)

Isle of Thanet (Kent)
E. 71,952

326*W. R. Rees-Davies, C.   29,453
H. A. Fountain, Lab.   17,555
G. E. MacDonald-Jones,
L.   6,998
C. maj.   11,898
(1955 C. maj. 12,289)

Isle of Wight
E. 66,939

327 H. F. M. Woodnutt, C.   31,228
E. C. Amey, Lab.   18,396
C. maj.   12,832
(1955 C. maj. 12,637)

Islington (3)

EAST   E. 48,613

328*E. G. M. Fletcher, Lab.   17,766
K. C. Burden, C.   13,097
Lab. maj.   4,669
(1955 Lab. maj. 6,702)

NORTH   E. 54,120

329*G. W. Reynolds, Lab.   18,718
R. D. Bartle, C.   14,820
Lab. maj.   3,898
(May 1958, by-election, Lab. maj.
7,461)
(1955 Lab. maj. 7,578)

SOUTH WEST   E. 56,620

330*A. Evans, Lab.   22,362
N. P. Scott, C.   11,974
Lab. maj.   10,388
(1955 Lab. maj. 13,268)

ITCHEN — See **Southampton**

Jarrow (English Borough)
E. 50,958

331*E. Fernyhough, Lab.	25,638	
T. T. Hubble, C.	15,286	
Lab. maj.		10,352
(1955 Lab. maj. 10,402)		

Keighley (English Borough)
E. 47,981

332 W. M. J. Worsley, C.	20,626	
*C. R. Hobson, Lab.	20,456	
C. maj.		170
(1955 Lab. maj. 3,403)		

KELVINGROVE – See **Glasgow**
KEMPTOWN – See **Brighton**

Kensington (2)

NORTH E. 51,492

333*G. H. R. Rogers, Lab.	14,925	
R. W. Dulbrook, C.	14,048	
M. Hydleman, L.	3,118	
Sir O. E. Mosley, Bt,		
Union Movement	2,021	
Lab. maj.		877
(1955 Lab. maj. 2,943)		

SOUTH E. 58,023

334 W. L. Roots, QC, C.	26,606	
G. C. H. Millar, L.	4,666	
I. S. Richard, Lab.	4,525	
C. maj.		21,940
(1955 C. maj. 25,247)		

Kent (13). See **Ashford, Canterbury, Chislehurst, Dartford, Dover, Faversham, Folkestone and Hythe, Gravesend, Isle of Thanet, Maidstone, Orpington, Sevenoaks** and **Tonbridge**

Kettering (Northants)
E. 74,696

335*G.R.Mitchison, CBE, QC,Lab.	32,933	
J. H. Lewis, C.	29,448	
Lab. maj.		3,485
(1955 Lab. maj. 5,903)		

Kidderminster (Worcestershire)
E. 58,223

336*Sir G. D. N. Nabarro, C.	27,699	
Mrs J. Tomlinson, Lab.	18,356	
C. maj.		9,343
(1955 C. maj. 8,224)		

Kilmarnock (Ayrshire)
E. 49,090

337*W. Ross, MBE, Lab.	25,379	
R. I. McNaught, C.	15,087	
Lab. maj.		10,292
(1955 Lab. maj. 8,341)		

King's Lynn (Norfolk)
E. 52,125

338 D. G. Bullard, C.	21,671	
G. C. Jackson, Lab.	19,906	
C. maj.		1,765
(1955 C. maj. 1,338)		

Kingston upon Thames
(English Borough)
E. 60,403

339*Rt Hon. J. A. Boyd-		
Carpenter, C.	31,649	
T. Braddock, Lab.	15,408	
C. maj.		16,241
(1955 C. maj. 14,965)		

Kinross and West Perthshire –
See **Perthshire and Kinross**

Kirkcaldy (Scottish Burgh)
E. 54,232

340 H. P. H. Gourlay, Lab.	25,428	
J. Law, C.	14,186	
D. Blyth, L.	4,020	
Lab. maj.		11,242
(1955 Lab. maj. 7,469)		

KIRKDALE – See **Liverpool**

Knutsford (Cheshire)
E. 52,999

341*Lt-Col Sir W. H. Bromley-		
Davenport, TD, C.	27,270	
F. R. Tetlow, L.	8,117	
N. Selwyn, Lab.	7,945	
C. maj.		19,153
(1955 C. maj. 19,486)		

LADYWOOD – See **Birmingham**

Lambeth (3)

BRIXTON E. 52,261

342*Lt-Col M. Lipton, OBE,		
Lab.	18,117	
Dr B. Warren, C.	16,005	
Lab. maj.		2,112
(1955 Lab. maj. 5,035)		

NORWOOD E. 57,807

343*Brig. Rt Hon. Sir J. G.		
Smyth, Bt, VC, MC, C.	22,958	
L. L. Reeves, Lab.	15,975	
D. Chapman, L.	4,744	
C. maj.		6,983
(1955 C. maj. 5,032)		

VAUXHALL E. 45,802

344*Rt Hon. G. R. Strauss, Lab.	18,437	
Miss A. E. O. Havers, C.	11,312	
Lab. maj.		7,125
(1955 Lab. maj. 8,728)		

Lanark (Lanarkshire)
E. 57,094

345	*Mrs J. C. M. Hart, Lab.*	25,171
	Hon P. F. Maitland, C.	24,631
	Lab. maj.	*540*

(1955   C. maj. 958)

Lanarkshire (6)

NORTH   E. 43,505

346	*Miss M. Herbison, Lab.*	21,152
	G. K. H. Younger, *C.*	14,883
	Lab. maj.	*6,269*

(1955   Lab. maj. 5,523)

See also **Bothwell, Hamilton, Lanark, Motherwell and Rutherglen.**

Lancashire (16). *See* **Chorley, Clitheroe, Darwen, Farnworth, Heywood and Royton, Huyton, Ince, Lancaster, Middleton and Prestwich, Morecambe and Lonsdale, Newton, North Fylde, Ormskirk, South Fylde, Westhoughton** and **Widnes**

Lancaster (Lancashire)
E. 43,714

347	H. J. Berkeley, *C.*	20,783
	E. Gardner, *Lab.*	15,255
	C. maj.	*5,528*

(1955   C. maj. 4,549)

LANGSTONE – *See* **Portmouth**

Leeds (6)

EAST   E. 66,074

348	*D. W. Healey,* MBE, *Lab.*	28,707
	J. A. Fawcett, *C.*	23,922
	Lab. maj.	*4,785*

(1955   Lab. maj. 4,939)

NORTH EAST   E. 54,594

349	*Rt Hon. Sir K. S. Joseph Bt, C.*	26,240
	H. M. Waterman, *Lab.*	14,709
	C. maj.	*11,531*

(Feb. 1956, by-election   C. maj.
5,869)

(1955   C. maj. 9,279)

NORTH WEST   E. 69,243

350	*Sir D. Kaberry, Bt,* TD, *C.*	35,210
	D. B. Matthews, *Lab.*	18,508
	C. maj.	*16,702*

(1955   C. maj. 15,329)

SOUTH   E. 52,822

351	*Rt Hon. H. T. N. Gaitskell,* CBE, *Lab.*	24,442
	J. F. W. Addey, *C.*	12,956
	J. B. Meeks, *L.*	4,340
	Lab. maj.	*11,486*

(By-election, 20 June 1963)

M. Rees, Lab.	18,785
J. Udal, *C.*	5,996
B. Walsh, *L.*	4,399
B. Ramelson, *Comm.*	670
Lab. maj.	*12,789*

(1955   Lab. maj. 12,016)

SOUTH EAST   E. 48,457

352	*Miss A. M. Bacon,* CBE, *Lab.*	21,795
	J. B. Womersley, *C.*	12,146
	Lab. maj.	*9,649*

(1955   Lab. maj. 12,572)

WEST   E. 60,269

353	*T. C. Pannell, Lab.*	25,878
	D. L. Crouch, *C.*	21,285
	Lab. maj.	*4,593*

(1955   Lab. maj. 6,264)

Leek (Staffordshire)
E. 72,777

354	*H. Davies, Lab.*	31,096
	Sir J. H. Wedgwood, Bt, TD, *C.*	29,947
	Lab. maj.	*1,149*

(1955   Lab. maj. 1,059)

Leicester (4)

NORTH EAST   E. 47,733

355	*Sir A. L. Ungoed-Thomas,* QC, *Lab.*	19,421
	Miss A. H. Spokes, *C.*	17,990
	Lab. maj.	*1,431*

(By-election, 12 July 1962)

T. G. Bradley, *Lab.*	11,274
D. Bond, *L.*	9,326
R. G. Marlar, *C.*	6,578
Lab. maj.	*1,948*

(1955   Lab. maj. 5,170)

NORTH WEST   E. 51,922

356	*Sir B. Janner, Lab.*	21,515
	F. A. Tomlinson, *C.*	19,742
	Lab. maj.	*1,773*

(1955   Lab. maj. 3,510)

SOUTH EAST   E. 53,810

357	*W. J. Peel, C.*	28,390
	D. J. Williams, *Lab.*	13,760
	C. maj.	*14,630*

(Nov. 1957, by-election, C. maj.
6,482)

(1955   C. maj. 11,541)

SOUTH WEST   *E.* 47,762

358*Rt Hon. H. W. Bowden,*
CBE, *Lab.*	17,395
A. D. Walder, *C.*	14,652
J. W. Ward, *L.*	5,438
Lab. maj.	*2,743*

(1955 Lab. maj. 4,489)

Leicestershire (4). *See* **Bosworth,
Harborough, Loughborough** and
Melton

Leigh (English Borough)
E. 58,911

359*H. Boardman, *Lab.*
H. Boardman, Lab.	31,672
W. Cameron, *C.*	16,897
Lab. maj.	*14,775*

(1955 Lab. maj. 11,956)

Leominster (Herefordshire)
E. 39,306

360 *Hon C. Bossom, C.*
Hon C. Bossom, C.	16,642
T. G. Jones, *L.*	6,905
F. W. Bowerman, *Lab.*	6,475
C. maj.	*9,737*

(1955 C. maj. 8,747)

Lewes (East Sussex)
E. 56,338

361*Col Sir T. V. H. Beamish,*
MC, *C.*	29,642
W. Reay, *Lab.*	13,065
C. maj.	*16,577*

(1955 C. maj. 12,546)

Lewisham (3)

NORTH   *E.* 52,415

362 *C. J. Chataway, C.*
C. J. Chataway, C.	22,125
*N. MacDermot, *Lab.*	17,512
K. J. Brookes, *L.*	2,921
C. maj.	*4,613*

(Feb. 1957, by-election, Lab. maj.
1,110)

(1955 C. maj. 3,236)

SOUTH   *E.* 53,962

363 *C. A. Johnson,* CBE, *Lab.*
C. A. Johnson, CBE, *Lab.*	22,354
J. L. Hunt, *C.*	19,273
G. Forrester, *Alert Party*	788
Lab. maj.	*3,081*

(1955 Lab. maj. 6,343)

WEST   *E.* 54,069

364*H. A. Price,* CBE, *C.*
H. A. Price, CBE, *C.*	22,466
R. C. Edmonds, *Lab.*	16,233
T. A. Smith, *L.*	4,721
C. maj.	*6,233*

(1955 C. maj. 4,325)

Leyton (English Borough)
E. 70,996

365*R. W. Sorensen, *Lab.*
R. W. Sorensen, Lab.	28,367
R. C. Buxton, *C.*	24,448
Lab. maj.	*3,919*

(1955 Lab. maj. 8,204)

Lichfield and Tamworth
(Staffordshire)   *E.* 50,240

366*J. W. Snow, *Lab.*
J. W. Snow, Lab.	21,341
Dr F. K. Roberts, *C.*	19,791
Lab. maj.	*1,550*

(1955 Lab. maj. 3,105)

Lincoln (English Borough)
E. 50,973

367*G. S. de Freitas, *Lab.*
G. S. de Freitas, Lab.	23,629
L. H. Priestley, *C.*	19,240
Lab. maj.	*4,389*

(By-election, 8 March 1962)
D. Taverne, *Lab.*	19,038
W. P. Grieve, *C.*	11,386
P. Furnell, *L.*	6,856
Capt A. Taylor, *Ind.*	412
Lab. maj.	*7,652*

(1955 Lab. maj. 5,222)

Lincolnshire and Rutland (7). *See*
**Brigg, Gainsborough, Grantham,
Holland with Boston, Horncastle,
Louth** and **Rutland and Stamford**

Liverpool (9)

EDGE HILL   *E.* 54,824

368*A. J. Irvine,* QC, *Lab.*
A. J. Irvine, QC, *Lab.*	19,725
J. Norton, *C.*	19,026
Lab. maj.	*699*

(1955 Lab. maj. 1,120)

EXCHANGE   *E.* 51,052

369*Mrs E. M. Braddock, *Lab.*
Mrs E. M. Braddock, Lab.	18,916
T. Beattie-Edwards, *C.*	11,945
Lab. maj.	*6,971*

(1955 Lab. maj. 7,186)

GARSTON   *E.* 65,506

370*R. M. Bingham,* TD, QC, *C.*
R. M. Bingham, TD, QC, *C.*	31,441
B. Crookes, *Lab.*	17,284
C. maj.	*14,157*

(Dec. 1957, by-election, C. maj.
4,304)

(1955 C. maj. 11,969)

KIRKDALE   *E.* 57,102

371*N. A. Pannell, *C.*
N. A. Pannell, C.	22,416
T. H. Hockton, *Lab.*	19,669
C. maj.	*2,747*

(1955 C. maj. 1,814)

SCOTLAND   E. 51,914

372*D. G. Logan, CBE, *Lab.*	20,051	
J. F. Bradley, *C.*	12,384	
Lab. maj.	*7,667*	
(1955 Lab. maj. 10,107)		

TOXTETH   E. 49,686

373*Rt Hon. *J. R. Bevins, C.*	19,575
W. H. Sefton, *Lab.*	15,660
C. maj.	*3,915*
(1955 C. maj. 4,539)	

WALTON   E. 57,312

374*Sir K. P. Thompson, Bt, C.	24,288
G. McCartney, *Lab.*	20,254
C. maj.	*4,034*
(1955 C. maj. 2,862)	

WAVERTREE   E. 55,679

375*J. D. Tilney, TD, C.	26,624
Mrs M. Aspin, *Lab.*	10,392
T. S. Rothwell, *L.*	5,161
C. maj.	*16,232*
(1955 C. maj. 15,620)	

WEST DERBY   E. 54,804

376*J. V. Woollam, C.	22,719
A. D. G. Paxton, *Lab.*	19,386
C. maj.	*3,333*
(1955 C. maj. 2,584)	

Llanelly (Carmarthenshire)
E. 64,048

377*Rt Hon. *J. Griffiths, Lab.*	34,625
H. Gardner, *C.*	10,128
Rev. D. E. Morgan, *Welsh*	
Nat.	7,176
Lab. maj.	*24,497*
(1955 Lab. maj. 23,381)	

Londonderry
E. 73,262

378*R. Chichester-Clark, U.U.	37,529
M. Canning, *S.F.*	13,872
U.U. maj.	*23,657*
(1955 U.U. maj. 16,033)	

Loughborough (Leicestershire)
E. 54,225

379*J. D. Cronin, *Lab.*	21,496
C. G. Waite, *C.*	17,749
R. E. Hancock, *L.*	6,303
Lab. maj.	*3,747*
(1955 Lab. maj. 4,263)	

Louth (Lincolnshire)
E. 51,773

380*Sir C. Osborne, *C.*	24,211
F. R. Macdonald, *Lab.*	15,408
C. maj.	*8,803*
(1955 C. maj. 6,520)	

Lowestoft (Suffolk)
E. 57,814

381 *J. M. L. Prior, C.*	24,324
*E. Evans, CBE, *Lab.*	22,835
C. maj.	*1,489*
(1955 Lab. maj. 1,915)	

Ludlow (Shropshire)
E. 46,735

382*C. J. Holland-Martin, C.	21,464
J. Garwell, *Lab.*	14,138
C. maj.	*7,326*
(By-election, 16 Nov. 1960)	
J. More, *C.*	13,777
D. Rees, *L.*	8,127
J. Garwell, *Lab.*	7,812
C. maj.	*5,650*
(1955 C. maj. 7,879)	

Luton (English Borough)
E. 59,769

383*Rt Hon. *C. Hill, MD, L. &	
C.*	27,153
C. R. Fenton, *Lab.*	22,134
L. & C. maj.	*5,019*
(By-election 7 November 1963)	
W. Howie, *Lab.*	21,108
Sir John Fletcher-Cooke,	
C.	17,359
M. Benjamin, *L.*	5,001
A. Chater, *Comm.*	490
Lab. maj.	*3,749*
(1955 L. & C. maj. 4,418)	

Macclesfield (Cheshire)
E. 58,892

384*Air Cdre Sir A. V. Harvey,	
CBE, C.	28,978
J. F. Bex, *Lab.*	19,652
C. maj.	*9,326*
(1955 C. maj. 9,189)	

Maidstone (Kent)
E. 63,304

385 J. J. Wells, *C.*	30,115
A. B. S. Soper, *Lab.*	19,652
C. maj.	*10,463*
(1955 C. maj. 7,406)	

Maldon (Essex)
E. 54,401

386*A. B. C. Harrison, C.	21,772
S. G. Richards, *Lab.*	19,532
L. C. M. Walsh, *L.*	3,860
C. maj.	*2,240*
(1955 C. maj. 550)	

Manchester (9)

ARDWICK E. 57,166

387*L. M. Lever, Lab.	24,134	
H. Sharp, C.	17,392	
Lab. maj.		6,742

(1955 Lab. maj. 2,082)

BLACKLEY E. 57,851

388*E. S. T. Johnson, MC, C.	22,163	
R. B. Chrimes, Lab.	17,790	
R. M. Hammond, L.	7,223	
C. maj.		4,373

(1955 C. maj. 5,436)

CHEETHAM E. 47,156

389*N. H. Lever, Lab.	20,941	
Miss M. P. O'Gara, C.	11,605	
Lab. maj.		9,336

(1955 Lab. maj. 8,531)

EXCHANGE E. 47,067

390*W. D. Griffiths, Lab.	19,328	
L. Smith, C.	10,604	
Lab. maj.		8,724

(1955 Lab. maj. 7,281)

GORTON E. 55,846

391*K. Zilliacus, Lab.	23,337	
D. H. Moore, C.	22,480	
Lab. maj.		857

(1955 Lab. maj. 269)

MOSS SIDE E. 51,271

392 J. Watts, C.	22,090	
N. Morris, Lab.	13,371	
C. maj.		8,719

(By-election, 7 Nov. 1961)

F. H. Taylor, C.	9,533	
R. H. Hargreaves, L.	6,447	
G. J. Oakes, Lab.	5,980	
W. Hesketh, Union Movement	1,212	
C. maj.		3,086

(1955 C. maj. 10,528)

OPENSHAW E. 54,610

393*W. R. Williams, Lab.	24,975	
M. B. Scholfield, C.	16,537	
Lab. maj.		8,438

(1955 Lab. maj. 8,042)

(By-election pending)

WITHINGTON E. 59,457

394*Sir R. A. Cary, Bt, C.	23,170	
R. E. Sheldon, Lab.	13,476	
G. V. Davies, L.	7,675	
C. maj.		9,694

(1955 C. maj. 12,653)

WYTHENSHAWE E. 69,925

395*Mrs E. Hill, C.	28,934	
A. Morris, Lab.	27,625	
C. maj.		1,309

(1955 C. maj. 2,822)

Mansfield (Nottinghamshire)
E. 56,674

396*H. B. Taylor, Lab.	31,066	
M. R. V. Eliot, C.	14,700	
Lab. maj.		16,366

(1955 Lab. maj. 16,033)

MARYHILL – See **Glasgow**

Melton (Leicestershire)
E. 70,233

397*Miss I. M. P. Pike, C.	34,997	
C. W. Shepherd, Lab.	22,176	
C. maj.		12,821

(Dec. 1956, by-election, C. maj. 2,362)

(1955 C. maj. 10,780)

Meriden (Warwickshire)
E. 62,449

398 G. R. Matthews, C.	26,498	
*R. Moss, Lab.	26,235	
C. maj.		263

(1955 Lab. maj. 1,105)

Merionethshire
E. 26,435

399*T. W. Jones, Lab.	9,095	
B. G. Jones, L.	8,119	
G. Evans, Welsh Nat.	5,127	
Lab. maj.		976

(1955 Lab. maj. 2,682)

Merthyr Tydfil
(Welsh Borough)
E. 42,153

400*S. O. Davies, Lab.	26,608	
Mrs M. M. M. Greenaway, C.	7,885	
Lab. maj.		18,723

(1955 Lab. maj. 18,082)

Merton and Morden
(English Borough)
E. 52,178

401*H. E. Atkins, C.	25,603	
R. W. Kerr, Lab.	17,444	
C. maj.		8,159

(1955 C. maj. 6,390)

Middlesbrough (2)

EAST E. 62,666

402*Rt Hon. H.A.Marquand, Lab.	29,391	
D. R. Chapman, C.	18,365	
Lab. maj.		11,026

(By-election, 14 March 1962)

†*Rt Hon. A. G. Bottomley,*
　OBE, *Lab.*　　　　　　　18,928
　G. Scott, *L.*　　　　　　7,145
　F. A. S. Wood, *C.*　　　4,613
　J. Hamm, *Union Movement*　550
　Lab. maj.　　　　　　　*11,783*
　(1955　Lab. maj. 10,758)

WEST　E. 53,059

403**Rt Hon. Sir J. E. S. Simon,*
　QC, *C.*　　　　　　　　24,602
　E. J. Fletcher, *Lab.*　　15,892
　G. W. I. Hodgson, *L.*　4,336
　C. maj.　　　　　　　　*8,710*

(By-election, 6 June 1962)

　Dr J. W. Bray, Lab.　　15,095
　B. Connelly, *C.*　　　　12,825
　G. Scott, *L.*　　　　　　9,829
　R. E. Eckley, *Ind.*　　　189
　M. Thompson, *Ind.*　　117
　Lab. maj.　　　　　　　*2,270*
　(1955　C. maj. 7,361)

Middlesex (2). *See* **Spelthorne** and
　Uxbridge

Middleton and Prestwich
　(Lancashire)
　E. 65,855

404**Sir J. D. Barlow, Bt, C.*　31,416
　F. G. Barton, *Lab.*　　21,248
　C. maj.　　　　　　　　*10,168*
　(1955　C. maj. 10,107)

Midlothian
　E. 58,092

405　*J. M. Hill, Lab.*　　28,457
　W. S. How, *C.*　　　　18,797
　Lab. maj.　　　　　　　*9,660*
　(1955　Lab. maj. 8,786)

Mid-Ulster
　E. 66,585

406**G. Forrest, Ind. U.U.*　33,093
　T. J. Mitchell, *S.F.*　　14,170
　Ind. U.U. maj.　　　　*18,923*
(May 1956, by-election, Ind. U.U.
　maj. 4,481)
　(1955　S.F. maj. 260)

Mitcham (English Borough)
　E. 70,463

407**Rt Hon. L. R. Carr, C.*　33,661
　E. J. C. Smythe, *Lab.*　23,845
　C. maj.　　　　　　　　*9,816*
　(1955　C. maj. 7,590)

Monmouth (Monmouthshire)
　E. 53,628

408**Rt Hon. G. E. P. Thorney-*
　croft, C.　　　　　　　25,422
　G. S. D. Parry, *Lab.*　19,165
　C. maj.　　　　　　　　*6,257*
　(1955　C. maj. 5,797)

Monmouthshire (5). *See* **Aber-**
tillery, Bedwellty, Ebbw Vale,
　Monmouth and **Pontypool**

Montgomeryshire
　E. 31,152

409**Rt Hon. E. Clement Davies,*
　QC, *L.*　　　　　　　　10,970
　F. L. Morgan, *C.*　　　8,176
　D. C. Jones, *Lab.*　　6,950
　L. maj.　　　　　　　　*2,794*

(By-election, 15 May 1962)

　H. E. Hooson, QC, *L.*　13,181
　R. H. Dawson, *C.*　　5,632
　T. Davies, *Lab.*　　　　5,299
　I. F. Elis, *Welsh Nat.*　1,594
　L. maj.　　　　　　　　*7,549*
　(1955　L. maj. 8,500)

Moray and Nairn
　E. 35,487

410　*G. T. C. Campbell,* MC, *C.*　13,742
　M. Mackay, *Lab.*　　　6,539
　D. C. MacDonald, *L.*　5,831
　C. maj.　　　　　　　　*7,203*
　(1955　C. maj. 5,129)

Morecambe and Lonsdale
　(Lancashire)　E. 57,654

411**B. R. Z. de Ferranti, C.*　30,228
　F. R. McManus, *Lab.*　14,253
　C. maj.　　　　　　　　*15,975*
(Nov. 1958, by-election, C. maj.
　11,231)
　(1955　C. maj. 17,701)

Morpeth (Northumberland)
　E. 45,361

412**W. J. Owen, Lab.*　　27,435
　D. Bloom, *C.*　　　　　10,716
　Lab. maj.　　　　　　　*16,719*
　(1955　Lab. maj. 14,833)

MOSS SIDE – *See* **Manchester**

Motherwell (Lanarkshire)
　E. 50,503

413**G. M. Lawson, Lab.*　22,009
　B. Brogan, *C.*　　　　17,613
　D. Murray *Ind.*　　　　1,331
　Lab. maj.　　　　　　　*4,396*
　(1955　Lab. maj. 2,885)

Nantwich (Cheshire)
E. 43,655

414*Wing-Cdr R. G. Grant-Ferris,		
C.		17,613
L. Knight, Lab.		10,876
G. M. Harvey, L.		7,983
C. maj.		6,737
(1955 C. maj. 7,366)		

Neath (Glamorgan)
E. 51,711

415*D. J. Williams, Lab.	30,469
D. N. I. Pearce, C.	10,263
J. J. David, Comm.	1,962
Lab. maj.	20,206
(1955 Lab. maj. 21,114)	

Nelson and Colne
E. 48,472

416*S. S. Silverman, Lab.	20,407
J. Crabtree, C.	19,143
T. C. Emmott, Ind.	1,889
Lab. maj.	1,264
(1955 Lab. maj. 2,291)	

Newark (Nottinghamshire)
E. 54,597

417*G. Deer, OBE, Lab.	24,072
P. Jenkin-Jones, C.	22,300
Lab. maj.	1,772
(1955 Lab. maj. 2,141)	

Newbury (Berkshire)
E. 62,854

418*Sir A. R. Hurd, C.	29,703
D. L. Stoddart, Lab.	19,787
C. maj.	9,916
(1955 C. maj. 7,237)	

Newcastle under Lyme
(English Borough)
E. 63,623

419*S. T. Swingler Lab.	29,840
T. Prendergast, C.	23,838
Lab. maj.	6,002
(1955 Lab. maj. 6,745)	

Newcastle upon Tyne (4)
CENTRAL E. 49,929

420*E. W. Short, Lab.	24,051
W. D. Rutter, C.	12,485
Lab. maj.	11,566
(1955 Lab. maj. 13,003)	

EAST E. 50,616

421 W. F. Montgomery, C.	21,457
*A. Blenkinsop, Lab.	21,359
C. maj.	98
(1955 Lab. maj. 1,822)	

NORTH E. 47,930

422*R. W. Elliott, C.	24,588
Mrs M. F. L. Prichard,	
Lab.	13,316
C. maj.	11,272
(March 1957. by-election, C. maj. 6,462)	
(1955 I. & C. maj. 10,933)	

WEST E. 64,509

423*E. Popplewell, CBE, Lab.	28,956
C. D. Larrow, C.	23,933
Lab. maj.	5,023
(1955 Lab. maj. 5,184)	

New Forest (Hampshire)
E. 58,958

424*Lt-Col Sir O. E. Crosthwaite	
Eyre, C.	29,949
R. C. Mitchell, Lab.	13,667
C. maj.	16,282
(1955 C. maj. 14,742)	

Newport (Welsh Borough)
E. 71,342

425*Rt Hon. Sir F. Soskice, QC,	
Lab.	31,125
A. D. Arnold, C.	27,477
Lab. maj.	3,648
(July 1956, by-election, Lab. maj. 8,485)	
(1955 Lab. maj. 4,360)	

Newton (Lancashire)
E. 65,124

426*F. Lee, Lab.	31,041
N. A. Miscampbell, C.	23,065
Lab. maj.	7,976
(1955 Lab. maj, 7,955)	

Norfolk (6)
CENTRAL E. 54,436

427 R. C. M. Collard, DSO,	
DFC, C. & Nat. L.	21,918
F. H. Stone, Lab.	15,131
G. M. Goode, L.	6,465
C. & Nat. L. maj.	6,787
(By-election, 22 Nov. 1962)	
I. H. J. Gilmour, C. & Nat.	
L.	13,268
G. Bennett, Lab.	13,048
G. M. Goode, L.	7,915
K. Coleman, Ind.	909
J. Andrews. Ind.	79
C. & Nat. L. maj.	220
(1955 C. & Nat. L. maj. 5,563)	

NORTH   *E.* 48,756
428**E. G. Gooch*, CBE, *Lab.*   19,784
 F. H. Easton, *C. & Nat. L.* 19,126
 Lab. maj.   *658*
 (1955   Lab. maj. 1,242)
SOUTH   *E.* 43,458
429**J. E. B. Hill*, *C.*   19,275
 J. M. Stewart, *Lab.*   16,542
 C. maj.   *2,733*
 (1955   C. maj. 1,475)
SOUTH WEST   *E.* 40,283
430**A. V. Hilton*, *Lab.*   16,858
 Mrs M. E. Kellett, *C.*   16,780
 Lab. maj.   *78*
(March 1959, by-election, Lab. maj.
 1,354)
 (1955   Lab. maj. 193)
See also **King's Lynn** and **Yarmouth**
 Normanton (Yorks, W.R.)
 E. 49,139
431**A. Roberts*, *Lab.*   29,672
 J. A. C. Briggs, *C.*   11,169
 Lab. maj.   *18,503*
 (1955   Lab. maj. 17,806)
 Northampton (English Borough)
 E. 72,521
432**R. T. Paget*, QC, *Lab.*   27,823
 Mrs J. C. J. Knight, *C.*   25,106
 A. T. Smith, *L.*   7,170
 Lab. maj.   *2,717*
 (1955   Lab. maj. 3,348)
 Northamptonshire (4)
SOUTH   *E.* 51,403
433**Rt Hon. Sir R. E. Manning-*
 ham-Buller, Bt, QC, *C.*   24,226
 A. Richardson, *Lab.*   18,292
 C. maj.   *5,934*
(By-election, 22 Nov. 1962)
 A. A. *Jones*, *C.*   14,921
 I. Wilde, *Lab.*   14,004
 N. Picarda, *L.*   7,002
 P. Buchan, *Ind.*   332
 C. maj.   *917*
 (1955   C. maj. 4,158)
See also **Kettering, Peterborough**
 and **Wellingborough**
NORTHFIELD – *See* **Birmingham**
 North Fylde (Lancashire)
 E. 53,864
434**Hon. R. O. Stanley*, *C.*   27,045
 J. Myerscough, *Lab.*   11,307
 C. maj.   *15,738*
 (1955   C. maj. 14,660)

Northumberland (3). *See* **Berwick**
 upon Tweed, Hexham and **Mor-**
 peth

 Northwich (Cheshire)
 E. 44,305
435**J. G. Foster*, QC, *C.*   20,396
 J. Crawford, *Lab.*   12,426
 R. E. Lewis, *L.*   4,602
 C. maj.   *7,970*
 (1955   C. maj. 6,555)

 Norwich (2)
NORTH   *E.* 41,221
436**J. Paton*, *Lab.*   19,092
 D. R. Chance, *C.*   12,609
 Lab. maj.   *6,483*
 (1955   Lab. maj. 6,595)

SOUTH   *E.* 43,789
437**Rt Hon. A. G. F. Rippon*, *C.* 19,128
 G. D. Wallace, *Lab.*   16,884
 C. maj.   *2,244*
 (1955   C. maj. 1,758)

 Nottingham (4)
CENTRAL   *E.* 52,491
438**Lt-Col J. K. Cordeaux*, CBE,
 C.   24,004
 I. Winterbottom, *Lab.*   21,869
 C. maj.   *2,135*
 (1955   C. maj. 758)

NORTH   *E.* 59,638
439   *W. C. Whitlock*, *Lab.*   24,005
 A. G. Blake, *C.*   18,952
 S. Thomas, *L.*   6,581
 J. Peck, *Comm.*   1,331
 Lab. maj.   *5,053*
 (1955   Lab. maj. 6,090)

SOUTH   *E.* 71,520
440   *W. G. A. Clark*, *C.*   29,607
 Hon J. E. Silkin, *Lab.*   22,235
 C. maj.   *7,372*
 (1955   C. maj. 7,053)

WEST   *E.* 62,030
441   *P. H. B. Tapsell*, *C.*   22,052
 **Sir T. O'Brien*, *Lab.*   21,888
 C. maj.   *164*
 (1955   Lab. maj. 3,908)

Nottinghamshire (6). *See* **Ash-**
 field, Bassetlaw, Carlton, Mans-
 field, Newark and **Rushcliffe**

Nuneaton (Warwickshire)
E. 58,038

442*F. G. Bowles, Lab.	24,894	
C. G. Miller, C.	15,354	
J. Campbell, L.	7,227	
Lab. maj.	9,540	

(1955 Lab. maj. 10,284)

Ogmore (Glamorgan)
E. 57,192

443*W. E. Padley, Lab.	35,170	
T. O. Ewart-James, C.	11,905	
Lab. maj.	23,265	

(1955 Lab. maj. 22,524)

Oldbury and Halesowen
E. 68,892

444*A. Moyle, CBE, Lab.	23,861	
J. F. Vernon, C.	21,478	
D. Mirfin, L.	10,343	
Lab. maj.	2,383	

(1955 Lab. maj. 5,055)

Oldham (2)

EAST   E. 54,520

445 C. Mapp, Lab.	19,329	
*Sir I. M. Horobin, C.	17,499	
D. Wrigley, L.	6,660	
Lab. maj.	1,830	

(1955 C. maj. 380)

WEST   E. 51,845

446*C. L. Hale, Lab.	22,624	
J. H. V. Sutcliffe, C.	18,505	
Lab. maj.	4,119	

(1955 Lab. maj. 3,899)

OPENSHAW – See **Manchester**

Orkney and Zetland
E. 26,435

447*Rt Hon. J. Grimond, TD, L.	12,099	
R. H. W. Bruce, C.	3,487	
R. S. McGowan, Lab.	3,275	
L. maj.	8,612	

(1955 L. maj. 7,993)

Ormskirk (Lancashire)
E. 61,420

448*Col Sir D. Glover, C.	32,952	
G. E. Roberts, Lab.	14,701	
C. maj.	18,251	

(1955 C. maj. 14,539)

Orpington (Kent)
E. 51,872

449*W. D. M. Sumner, OBE, QC, C.	24,303	
N. J. Hart, Lab.	9,543	
J. O. Galloway, L.	9,092	
C. maj.	14,760	

(By-election, 14 March 1962)

E. R. Lubbock, L.	22,846	
P. Goldman, C.	14,991	
A. Jinkinson, Lab.	5,350	
L. maj.	7,855	

(1955 C. maj. 11,936)

Oswestry (Shropshire)
E. 50,772

450*Rt Hon. W. D. Ormsby-Gore, C.	21,055	
G. Thomas, Lab.	10,531	
D. G. Rees, L.	6,068	
C. maj.	10,524	

(By-election, 8 Nov. 1961)

W. J. Biffen, C.	12,428	
J. Buchanan, L.	8,647	
A. B. Walden, Lab.	8,519	
J. A. Dayton, Ind.	839	
C. maj.	3,781	

(1955 C. maj. 10,425)

Oxford (English Borough)
E. 66,655

451 Hon. C. M. Woodhouse, DSO, OBE, C.	26,798	
L. N. Anderton, Lab.	18,310	
I. R. M. Davies, L.	7,491	
C. maj.	8,488	

(1955 C. maj. 7,778)

Oxfordshire (2). See **Banbury** and **Henley**

Paddington (2)

NORTH   E. 40,952

452*B. T. Parkin, Lab.	14,397	
H. H. S. Montefiore, C.	13,629	
Lab. maj.	768	

(1955 Lab. maj. 2,092)

SOUTH   E. 40,951

453*R. A. Allan, DSO, OBE, C.	16,006	
D. J. Nisbet, Lab.	8,719	
C. maj.	7,287	

(1955 C. maj. 7,047)

Paisley (Scottish Burgh)
E. 63,097

454*D. H. Johnston, QC, Lab.	28,519	
G. R. Rickman, C.	21,250	
Lab. maj.	7,269	

(By-election, 20 April 1961)

J. Robertson, Lab.	19,200	
J. M. Bannerman, L.	17,542	
G. R. Rickman, C.	5,597	
Lab. maj.	1,658	

(1955 Lab. maj. 6,098)

PARK – See **Sheffield**

PAVILION – *See* **Brighton**
PECKHAM – *See* **Camberwell**

Pembrokeshire
E. 62,372

455*D. L. Donnelly, *Lab.*	27,623	
H. G. Partridge, *C.*	22,301	
W. Williams, *Welsh Nat.*	2,253	
Lab. maj.		*5,322*

(1955   Lab. maj. 1,592)

Penistone (Yorks, W.R.)
E. 61,397

456*J. J. Mendelson, *Lab.*	31,117	
J. B. Deby, *C.*	19,809	
Lab. maj.		*11,308*

(June 1959, by-election, Lab. maj. 11,119)

(1955   Lab. maj. 11,636)

Penrith and the Border
(Cumberland)
E. 51,190

457*W. S. I. Whitelaw, MC, *C.*	23,551	
B. P. Atha, *Lab.*	9,342	
B. G. Ashmore, *L.*	7,602	
C. maj.		*14,209*

(1955   C. maj. 13,672)

PENTLANDS – *See* **Edinburgh**
PERRY BARR – *See* **Birmingham**

Perthshire and Kinross (2)
KINROSS AND WEST   E. 33,582

458*W. G. Leburn, TD, *C.*	16,256	
J. G. Mackenzie, *Lab.*	4,008	
A. Donaldson, *Scot. Nat.*	3,568	
C. maj.		*12,248*

(By-election, 7 November 1963)

Sir Alec Douglas-Home, Kt, *C.*	14,147	
A. D. Millar, *L.*	4,819	
A. Forrester, *Lab.*	3,752	
A. Donaldson, *Scot. Nat.*	1,801	
I. Smith, *Ind.*	78	
W. Rushton, *Ind.*	45	
R. Wort, *Ind.*	23	
C. maj.		*9,328*

(1955   C. maj. 12,158)

PERTH AND EAST   E. 55,064

459 I. MacArthur, *C.*	24,217	
Dr R. D. McIntyre, *Scot. Nat.*	9,637	
T. W. Moore, *Lab.*	7,781	
C. maj.		*14,580*

(1955   C. maj. 13,721)

Peterborough
(Northamptonshire)
E. 60,545

460*Sir H. Nicholls, Bt, *C.*	27,414	
Miss B. Boothroyd, *Lab.*	22,830	
C. maj.		*4,584*

(1955   C. maj. 3,238)

Petersfield (Hampshire) E. 52,796

461*Hon. P. R. Legh, *C.*	23,687	
J. S. P. Davey, *Lab.*	8,278	
Lt-Col R. M. Digby, *L.*	6,912	
C. maj.		*15,409*

(By-election, 16 Nov. 1960)

Miss J. M. Quennell, *C.*	15,613	
Lt-Col R. M. Digby, *L.*	8,310	
W. Royle, *Lab.*	4,777	
C. maj.		*7,303*

(1955   C. maj. 14,090)

Plymouth (2)
DEVONPORT   E. 64,236

462*Miss J. H. Vickers, MBE, *C. & Nat. L.*	28,481	
M. M. Foot, *Lab.*	22,027	
C. & Nat. L. maj.		*6,454*

(1955   C. & Nat. L. maj. 100)

SUTTON   E. 74,078

463 I. M. Fraser, MC, *C.*	32,752	
J. D. Richards, *Lab.*	25,991	
C. maj.		*6,761*

(1955   C. maj. 3,810)

POLLOK – *See* **Glasgow**

Pontefract (English Borough)
E. 54,677

464*G. O. Sylvester, *Lab.*	35,194	
E. T. Bowman, *C.*	10,884	
Lab. maj.		*24,310*

(By-election, 22 March 1962)

J. Harper, *Lab.*	26,461	
P. Dean, *C.*	6,633	
R. E. Eckley, *Ind.*	1,146	
Lab. maj.		*19,828*

(1955   Lab. maj. 22,463)

Pontypool (Monmouthshire)
E. 47,452

465*L. Abse, *Lab.*	26,755	
P. S. Thomas, *C.*	8,903	
B. C. L. Morgan, *Welsh Nat.*	2,519	
Lab. maj.		*17,852*

(Nov. 1958, by-election, Lab. maj. 13,727)

(1955   Lab. maj. 16,572)

Pontypridd (Glamorgan)
E. 53,903

466*A. Pearson, CBE, Lab.		29,853
Sir B. M. Rhys-Williams, Bt, C.		13,896
Lab. maj.		*15,957*
(1955 Lab. maj. 17,163)		

Poole (English Borough)
E. 63,554

467*Capt. Sir R. A. Pilkington, KBE, MC, C.		26,956
A. J. Williams, Lab.		15,325
J. C. Holland, L.		8,735
C. maj.		*11,631*
(1955 C. maj. 9,562)		

Poplar (London Borough)
E. 44,412

468*Rt Hon. C. W. Key, Lab.		22,506
P. B. Black, C.		6,635
Lab. maj.		*15,871*
(1955 Lab. maj. 19,828)		

Portsmouth (3)
LANGSTONE E. 79,885

469*G. P. Stevens, C.		38,834
D. G. Reynolds, Lab.		20,553
C. maj.		*18,281*
(1955 C. maj. 14,155)		

SOUTH E. 55,121

470*Sir J. M. Lucas, Bt, KBE, MC, C.		27,892
F. Towell, Lab.		11,979
C. maj.		*15,913*
(1955 C. maj. 14,287)		

WEST E. 53,206

471*Brig. T. H. Clarke, CBE, C.		23,600
Dr M. Bresler, Lab.		17,334
C. maj.		*6,266*
(1955 C. maj. 3,669)		

Preston (2)
NORTH E. 52,212

472*Rt Hon. J. Amery, C.		23,990
A. Davidson, Lab.		19,529
C. maj.		*4,461*
(1955 C. maj. 2,903)		

SOUTH E. 49,809

473*A. Green, C.		21,954
T. G. Bradley, Lab.		18,935
C. maj.		*3,019*
(1955 C. maj. 474)		

PROVAN – *See* **Glasgow**

Pudsey (English Borough)
E. 52,285

474 J. Hiley, C.		22,752
V. P. Richardson, Lab.		16,241
J. S. Snowden, L.		6,429
C. maj.		*6,511*
(1955 C. maj. 4,564)		

PUTNEY – *See* **Wandsworth**

Reading (English Borough)
E. 58,772

475 P. F. H. Emery, C.		26,314
*I. Mikardo, Lab.		22,372
C. maj.		*3,942*
(1955 Lab. maj. 238)		

Reigate (Surrey)
E. 60,266

476*Rt Hon. Sir J. K. Vaughan-Morgan, Bt, C.		26,966
C. J. Garnsworthy, Lab.		14,465
Mrs A. H. Scott, L.		8,205
C. maj.		*12,501*
(1955 C. maj. 10,307)		

Renfrewshire (2)
EAST E. 61,060

477 Miss M. B. H. Anderson, OBE, C.		29,672
A. J. Houston, Lab.		14,579
D. M. H. Starforth, L.		6,339
C. maj.		*15,093*
(1955 C. maj. 16,588)		

WEST E. 47,395

478*Rt Hon. J. S. Maclay, CH, CMG, L. & C.		20,959
C. Minihan, Lab.		18,206
L. & C. maj.		*2,753*
(1955 L. & C. maj. 4,040)		

Rhondda (2)
EAST E. 37,908

479 G. E. Davies, Lab.		20,565
Mrs A. Powell, Comm.		4,580
D. H. Peace, C.		3,629
N. Williams, Welsh Nat.		2,776
Lab. maj.		*15,985*
(1955 Lab. maj. 17,315)		

WEST E. 34,450

480*I. R. Thomas, Lab.		21,130
G. P. James, Welsh Nat.		4,978
F. L. Pym, C.		3,242
Lab. maj.		*16,152*
(1955 Lab. maj. 16,864)		

Richmond, Surrey
(English Borough)
E. 59,852)

481	A. H. F. *Royle*, C.	27,161
	C. H. Archibald, *Lab.*	12,975
	J. A. Baker, *L.*	7,359
	C. maj.	*14,186*

(1955   C. maj. 12,955)

Richmond (Yorkshire, N.R.)
E. 52,416

482	T. P. G. *Kitson*, C.	28,270
	Mrs M. McMillan, *Lab.*	9,203
	C. maj.	*19,067*

(1955   C. maj. 16,005)

Ripon (Yorkshire, W.R.)
E. 41,184

483*	Col Sir M. *Stoddart-Scott*, OBE, TD, MD, C.	22,757
	J. H. Swann, *Lab.*	9,791
	C. maj.	*12,966*

(1955   C. maj. 12,065)

Rochdale (English Borough)
E. 61,191

484*	J. *McCann*, *Lab.*	21,689
	L. H. C. Kennedy, *L.*	18,949
	T. Normanton, C.	11,665
	Lab. maj.	*2,740*

(Feb. 1958, by-election, Lab. maj. 4,530)
(1955   C. maj. 1,590)

Rochester and Chatham
(English Borough)
E. 64,386

485	J. M. G. *Critchley*, C.	26,510
	Rt Hon. A. G. Bottomley, OBE, Lab.	25,487
	C. maj.	*1,023*

(1955   Lab. maj. 2,447)

Romford (English Borough)
E. 73,082

486*	R. J. *Ledger*, *Lab.*	25,558
	R. J. S. Harvey, C.	24,951
	D. Geary, *L.*	8,228
	Lab. maj.	*607*

(1955   Lab. maj. 2,625)

Ross and Cromarty – *See* **Inverness-shire and Ross and Cromarty**

Rossendale (English Borough)
E. 50,577

487*	A. W. J. *Greenwood*, *Lab.*	20,743
	J. R. T. Holt, C.	18,152
	A. Cooper, *L.*	4,752
	Lab. maj.	*2,591*

(1955   Lab. maj. 2,911)

Rotherham (English Borough)
E. 57,080

488*	J. H. *Jones*, *Lab.*	28,298
	R. Hall, C.	16,759
	Lab. maj.	*11,539*

(By-election, 28 March 1963)

	B. K. O'*Malley*, *Lab.*	22,441
	M. Barrass, C.	9,209
	R. E. Eckley, *Ind.*	742
	Lab. maj.	*13,232*

(1955   Lab. maj. 11,541)

Rother Valley (Yorks, W.R.)
E. 71,652

489*	D. *Griffiths*, *Lab.*	43,962
	W. A. V. Hoskins, C.	15,369
	Lab. maj.	*28,593*

(1955   Lab. maj. 27,052)

Rowley Regis and Tipton
E. 59,895

490*	Rt Hon. A. *Henderson*, QC, *Lab.*	27,151
	A. Taylor, C.	17,174
	Lab. maj.	*9,977*

(1955   Lab. maj. 13,168)

Roxburgh, Selkirk and Peebles
E. 55,459

491*	Cmdr C. E. M. *Donaldson*, VRD, C.	22,275
	Dr J. M. MacCormick, *L.*	12,762
	T. Dalyell, *Lab.*	9,336
	C. maj.	*9,513*

(1955   C. maj. 7,170)

Rugby (Warwickshire)
E. 47,809

492	Lt-Col A. R. *Wise*, MBE, TD, C.	17,429
	*J. Johnson, *Lab.*	16,959
	S. Goldblatt, *L.*	6,413
	A. S. Frost, *Ind.*	142
	C. maj.	*470*

(1955   Lab. maj. 1,378)

Ruislip-Northwood
(English Borough)
E. 49,198

493*	F. P. Crowder, C.	23,480
	J. L. King, Lab.	10,424
	R. A. Walker, L.	7,295
	C. maj.	13,056
	(1955 C. maj. 11,555)	

Runcorn (Cheshire)
E. 49,584

494*	Rt Hon. D. F. Vosper, TD, C.	26,615
	J. Barnett, Lab.	13,837
	C. maj.	12,778
	(1955 C. maj. 10,830)	

Rushcliffe (Nottinghamshire)
E. 58,971

495*	Rt Hon. M. Redmayne, DSO, C.	27,392
	N. D. Sandelson, Lab.	22,952
	C. maj.	4,440
	(1955 C. maj. 1,643)	

Rutherglen (Lanarkshire)
E. 42,833

496*	R. C. Brooman-White, C.	19,146
	E. J. Milne, Lab.	17,624
	C. maj.	1,522
	(1955 C. maj. 2,101)	

Rutland and Stamford
(Lincolnshire and Rutland)
E. 41,061

497	K. Lewis, C.	19,078
	C. S. B. Attlee, Lab.	14,137
	C. maj.	4,941
	(1955 C. maj. 2,819)	

Rye (East Sussex)
E. 54,599

498*	B. G. Irvine, C.	27,465
	J. R. Murray, L.	7,549
	D. S. Tilbé, Lab.	7,359
	C. maj.	19,916
	(1955 C. maj. 17,940)	

Saffron Walden (Essex)
E. 48,454

499*	Rt Hon. R. A. Butler, CH, C.	20,955
	Rev. H. N. Horne, Lab.	14,173
	D. J. Ridley, L.	4,245
	C. maj.	6,782
	(1955 C. maj. 6,418)	

St. Albans (Hertfordshire)
E. 52,823

500	V. H. Goodhew, C.	23,157
	L. W. Carroll, Lab.	14,650
	W. A. N. Jones, L.	5,948
	C. maj.	8,507
	(1955 C. maj. 5,721)	

St. Helens (English Borough)
E. 75,280

501*	L. Spriggs, Lab.	35,961
	M. Carlisle, C.	21,956
	Lab. maj.	14,005
	(June 1958, by-election, Lab. maj. 11,994)	
	(1955 Lab. maj. 15,883)	

St. Ives (Cornwall)
E. 44,010

502*	G. R. Howard, C. & Nat. L.	15,700
	D. Longden, Lab.	8,802
	G. E. L. Whitmarsh, L.	8,258
	C. & Nat. L. maj.	6,898
	(1955 C. & Nat. L. maj. 7,335)	

St. Marylebone
(London Borough)
E. 55,080

503*	Sir W. W. Wakefield, C.	23,278
	B. Hooberman, Lab.	8,507
	E. M. Wheeler, L.	4,304
	C. maj.	14,771
	(1955 C. maj. 15,399)	
	(By-election pending.)	

St. Pancras, North
(London Borough)
E. 59,194

504*	K. Robinson, Lab.	22,256
	D. B. Mitchell, C.	15,949
	W. Webster, Ind.	1,685
	J. Nicolson, Comm.	1,230
	Lab. maj.	6,307
	(1955 Lab. maj. 7,082)	

Salford (2)
EAST E. 51,231

505*	F. Allaun, Lab.	20,639
	J. H. Franks, C.	17,171
	Lab. maj.	3,468
	(1955 Lab. maj. 1,728)	

WEST E. 56,490

506*	C. Royle, Lab.	23,167
	H. H. Davies, C.	20,306
	Lab. maj.	2,861
	(1955 Lab. maj. 859)	

Salisbury (Wiltshire)
E. 49,997

507*J. G. Morrison, TD, C.	20,641	
Dr J. A. Cannon, Lab.	12,932	
J. M. Booker, L.	5,516	
C. maj.	7,709	

(1955   C. maj. 7,639)

Scarborough and Whitby
(Yorkshire, N.R.)
E. 63,938

508*Sir A. C. M. Spearman, C.	25,226	
G. Gray, L.	10,759	
N. G. Barnett, Lab.	10,468	
C. maj.	14,467	

(1955   C. maj. 16,645)

SCOTLAND – See **Liverpool**
SCOTSTOUN – See **Glasgow**

Sedgefield (Durham)
E. 63,535

509*J. Slater, BEM, Lab.	30,642	
D. F. M. Appleby, C.	21,771	
Lab. maj.	8,871	

(1955   Lab. maj. 8,853)

SELLY OAK – See **Birmingham**

Sevenoaks (Kent)
E. 62,701

510*J. C. Rodgers, C.	28,186	
R. C. Ogley, Lab.	14,265	
Mrs N. Penman, L.	7,819	
C. maj.	13,921	

(1955   C. maj. 11,078)

Sheffield (6)
ATTERCLIFFE   E. 65,024

511*J. B. Hynd, Lab.	33,676	
Lt-Col H. L. Lambert,		
C. & L.	15,304	
Lab. maj.	18,372	

(1955   Lab. maj. 19,568)

BRIGHTSIDE   E. 57,090

512*R. E. Winterbottom, Lab.	28,302	
H. C. Holmes, C. & L.	12,269	
H. Hill, Comm.	1,373	
Lab. maj.	16,033	

(1955   Lab. maj. 15,404)

HALLAM   E. 60,225

513 J. H. Osborn, C. & L.	28,747	
E. S. Sachs, Lab.	11,938	
B. Roseby, L.	5,119	
C. & L. maj.	16,809	

(1955   C. & L. maj. 14,739)

HEELEY   E. 72,648
514*Sir P. G. Roberts, Bt, C. &

L.	33,236	
Miss J. Mellors, Lab.	23,109	
C. & L. maj.	10,127	

(1955   C. & L. maj. 11,051)

HILLSBOROUGH   E. 51,023

515*G. Darling, Lab.	21,888	
S. K. Arnold, C.	16,845	
Lab. maj.	5,043	

(1955   Lab. maj. 7,010)

PARK   E. 51,533

516*F. W. Mulley, Lab.	26,078	
J. Neill, C. & L.	10,598	
Lab. maj.	15,480	

(1955   Lab. maj. 18,339)

SHETTLESTON – See **Glasgow**

Shipley (Yorkshire, W.R.)
E. 45,460

517*G. A. N. Hirst, TD, C.	22,536	
M. R. English, Lab.	17,025	
C. maj.	5,511	

(1955   C. maj. 5,331)

Shoreditch and Finsbury
(London Borough)
E. 53,210

518*M. Cliffe, Lab.	22,744	
T. H. M. Whipham, C.	11,178	
Lab. maj.	11,566	

(Nov. 1598, by-election, Lab. maj.
6,995)

(1955   Lab. maj. 16,284)

Shrewsbury (Shropshire)
E. 46,846

519*Sir J. A. Langford-Holt, C.	19,970	
K. V. Russell, Lab.	11,338	
H. Shaw, L.	6,387	
C. maj.	8,632	

(1955   C. maj. 7,593)

Shropshire (4) See **Ludlow, Oswestry, Shrewsbury and Wrekin**

Skipton (Yorkshire, W.R.)
E. 49,037

520*G. B. Drayson, TD, C.	20,278	
F. O. Hooley, Lab.	11,178	
Miss K. C. Graham, L.	10,543	
C. maj.	9,100	

(1955   C. maj. 9,182)

SMALL HEATH – See **Birmingham**

Smethwick (English Borough)
E. 49,794

521*Rt Hon. P. C. Gordon-Walker,
Lab.   20,670
P. H. S. Griffiths, C.   17,126
Lab. maj.   *3,544*
(1955 Lab. maj. 6,495)

Solihull (Warwickshire)
E. 60,227

522*Sir M. A. Lindsay, Bt,
CBE, DSO, C.   35,862
E. J. Bowen, Lab.   12,682
C. maj.   *23,180*
(1955 C. maj. 18,023)

Somerset (6)

NORTH E. 63,231

523*Sir E. H. C. Leather, C.   30,432
E. F. Wilde, Lab.   23,649
C. maj.   *6,783*
(1955 C. maj. 4,183)

See also **Bridgwater, Taunton, Wells, Weston-super-Mare and Yeovil**

Southall (English Borough)
E. 55,290

524*G. A. Pargiter, Lab.   22,285
M. T. B. Underhill, C.   19,966
Lab. maj.   *2,319*
(1955 Lab. maj. 6,335)

Southampton (2)

ITCHEN E. 69,886

525*H. M. King, DPhil, Lab.   29,123
E. M. King, C.   25,390
Lab. maj.   *3,733*
(1955 Lab. maj. 5,771)

TEST E. 67,087

526*J. M. Howard, C.   30,176
Mrs S. V. T. B. Williams,
Lab.   23,410
C. maj.   *6,766*
(1955 C. maj. 3,842)

Southend (2)

EAST E. 55,265

527*Sir S. J. McAdden, CBE, C.   24,712
E. J. Trevett, Lab.   16,987
C. maj.   *7,725*
(1955 C. maj. 6,758)

WEST E. 60,999

528*H. P. G. Channon, C.   27,612
Miss H. J. Harvey, L.   10,577
A. Pearson-Clarke, Lab.   9,219
C. maj.   *17,035*

(Jan. 1959, by-election, C. maj. 8,179)
(1955 C. maj. 18,460)

South Fylde (Lancashire)
E. 65,310

529*Col C. G. Lancaster, C.   36,988
N. Holding, Lab.   12,521
C. maj.   *24,467*
(1955 C. maj. 22,395)

Southgate (English Borough)
E. 54,869

530*Sir A. Beverley Baxter, C.   25,704
G. J. Bridge, L.   8,968
S. J. Chapman, Lab.   7,613
C. maj.   *16,736*
(1955 C. maj. 18,210)

Southport (English Borough)
E. 62,466

531 W. I. Percival, QC, C.   26,905
S. Goldberg, L.   11,292
C. W. Hadfield, Lab.   9,805
C. maj.   *15,613*
(1955 C. maj. 17,441)

South Shields (English Borough)
E. 75,538

532*Rt Hon. J. C. Ede, CH, Lab. 32,577
J. Chalmers, C.   23,638
Lab. maj.   *8,939*
(1955 Lab. maj. 10,252)

Southwark (London Borough)
E. 61,747

533 R. J. Gunter, Lab.   25,036
J. M. Greenwood, C.   12,696
S. P. Bent, Comm.   1,395
Lab. maj.   *12,340*
(1955 Lab. maj. 17,230)

Sowerby (Yorkshire, W.R.)
E. 52,560

534*A. L. N. D. Houghton, Lab. 18,949
R. K. McKim, C.   16,993
J. G. Walker, L.   7,654
Lab. maj.   *1,956*
(1955 Lab. maj. 2,783)

SPARKBROOK – See **Birmingham**

Spelthorne (Middlesex)
E. 52,115

535*Sir G. B. Craddock, C.   25,221
J. P. Carruthers, Lab.   17,128
C. maj.   *8,093*
(1955 C. maj. 5,982)

SPRINGBURN – See **Glasgow**

Stafford and Stone
(Staffordshire)
E. 57,078

536*Rt Hon. H. C. P. J. Fraser, MBE, C.	28,107	
A. Gregory, Lab.	18,034	
C. maj.		10,073
(1955 C. maj. 8,656)		

Staffordshire (6). See **Brierley Hill, Burton, Cannock, Leek, Lichfield and Tamworth** and **Stafford and Stone**

Stalybridge and Hyde
(Cheshire)
E. 55,183

537*F. Blackburn, Lab.	23,732	
E. J. Brown, C.	22,309	
Lab. maj.		1,423
(1955 Lab. maj. 155)		

STECHFORD – See **Birmingham**

Stepney (London Borough)
E. 63,932

538*W. J. Edwards, Lab.	26,875	
P. B. Calwell, C.	8,566	
S. Kaye, Comm.	2,548	
Lab. maj.		18,309
(1955 Lab. maj. 21,944)		

Stirling and Clackmannan (2)
CLACKMANNAN AND EAST
E. 52,200

539*Rt Hon. A. Woodburn, Lab.	25,004	
R. C. Aitchison, C.	17,132	
Lab. maj.		7,872
(1955 Lab. maj. 7,009)		

WEST   E. 43,686

540 W. Baxter, Lab.	21,008	
W. A. Gay, C.	15,497	
Lab. maj.		5,511
(1955 Lab. maj. 3,167)		

Stirling and Falkirk
(Scottish Burgh) E. 55,759

541*M. MacPherson, MBE, Lab.	22,423	
R. S. Johnston, C.	19,797	
J. Halliday, Scot. Nat.	2,983	
Lab. maj.		2,626
(1955 Lab. maj. 1,306)		

Stockport (2)
NORTH   E. 53,287

542*Wing-Cdr Sir N. J. Hulbert, C.	23,487	
M. E. J. Swain, Lab.	20,265	
C. maj.		3,222
(1955 C. maj. 4,567)		

SOUTH   E. 47,265

543*H. M. Steward, C.	20,522	
S. Orme, Lab.	17,982	
C. maj.		2,540
(1955 C. maj. 4,086)		

Stockton on Tees
(English Borough)
E. 53,224

544*G. R. Chetwynd, Lab.	23,961	
G. J. K. Coles, C.	20,684	
Lab. maj.		3,277
(By-election, 5 April, 1962)		
W. T. Rodgers, Lab.	19,694	
G. J. K. Coles, C.	12,112	
J. H. Mulholland, L.	11,722	
Lab. maj.		7,582
(1955 Lab. maj. 3,815)		

Stoke Newington and Hackney, North (London Borough)
E. 64,723

545*D. Weitzman, QC, Lab.	22,950	
R. L. White, C.	14,515	
P. Phillips, L.	6,076	
Lab. maj.		8,435
(1955 Lab. maj. 10,088)		

Stoke on Trent (3)
CENTRAL   E. 62,220

546*Dr B. Stross, Lab.	28,630	
J. P. H. Harrison, C.	18,205	
Lab. maj.		10,425
(1955 Lab. maj. 12,355)		

NORTH   E. 58,336

547*Mrs H. Slater, Lab.	29,336	
S. F. Middup, MBE, C.	16,522	
Lab. maj.		12,814
(1955 Lab. maj. 14,874)		

SOUTH   E. 63,777

548*E. Smith, Lab.	29,578	
G. S. Tucker, C.	20,318	
Lab. maj.		9,260
(1955 Lab. maj. 13,264)		

Stratford (Warwickshire)
E. 49,660

549 J. D. Profumo, OBE, C.	26,146	
J. Stretton, Lab.	12,017	
C. maj.		14,129

(By-election 15 August 1963)

A. E. O. Maude, TD, C.	15,846
A. Faulds, Lab.	12,376
D. Mirfin, L.	7,622
M. Blair, Ind.	281
D. Sutch, Ind.	209
C. maj.	*3,470*

(1955   C. maj. 13,312)

STREATHAM – See **Wandsworth**

Stretford (English Borough)
E. 71,304

550*Sir S. Storey, Bt, C.	32,888
E. Reid, Lab.	23,538
C. maj.	*9,350*

(1955   C. maj. 11,834)

Stroud (Gloucestershire)
E. 57,222

551*J. A. Kershaw, MC, C.	23,448
A. T. Evans, Lab.	18,336
C. J. McNair, L.	6,988
C. maj.	*5,112*

(1955   C. maj. 3,943)

Sudbury and Woodbridge
(Suffolk)
E. 60,756

552*Rt Hon. J. H. Hare, OBE, C.	26,130
R. B. Stirling, Lab.	16,248
A. Herbert, L.	6,914
C. maj.	*9,882*

(1955   C. maj. 7,190)
(By-election pending.)

Suffolk (4). *See* **Bury St. Edmunds, Eye, Lowestoft and Sudbury and Woodbridge**

Sunderland (2)
NORTH   E. 57,763

553*F. T. Willey, Lab.	24,341
P. E. Heselton, C.	22,133
Lab. maj.	*2,208*

(1955   Lab. maj. 2,836)

SOUTH   E. 68,014

554*P. G. Williams, C.	27,825
E. Armstrong, Lab.	26,835
C. maj.	*990*

(1955   C. maj. 1,774)

Surbiton (English Borough)
E. 45,165

555*N. T. L. Fisher, MC, C.	24,058
A. Imisson, Lab.	11,633
C. maj.	*12,425*

(1955   C. maj. 10,483)

Surrey (10)
EAST   E. 69,996

556*C. J. A. Doughty, QC, C.	36,310
K. S. Vaus, L.	10,376
J. C. Hunt, Lab.	10,102
C. maj.	*25,934*

(1955   C. maj., 24,709)

See also **Carshalton, Chertsey, Dorking, Epsom, Esher, Farnham Guildford, Reigate** and **Woking**

East Sussex (4). *See* **Eastbourne East Grinstead, Lewes and Rye**

West Sussex (3). *See* **Arundel and Shoreham, Chichester and Horsham**

SUTTON – See **Plymouth**

Sutton and Cheam
(English Borough)
E. 58,898

557*R. C. Sharples, OBE, MC, C.	27,344
F. A. Judd, Lab.	11,946
J. Montgomerie, L.	7,600
C. maj.	*15,398*

(1955   C. maj. 14,333)

Sutton Coldfield
(English Borough)
E. 65,347

558*Rt Hon. G. W. Lloyd, C.	33,064
R. S. G. Hattersley, Lab.	11,310
K. J. Hovers, L.	7,543
C. maj.	*21,754*

(1955   C. maj. 17,987)

Swansea (2)
EAST   E. 55,301

559*D. L. Mort, Lab.	29,884
H. J. F. Crum Ewing, C.	9,754
E. C. Rees, Welsh Nat.	4,651
Lab. maj.	*20,130*

(By-election 28 March 1963)

N. McBride, Lab.	18,909
R. Owens, L.	4,895
Rev. L. Atkin, Ind.	2,462
Miss A. P. Thomas, C.	2,272
E. C. Rees, Welsh Nat.	1,620
B. Pearce, Comm.	773
Lab. maj.	*14,014*

(1955   Lab. maj. 17,472)

WEST   E. 58,045

560 J. E. H. Rees, C.	24,043
*P. Morris, Lab.	23,640
C. maj.	*403*

(1955   Lab. maj. 1,021)

Swindon (English Borough)
E. 55,339

561*F. E. Noel-Baker, Lab.	24,087
G. L. Pears, C.	20,178
Lab. maj.	3,909
(1955 Lab. maj. 3,939)	

Taunton (Somerset)
E. 52,675

562*E. D. L. du Cann, C.	22,680
L. V. Pike, Lab.	16,182
C. M. K. Bruton, L.	7,031
C. maj.	6,498
(Feb. 1956, by-election, C. maj. 657)	
(1955 C. maj. 5,542)	

Tavistock (Devonshire)
E. 46,908

563*Sir H. G. Studholme, Bt, cvo, C.	19,778
R. G. Moore, L.	9,008
B. R. Weston, Lab.	8,022
C. maj.	10,770
(1955 C. maj. 10,236)	

TEST – See **Southampton**

Thirsk and Malton
(Yorkshire, N.R.)
E. 52,517

564*Rt Hon. R. H. Turton, MG, C.	27,413
Dr J. W. Bray, Lab.	12,318
C. maj.	15,095
(1955 C. maj. 14,085)	

Thurrock (Essex)
E. 67,054

565*H. J. Delargy, Lab.	32,270
W. E. McNamara, C.	20,188
Lab. maj.	12,082
(1955 Lab. maj. 15,329)	

Tiverton (Devonshire)
E. 48,416

566*Rt Hon. D. Heathcoat Amory, TD, C.	21,714
Dr J. E. O. Dunwoody, Lab.	9,836
J. J. Collier, L.	7,504
C. maj.	11,878
(By-election 16 Nov. 1960)	
R. J. Maxwell-Hyslop, C.	15,308
J. J. Collier, L.	12,268
R. F. H. Dobson, Lab.	5,895
C. maj.	3,040
(1955 C. maj. 10,424)	

Tonbridge (Kent)
E. 67,320

567*R. P. Hornby, C.	31,687
K. W. May, Lab.	21,181
C. maj.	10,506
(June 1956, by-election, C. maj. 1,602)	
(1955 C. maj. 10,196)	

Torquay (English Borough)
E. 67,608

568*F. M. Bennett, C.	29,527
W. V. Cooper, Lab.	11,784
T. O. Kellock, L.	10,685
C. maj.	17,743
(Dec. 1955 by-election, C. maj. 10,581)	
(1955 C. maj. 17,230)	

Torrington (Devonshire)
E. 44,029

569 P. B. Browne, C.	17,283
*M. R. Bonham-Carter, L.	15,018
R. F. H. Dobson, Lab.	5,633
C. maj.	2,265
(March 1958, by-election, L. maj. 219)	
(1955 Nat. L. & C. maj. 9,312)	

Totnes (Devonshire)
E. 63,071

570*R. L. Mawby, C.	26,925
T. J. B. Heelas, Lab.	13,116
T. C. Jones, L.	10,719
C. maj.	13,809
(1955 C. maj. 11,594)	

Tottenham (English Borough)
E. 59,794

571 A. G. Brown, Lab. (now Ind.)	22,325
D. J. G. Hennessy, C.	15,688
L. G. Lepley, L.	5,030
Lab. maj.	6,637
(1955 Lab. maj. 8,883)	

TOXTETH – See **Liverpool**

Truro (Cornwall)
E. 55,185

572*H. G. B. Wilson, C.	19,544
R. J. R. Blindell, Lab.	15,057
Miss B. N. Seear, L.	9,637
C. maj.	4,487
(1955 C. maj. 4,717)	

Twickenham (English Borough)
E. 73,852

573*R. G. Cooke, CBE, C.	33,677
Mrs A. P. Clark, Lab.	16,638
K. A. Powell, L.	8,589
C. maj.	17,039

(1955 C. maj. 16,276)

Tynemouth (English Borough)
E. 72,273

574*Dame I. M. B. Ward, DBE, C.	32,810
W. H. Hutchison, Lab.	18,866
D. N. Thompson, L.	6,525
C. maj.	13,944

(1955 C. maj. 10,836)

Uxbridge (Middlesex)
E. 56,997

575 C. Curran, C.	22,360
*F. Beswick, Lab.	20,970
G. R. Goodall, L.	4,746
C. maj.	1,390

(1955 Lab. maj. 876)

VAUXHALL – See **Lambeth**

Wakefield (English Borough)
E. 60,790

576*Rt Hon. A. Creech Jones, Lab.	29,705
T. M. Jopling, C.	20,114
Lab. maj.	9,591

(1955 Lab. maj. 9,745)

Wallasey (English Borough)
E. 72,660

577*Rt Hon. A. E. Marples, C.	35,567
G. Woodburn, Lab.	20,501
C. maj.	15,066

(1955 C. maj. 14,218)

Wallsend (English Borough)
E. 80,235

578*J. McKay, Lab.	37,862
R. B. Baird, C.	29,096
Lab. maj.	8,766

(1955 Lab. maj. 9,350)

Walsall (2)

NORTH E. 59,257

579*W. T. Wells, QC, Lab.	27,693
J. G. Ackers, C.	17,741
Lab. maj.	9,952

(1955 Lab. maj. 10,695)

SOUTH E. 62,804

580*Sir H. J. d'Avigdor Gold-smid, Bt, DSO, MC, C.	30,471
J. A. F. Ennals, Lab.	21,689
C. maj.	8,782

(1955 C. maj. 2,426)

Walthamstow (2)

EAST E. 43,892

581*J. E. Harvey, C.	16,622
Mrs M. McKay, Lab.	13,721
N. H. Cork, L.	4,974
W. H. Christopher, I.L.P.	183
C. maj.	2,901

(1955 C. maj. 1,129)

WEST E. 38,226

502*E. C. Redhead, Lab.	15,980
H. C. Midgley, C.	7,872
W. O. Smedley, L.	5,229
Lab. maj.	8,108

(March 1956, by-election, Lab. maj. 9,204)

(1955 Lab. maj. 9,250)

WALTON – See **Liverpool**

Wandsworth (4)

CENTRAL E. 61,831

583*M. H. C. Hughes-Young, MC, C.	23,655
Mrs A. P. Llewelyn Davies, Lab.	21,683
R. A. Locke, L.	4,287
C. maj.	1,972

(1955 C. maj. 1,093)

CLAPHAM E. 55,894

584 Dr A. J. Glyn, C.	22,266
*C. W. Gibson, Lab.	20,390
C. maj.	1,876

(1955 Lab. maj. 225)

PUTNEY E. 71,772

585*Sir H. N. Linstead, OBE, C.	28,236
D. Taverne, Lab.	23,115
M. F. Burns, L.	6,166
C. maj.	5,121

(1955 C. maj. 7,195)

STREATHAM E. 50,916

586*Rt Hon. D. Sandys, C.	23,479
Dr D. L. Kerr, Lab.	10,773
R. S. Rubin, L.	5,039
C. maj.	12,706

(1955 C. maj. 12,268)

Warrington (English Borough)
E. 52,884

587*Rt Hon. Edith Summerskill, Lab.	22,890
F. O. Stansfield, C.	17,791
Lab. maj.	5,099

(By-election 20 April 1961)

†*W. T. Williams, Lab.*	16,149
Mrs B. A. Arnold, *C.*	9,149
F. R. Tetlow, *L.*	3,623
Lab. maj.	*7,000*

(1955 Lab. maj. 5,646)

Warwick and Leamington
(Warwickshire)
E. 62,849

588 *Rt Hon. Sir J. G. S. Hobson,*	
OBE, TD, QC, *C.*	32,513
W. Wilson, *Lab.*	19,434
C. maj.	*13,079*

(March 1957, by-election, C. maj.
2,157)
(1955 C. maj. 13,466)

Warwickshire (6). *See* **Meriden, Nuneaton, Rugby, Solihull, Stratford** and **Warwick and Leamington**

Watford (English Borough)
E. 53,388

589**F. W. Farey-Jones, C.*	21,216
Mrs R. Short, *Lab.*	18,315
I. S. Steers, *L.*	5,753
C. maj.	*2,901*

(1955   C. maj. 1,717)

WAVERTREE – *See* **Liverpool**

Wednesbury (English Borough)
E. 60,297

590**J. T. Stonehouse, Lab.*	24,147
E. Knight, *C.*	17,464
F. B. Willmott, *L.*	4,780
Lab. maj.	*6,683*

(Feb. 1957, by-election, Lab. maj.
12,236)
(1955   Lab. maj. 8,944)

Wellingborough
(Northamptonshire)
E. 52,261

591 *M. C. Hamilton, C.*	22,964
*G. S. Lindgren, Lab.	22,358
C. maj.	*606*

(1955   Lab. maj. 926)

Wells (Somerset)
E. 57,455

592**Lt-Cmdr S. L. C. Maydon,*	
DSO, DSC, *C.*	23,357
J. A. A. Evans, *Lab.*	16,452
P. R. Hobhouse, *L.*	8,220
C. maj.	*6,905*

(1955   C. maj. 5,879)

Wembley (2)

NORTH   E. 47,554

593**Wing-Cdr E. E. Bullus, C.*	22,211
R. M. Lewis, *Lab.*	11,131
Dr D. G. Valentine, *L.*	6,171
C. maj.	*11,080*

(1955   C. maj. 10,109)

SOUTH   E. 45,150

594**R. S. Russell, C.*	19,733
E. Mackenzie, *Lab.*	12,166
J. E. C. Perry, *L.*	5,403
C. maj.	*7,567*

(1955   C. maj. 6,456)

West Bromwich
(English Borough)
E. 64,111

595**Rt Hon .J. Dugdale, Lab.*	26,702
A. H. Windrum, *C.*	19,809
Lab. maj.	*6,893*

(By-election 4 July 1963)

M. A. Foley, *Lab.*	20,510
G. Hawkins, *C.*	8,246
N. R. W. Mawle, *L.*	6,161
Lab. maj.	*12,264*

(1955   Lab. maj. 10,020)

Westbury (Wiltshire)
E. 53,238

596**Sir R. V. Grimston, Bt, C.*	20,396
J. G. Ridley, *Lab.*	14,570
B. T. Wigoder, *L.*	9,816
C. maj.	*5,826*

(1955   C. maj. 3,389)

WEST DERBY – *See* **Liverpool**

Western Isles
(Inverness-shire and Ross and
Cromarty)
E. 25,178

597**M. K. Macmillan, Lab.*	8,663
D. Macleod, *L. & C.*	7,496
Lab. maj.	*1,167*

(1955   Lab. maj. 2,172)

West Ham (2)

NORTH   E. 57,828

598**A. W. J. Lewis, Lab.*	24,096
J. G. Jones, *C.*	9,318
D. A. S. Brooke, *L.*	7,271
Lab. maj.	*14,778*

(1955   Lab. maj. 16,537)

SOUTH E. 52,341

599*F. E. *Jones*, QC, *Lab.*	28,017	
P. Goldman, *C.*	5,188	
O. French, *L.*	4,020	
Lab. maj.	*22,829*	

(1955 Lab. maj. 23,454)

Westhoughton (Lancashire)
E. 56,948

600*J. T. *Price*, *Lab.*	29,359	
Lt-Col J. E. Gouldbourn, *C.*	18,634	
Lab. maj.	*10,725*	

(1955 Lab. maj. 10,052)

West Lothian
E. 58,457

601*J. *Taylor*, *Lab.*	27,454	
W. I. Stewart, *C.*	18,083	
Lab. maj.	*9,371*	

(By-election, 14 June 1962)

T. Dalyell, *Lab.*	21,266	
W. C. Wolfe, *Scot. Nat.*	9,750	
W. I. Stewart, *C.*	4,784	
D. Bryce, *L.*	4,537	
G. McLennan, *Comm.*	1,511	
Lab. maj.	*11,516*	

(1955 Lab. maj. 8,307)

Westmorland
E. 46,991

602*W. M. F. *Vane*, TD, *C.*	20,676	
A. G. D. Acland, *L.*	8,984	
C. Hughes-Stanton, *Lab.*	7,359	
C. maj.	*11,692*	

(1955 C. maj. 13,147)

Weston-super-Mare
(Somerset)
E. 60,795

603*D. W. E. *Webster*, *C.*	27,881	
S. E. Hampton, *Lab.*	10,977	
E. B. Taylor, *L.*	9,609	
C. maj.	*16,904*	

(June 1958, by-election, C. maj. 9,976)

(1955 C. maj. 11,082)

Whitehaven (Cumberland)
E. 46,650

604*J. B. *Symonds*, *Lab.*	22,783	
H. J. Pedraza, *C.*	16,653	
Lab. maj.	*6,130*	

(June 1959, by-election, Lab. maj. 6,324)

(1955 Lab. maj. 6,194)

Widnes (Lancashire)
E. 48,966

605*J. E. *MacColl*, *Lab.*	21,218	
Lt-Cdr B. L. Butcher, *C.*	19,620	
Lab. maj.	*1,598*	

(1955 Lab. maj. 1,449)

Wigan (English Borough)
E. 55,155

606*E. A. *Fitch*, *Lab.*	30,664	
J. J. Hodgson, *C.*	14,615	
M. Weaver, *Comm.*	945	
Lab. maj.	*16,049*	

(June 1958, by-election, Lab. maj. 17,167)

(1955 Lab. maj. 14,872)

Willesden (2)

EAST E. 58,865

607 T. H. H. *Skeet*, *C.*	22,709	
*M. Orbach, *Lab.*	20,499	
C. maj.	*2,210*	

(1955 Lab. maj. 659)

WEST E. 61,534

608 L. A. *Pavitt*, *Lab.*	25,680	
Mrs P. S. Brookes, *C.*	17,946	
L. Burt, *Comm.*	1,324	
Lab. maj.	*7,734*	

(1955 Lab. maj. 11,111)

Wiltshire (4). *See* **Chippenham, Devizes, Salisbury** and **Westbury**

Wimbledon (English Borough)
E. 42,151

609*Sir C. W. *Black*, *C.*	21,538	
L. M. Kershaw, *Lab.*	10,678	
C. maj.	*10,860*	

(1955 C. maj. 10,490)

Winchester (Hampshire)
E. 48,321

610*P. H. B. O. *Smithers*, VRD, D.Phil, *C.*	24,924	
Mrs M. J. Manning, *Lab.*	12,132	
C. maj.	*12,792*	

(1955 C. maj. 11,236)

Windsor (Berkshire)
E. 60,673

611*Sir C. E. *Mott-Radclyffe*, *C.*	29,942	
W. E. Robinson, *Lab.*	15,864	
C. maj.	*14,078*	

(1955 C. maj. 10,724)

Wirral (Cheshire)
E. 71,025
612*Rt Hon. *J. S. B. Lloyd*, CH,
   CBE, TD, QC, *C.*   39,807
   F. W. Venables, *Lab.* 18,805
   C. maj.   *21,002*
   (1955   C. maj. 17,051)

WITHINGTON – *See* **Manchester**

Woking (Surrey)
E. 64,295
613*Rt Hon. *H. A. Watkinson*,
   CH, *C.*   33,521
   R. D. V. Williams, *Lab.* 16,210
   C. maj.   *17,311*
   (1955   C. maj. 12,467)

Wokingham (Berkshire)
E. 67,144
614 *W. R. van Straubenzee*, MBE,
   C.   30,896
   T. G. Boston, *Lab.* 14,905
   C. W. J. Rout, *L.*   7,899
   C. maj.   *15,991*
   (1955   C. maj. 12,948)

Wolverhampton (2)
NORTH EAST   E. 51,217
615**J. Baird*, *Lab.*   20,436
   O. A. Pomeroy, *C.* 16,639
   Lab. maj.   *3,797*
   (1955   Lab. maj. 9,209)
SOUTH WEST   E. 51,293
616*Rt Hon. *J. E. Powell*, MBE,
   C.   25,696
   E. L. J. Thorne, *Lab.* 14,529
   C. maj.   *11,167*
   (1955   C. maj. 8,420)

Woodford (English Borough)
E. 45,070
617*Rt Hon. *Sir W. S. Churchill*,
   KG, OM, CH, *C.* 24,815
   A. C. Latham, *Lab.* 10,018
   C. maj.   *14,797*
   (1955   C. maj. 15,808)

Wood Green (English Borough)
E. 59,380
618*Mrs *J. S. Butler*, *Lab.* 22,869
   R. G. Shillingford, *C.* 21,735
   Lab. maj.   *1,134*
   (1955   Lab. maj. 3,712)

WOODSIDE – *See* **Glasgow**

Woolwich (2)
EAST   E. 46,349
619**C. P. Mayhew*, *Lab.* 22,353
   E. J. Porter, *C.*   12,638
   Lab. maj.   *9,715*
   (1955   Lab. maj. 10,346)
WEST   E. 54,563
620 *C. W. C. Turner*, *C.* 24,373
   W. Hamling, *Lab.* 20,678
   R. S. Mallone, *Fellowship
   Party*   1,189
   C. maj.   *3,695*
   (1955   C. maj. 1,880)

Worcester (English Borough)
E. 59,117
621*Rt Hon. *G. R. Ward*, *C.* 27,024
   B. C. Stanley, *Lab.* 19,832
   C. maj.   *7,192*
(By-election, 16 March 1961)
   P. E. Walker, *C.*   15,087
   B. C. Stanley, *Lab.* 11,490
   R. Glenton, *L.*   11,435
   C. maj.   *3,597*
   (1955   C. maj. 6,102)

Worcestershire (3)
SOUTH   E. 57,657
622*Comdr *Sir P. G. Agnew*, Bt,
   C.   25,824
   D. W. Young, *Lab.* 10,884
   Dr E. H. L. Harries, *L.* 6,890
   C. maj.   *14,940*
   (1955   C. maj. 12,980)

See also **Bromsgrove and Kidder-minster**

Workington (Cumberland)
E. 49,401
623**T. F. Peart*, *Lab.* 25,537
   T. M. Brannan, *C.* 16,894
   Lab. maj.   *8,643*
   (1955   Lab. maj. 7,928)

Worthing (English Borough)
E. 60,505
624*Brig. *Sir O. L. Prior-Palmer*, DSO, *C.* 31,396
   F. R. Mason, *Lab.*   7,618
   D. R. E. Abel, *L.*   7,045
   C. maj.   *23,778*
   (1955   C. maj. 21,875)

The Wrekin (Shropshire)
E. 48,789

625*W. Yates, C.		22,030
D. W. T. Bruce, Lab.		19,052
C. maj.		2,978
(1955 C. maj. 478)		

Wrexham (Denbighshire)
E. 66,150

626*J. I. J. Jones, Lab.		30,101
G. H. Pierce, C. & Nat. L.		17,144
D. E. Morgan, Welsh Nat.		6,579
Lab. maj.		12,957
(1955 Lab. maj. 11,659)		

Wycombe (Buckinghamshire)
E. 68,199

627*J. Hall, OBE, TD, C.		30,774
W. G. Fordham, Lab.		19,904
A. D. Dennis, L.		7,068
C. maj.		10,870
(1955 C. maj. 7,940)		

WYTHENSHAWE – See **Manchester**

YARDLEY – See **Birmingham**

Yarmouth (Norfolk)
E. 52,847

628*A. Fell, C.		22,827
S. C. Davis, Lab.		19,248
C. maj.		3,579
(1955 C. maj. 917)		

Yeovil (Somerset)
E. 59,739

629*J. W. W. Peyton, C.		23,771
W. A. Baker, Lab.		17,638
Col G. F. Taylor, L.		9,484
C. maj.		6,133
(1955 C. maj. 4,266)		

York (English Borough)
E. 73,717

630 C. B. Longbottom, C.		33,099
Dr D. R. L. M. Poirier, Lab.		29,025
C. maj.		4,074
(1955 C. maj. 1,104)		

Yorkshire, East Riding (3). See **Bridlington, Haltemprice** and **Howden**

Yorkshire, North Riding (4). See **Cleveland, Richmond, Scarborough and Whitby** and **Thirsk and Malton**

Yorkshire, West Riding (14). See **Barkston Ash, Colne Valley, Dearne Valley, Don Valley, Goole, Harrogate, Hemsworth, Normanton, Penistone, Ripon, Rother Valley, Shipley, Skipton** and **Sowerby**

BY-ELECTIONS PENDING

in November 1963 at Dumfries, Openshaw (Manchester), St Marylebone and Sudbury and Woodbridge.

ADDENDUM

By-election at Bristol, South-East, August 1963

A. N. W. Benn, Lab.		20,313
E. Martell, Nat. Fellowship		1,834
Mrs. M. Lloyd, Ind.		287
J. Pearl, Ind.		44
Lab. maj.		15,479

INDEX